Global and Transnational Sport

This book is a multidisciplinary exploration into the development of modern sporting culture from global and transnational history perspectives. The eight chapters in this book explore more than 150 years of the development of several modern sports – baseball, basketball, cricket, football, handball, ice hockey and lacrosse – across the two Americas, Asia, Australia and Europe, some analysing events since the mid-nineteenth century and some analysing only a few years in the very present. Drawing on the methods of history, international relations, political science and sociology, the contributing authors examine various theories of sporting globalization. The chapters take a balanced look at the concepts of the nation state and the connected world, which are the substantive core around which modern human society is ordered. They construct stories of entanglements and convergences, from within and without the nation state, in which the national and the non-national are not mutually exclusive. The key features of this collection are how cultural elements are introduced to sport; how changes are perceived; how sporting practices and institutions can be defined at geopolitical and other levels; how we might conceptualize the perimeter of judging the national–transnational or the local–translocal paradigms; and how we could complicate the understanding of sport/knowledge transfer by ascribing different degrees of importance to origin, process, purpose, outcome, personnel and network. The chapters in this book were originally published as a special issue of *Sport in Society: Cultures, Commerce, Media, Politics.*

Souvik Naha has a PhD in History from the ETH Zurich, Switzerland. His research has been published in journals such as *International Journal of the History of Sport, Sport in Society, Soccer & Society, Sport in History* and *Economic and Political Weekly,* as well as in various edited volumes. He is currently a Guest Lecturer in History at West Bengal State University, India, and the book review editor of *Soccer & Society.*

Sport in the Global Society: Contemporary Perspectives
Series Editor: Boria Majumdar
University of Central Lancashire, UK

The social, cultural (including media) and political study of sport is an expanding area of scholarship and related research. While this area has been well served by the *Sport in the Global Society* series, the surge in quality scholarship over the last few years has necessitated the creation of *Sport in the Global Society: Contemporary Perspectives*. The series will publish the work of leading scholars in fields as diverse as sociology, cultural studies, media studies, gender studies, cultural geography and history, political science and political economy. If the social and cultural study of sport is to receive the scholarly attention and readership it warrants, a cross-disciplinary series dedicated to taking sport beyond the narrow confines of physical education and sport science academic domains is necessary. *Sport in the Global Society: Contemporary Perspectives* will answer this need.

For a complete list of titles in this series, please visit https://www.routledge.com/series/SGSC

Recent titles in the series include:

Young People and Sport
From Participation to the Olympics
Edited by Berit Skirstad, Milena M. Parent and Barrie Houlihan

Reviewing the AFL's Vilification Laws
Rule 35, reconciliation and racial harmony in Australian Football
Sean Gorman, Dean Lusher and Keir Reeves

The State of the Field
Ideologies, Identities and Initiatives
Edited by David Kilpatrick

Global and Transnational Sport
Ambiguous Borders, Connected Domains
Edited by Souvik Naha

New Perspectives on Association Football in Irish History
Going beyond the "Garrison Game"
Edited by Conor Curran and David Toms

Major Sporting Events
Beyond the Big Two
Edited by John Harris, Fiona Skillen and Matthew McDowell

Global and Transnational Sport
Ambiguous Borders, Connected Domains

Edited by
Souvik Naha

LONDON AND NEW YORK

First published 2018
by Routledge
2 Park Square, Milton Park, Abingdon, Oxon, OX14 4RN, UK

and by Routledge
711 Third Avenue, New York, NY 10017, USA

Routledge is an imprint of the Taylor & Francis Group, an informa business

© 2018 Taylor & Francis

All rights reserved. No part of this book may be reprinted or reproduced or utilised in any form or by any electronic, mechanical, or other means, now known or hereafter invented, including photocopying and recording, or in any information storage or retrieval system, without permission in writing from the publishers.

Trademark notice: Product or corporate names may be trademarks or registered trademarks, and are used only for identification and explanation without intent to infringe.

British Library Cataloguing in Publication Data
A catalogue record for this book is available from the British Library

ISBN13: 978-0-8153-9668-0

Typeset in Minion Pro
by codeMantra

Publisher's Note
The publisher accepts responsibility for any inconsistencies that may have arisen during the conversion of this book from journal articles to book chapters, namely the possible inclusion of journal terminology.

Disclaimer
Every effort has been made to contact copyright holders for their permission to reprint material in this book. The publishers would be grateful to hear from any copyright holder who is not here acknowledged and will undertake to rectify any errors or omissions in future editions of this book.

Contents

Citation Information	vii
Notes on Contributors	ix

1   Introduction: 'Over the border and the gates'?
Global and transnational sport   1
Souvik Naha

2   Playing on the border: sport, borderlands and the
North Atlantic, 1850–1950   8
Colin D. Howell and Daryl Leeworthy

3   The intercultural transfer of football: the contexts of
Germany and Argentina   25
Thomas Adam

4   Sport transfer over the channel: elitist migration and the advent
of football and ice hockey in Switzerland   44
Christian Koller

5   With or without cricket? The two lives of the English game
in a decolonizing India   59
Souvik Naha

6   Did South America foster European football?: transnational influences
on the continentalization of FIFA and the creation of UEFA, 1926–1959   78
Philippe Vonnard and Grégory Quin

7   'Yes to Football, No to Torture!' The politics of the 1978 Football
World Cup in West Germany   94
Felix A. Jiménez Botta

CONTENTS

8 Learning in landscapes of professional sports: transnational
   perspectives on talent development and migration into Danish
   women's handball around the time of the financial crisis, 2004–2012   111
   Sine Agergaard

9 We're all transnational now: sport in dynamic sociocultural environments   124
   David Rowe

   Index   139

Citation Information

The chapters in this book were originally published in *Sport in Society: Cultures, Commerce, Media, Politics*, volume 20, issue 10 (October 2017). When citing this material, please use the original page numbering for each article, as follows:

Chapter 1
Introduction: 'Over the border and the gates'? Global and transnational sport
Souvik Naha
Sport in Society: Cultures, Commerce, Media, Politics, volume 20, issue 10 (October 2017)
pp. 1347–1353

Chapter 2
Playing on the border: sport, borderlands and the North Atlantic, 1850–1950
Colin D. Howell and Daryl Leeworthy
Sport in Society: Cultures, Commerce, Media, Politics, volume 20, issue 10 (October 2017)
pp. 1354–1370

Chapter 3
The intercultural transfer of football: the contexts of Germany and Argentina
Thomas Adam
Sport in Society: Cultures, Commerce, Media, Politics, volume 20, issue 10 (October 2017)
pp. 1371–1389

Chapter 4
Sport transfer over the channel: elitist migration and the advent of football and ice hockey in Switzerland
Christian Koller
Sport in Society: Cultures, Commerce, Media, Politics, volume 20, issue 10 (October 2017)
pp. 1390–1404

Chapter 5
With or without cricket? The two lives of the English game in a decolonizing India
Souvik Naha
Sport in Society: Cultures, Commerce, Media, Politics, volume 20, issue 10 (October 2017)
pp. 1405–1423

CITATION INFORMATION

Chapter 6
Did South America foster European football?: transnational influences on the continental-ization of FIFA and the creation of UEFA, 1926–1959
Philippe Vonnard and Grégory Quin
Sport in Society: Cultures, Commerce, Media, Politics, volume 20, issue 10 (October 2017)
pp. 1424–1439

Chapter 7
'Yes to Football, No to Torture!' The politics of the 1978 Football World Cup in West Germany
Felix A. Jiménez Botta
Sport in Society: Cultures, Commerce, Media, Politics, volume 20, issue 10 (October 2017)
pp. 1440–1456

Chapter 8
Learning in landscapes of professional sports: transnational perspectives on talent develop-ment and migration into Danish women's handball around the time of the financial crisis, 2004–2012
Sine Agergaard
Sport in Society: Cultures, Commerce, Media, Politics, volume 20, issue 10 (October 2017)
pp. 1457–1469

Chapter 9
We're all transnational now: sport in dynamic sociocultural environments
David Rowe
Sport in Society: Cultures, Commerce, Media, Politics, volume 20, issue 10 (October 2017)
pp. 1470–1484

For any permission-related enquiries please visit:
http://www.tandfonline.com/page/help/permissions

Notes on Contributors

Thomas Adam is Professor of Transnational History at the University of Texas at Arlington, USA. He specializes in Transnational History, Philanthropy and Civil Society Studies, Intercultural Transfer and History of Higher Education.

Sine Agergaard is Associate Professor at the Department of Public Health, Aarhus University, Denmark.

Colin D. Howell is Emeritus Professor at the Department of History, Saint Mary's University, Canada. He serves on the editorial advisory board for *Sport History Review*.

Felix A. Jiménez Botta is a PhD candidate in the History Department at Boston College, USA. He has a particular interest in transnational histories linking the German-speaking world and Latin America.

Christian Koller is Director of the Swiss Social Archives, Switzerland. He is also Titular Professor of History at the University of Zurich, Switzerland.

Daryl Leeworthy teaches History in the Department for Adult and Continuing Education at Swansea University, UK. His research focuses on the social and labour history of South Wales.

Souvik Naha has a PhD in History from the ETH Zurich, Switzerland. He is currently a Guest Lecturer in History at West Bengal State University, India, and the book review editor of *Soccer & Society*.

Grégory Quin is an Honorary Visiting Research Fellow in the International Centre for Sports History and Culture at De Montfort University, UK. He has a wide range of interests around sports history, especially in an international framework.

David Rowe is a Professor at the Institute for Culture and Society, Western Sydney University, Australia. He has published extensively in the areas of media and popular culture, especially sport, music and journalism.

Philippe Vonnard is an Associate Researcher at the Institute for Sport Sciences, University of Lausanne, Switzerland.

INTRODUCTION

'Over the border and the gates'? Global and transnational sport[1]

Souvik Naha

In his introduction to a *Sport in Society* special issue, about a decade ago, Klein (2007) warned fellow sport studies scholars against misdirecting their energy towards winning recognition for their work from the respective parent disciplines. Only within two disciplines, he contended, could case studies from the world of sport receive more respect than they were usually accorded – studies of gender and globalization. Incidentally, earlier that year, Giulianotti and Robertson (2007) edited a special issue for the journal *Global Networks*, assembling 'leading mainstream scholars' to examine, with a focus on sport, the new angle of globalization studies – transnational history. Transnational networks are hardly any new and unnoticed progeny of global connections. Concepts such as the Atlantic Empire, the British World and Overseas History have been around for a century, but the range of entanglements that underwrote these histories, set up by agents as diverse as navigation companies and touring sportspersons, have only started to be explored in the last few decades (Bridge and Fedorowich 2003). Although scholars have lamented the dearth of 'the trans-national (as opposed to international) treatment' for sports in Europe (Young, Hilbrenner, and Tomlinson 2011), compared to other disciplines, a global turn flourished early in sport studies, probably due to the inherently international nature of sport.

The global 'diffusion' of sporting ideals, the nation's role in international competitions, sport and diplomacy, development of mega-events (World Cups) and recurring tournaments (Tennis Opens), international sport administration, media coverage and finally, migration of elite athletes have drawn substantial scholarly attention since the 1980s (Taylor 2013a). The concepts of 'flows' and 'boundaries', so integral to the recent debates on global and transnational history, have found its way into sport studies since the beginning of the 2000s (Maguire 1999, 2005; Millward 2011; Rowe 2011). Nearly all of these works dwell on the contemporary landscape of sport, and only a few examine the beginning of sport's 'globality' from a long-term perspective (Bale and Maguire 1994; Dyreson 2003; Keys 2003; Taylor 2006, 2013b; Huggins 2009; Collins 2013). On the contrary, quite a few studies on circulation and appropriation of sport to have not used any of these frameworks (Odendaal 1988; Hibbins 1989; Nandy 1989) can yet be considered as the precursor to the recent output due to thematic similarity. This lack of a theoretical approach to long-term history, except for among the articles from a *Journal of Global History* special issue, edited by Taylor (2013a), has restricted all theoretical flourish in studies of sport's global issues to the realm of the recent.

Understandably what transpires at a sport event sometimes takes a backseat to its mediated meanings, which is particularly true for transferred codes. This is where the process, which implies a flow of events in time, is prioritized over anything that is fixed in time. The importance of studying single moments in the process cannot be overridden, especially as it is a chain of moments/events that empirically supports any process. Most of the research on sporting transnationalism have been informed by events and not processes. Despite the comparatively recent emergence of this analytical method and short-term structuring of research questions, the

---

[1] Dylan Thomas, 'A Refusal to Mourn the Death, by Fire, of a Child in London', *Collected Poems 1934–1952*, London: J M Dent, 1959, p. 102.

historiography of studying sport from a transnational perspective is surprisingly diverse. This is particularly evidenced in the outpour of research on athlete migration, which has received by far the maximum attention (Maguire and Pearton 2000; Maguire and Falcous 2010; Carter 2011; Agergaard and Tiesler 2014). Transnational fandom too has been a popular topic, with research involving actors and dynamics as diverse as English football clubs in Norway (Hognestad 2006), European football in Nigeria (Onwumechili and Oloruntola 2014), Italians settled in Sydney (Ricatti and Klugman 2013), South American migrants in Spain (Müller 2014), marketing a local team to Lusophone migrants in America (Moniz 2007) and local fans' response to foreign owners (Bi 2015).

The eight articles in this volume take a step towards bridging the worlds of history, sociology and international relations. They cumulatively explore more than 150 years of the development of several modern sports – baseball, basketball, cricket, football, handball, ice hockey and lacrosse – across the two Americas, Asia, Australia and Europe, some analysing a century of events since the mid-nineteenth century and some only a few years in the very present. The sheer variety and compositeness of scopes and methods among what is a relatively small collection of articles delimit some of the hitherto vague perimeters of the theories of sporting globalization. They avoid being over-determined by either the nation state or the connected world as the substantive core around which human society is ordered. They respond to, in varying degrees, the assumptions of 'methodological cosmopolitanism' (Beck 2002) and 'methodological glocalism' (Giulianotti and Klauser 2012). Beck's (2002, 19) ideas of 'the implosion of the dualism between the national and the international' and 'the incongruity of borders' resonate with some of the articles, while others refer to existing hierarchies that defy the drive towards cosmopolitanism. Thus, the articles are rather invested in constructing stories of entanglements and convergences, from within and without the nation state, in which the national and the non-national are not mutually exclusive (Sassen 2000).

Events involving simultaneous action performed by multiple actors across several sites have periodically emerged from the crucible of theory as comparative, connected, international, world, global, transnational, transcultural, intercultural and many other, some quite obscure, sorts of history. These perspectives frequently overlap. The fan frenzy for David Beckham in China as a self-contained national phenomenon can be explained as global or international fandom. The diffusion of the Beckham ideal, defined by addition of charisma and glamour to sporting excellence, into the Chinese popular culture market is an example of transnational and transcultural dispersion of celebrity culture. At the same time, the Chinese experience can be contrasted and compared to any other spatial context for understanding appropriation from an intercultural perspective. In recognition of the plausible multiplicity of approaches towards analysing an event, it seems rather rewarding to consider these terms as complementary interpretative tools instead of as paradigms. The contributors to this volume have likewise integrated several approaches in their attempts to probe the complex connections constituted by networks, institutions, ideas and processes, considering geographically bounded, localized histories alongside transnational activities.

Global history is closely linked with globalization. Although it may not be actually 'global' in scope, it is a concept that examines particular regions connected by particular networks. Transnational history describes interconnectivity in a more qualified, specific way since the term global implies a 'single system of connection' and disregards the sheer diversity of the systems in interaction (Cooper 2001). Compared to international history, use of the term transnational generates 'a sense of movement and interpenetration' (Bayly et al. 2006, 1442). A transnational approach helps to track the movement of people and products at every recorded step (Clavin 2005). According to Isabel Hofmeyr (Bayly et al. 2006), movements, flows and circulation are not simply themes or motifs in transnational history, but are self-sufficient analytic methods which illuminate both historic events and processes at various spatial intersections. Nevertheless, the analytical methods of global history are much more complex than the universality the name suggests. In contrast with global history, existence of nations is a precondition for international and transnational history (Sachsenmaier 2011). Even though 'cultural nations' (Glatz 1993) may theoretically prevail over geopolitical nations in terms of global appeal, the latter are still undeniably important for organized sport (Polley 1998; Rowe 2003). Hence, the need for the umbrella term to be replaced by something that explicitly reflects, for instance, cross-border connections and yet does not deny nation states of their agency.

Colin Howell and Daryl Leeworthy's article traces the parallel transfer of sports across the North Atlantic, destabilizing the British Isle's position as the primary distribution centre of sport in the nineteenth century. They propose a borderlands approach, a concept well known in American history, as an alternative model for understanding asymmetric shifts from the periphery to the core. By no means do borderlands refer to a geographical boundary separating territories, neither is it the permeable membrane that allows diffusion to happen. It is more of a sieve that factors in the local circumstances of cultural exchange that underpin patterns of internationalization of sports. Based on a study of the transfer of lacrosse, a traditional tribal sport, and basketball, invented by a Canadian doctor, to Great Britain, the authors successfully repudiate the top-down approaches to sporting diffusion.

Britain's importance in the diffusion narrative cannot be underestimated, but the agency of British actors in the process comes under scrutiny in Thomas Adam's article. Adam investigates the transfer of football from English public schools to German and Argentine high schools, highlighting the significant modifications the game underwent due to the subjectivity of the personnel and methods of transfer, and the requirements of the receiving society. Football became indigenized in these countries to such an extent that its English origin disappeared in translation, almost denying the existence of any transfer as it happened. The study of Germany, in particular, illustrates the pitfall of applying common sense and taking the country of a sport's origin as the nodal point of diffusion. In Germany, the person who masterminded the inclusion of football in the school curriculum had never travelled to England, and learnt about the game from German travelogues and the works of Thomas Hughes. Transplanted British people were instrumental in organizing football in South America, but a subsequent drive to enhance national identity led to a nationalist reinterpretation of the sport's origin, thereby writing England out of the English game's history. The internal development of the sport in Germany and Argentina followed different trajectories due to the circumstances of class and ideology, which again were quite different from how football evolved in Britain.

Even when the British did take the initiative to introduce sports to a country, the intention was not always justified by the outcome. As Christian Koller shows in his comparative analysis of the import of football and ice hockey to Switzerland by British students, tourists, and merchants and homecoming Swiss migrants, the sociocultural context determined the image and clientele of these sports. Football and ice hockey's success story in Switzerland contradicts Maarten Van Bottenburg's (2001) argument about the games stemming from German tradition having been more popular than English games in the German-speaking region. Despite the involvement of social elites in the propagation of the sports, local appropriation reinvented their nature. Football became the sport of the urban, working-class Swiss public, whereas ice hockey represented a rural, alpine Switzerland. Yet, unlike the cases of German and Argentine football, Swiss football and ice hockey retained British character and vocabulary, thereby manifesting another aspect of cultural transfer – selective appropriation, which is not necessarily resistance but rather reinscription.

The theme of reinscription is examined further by Souvik Naha in the context of cricket's contested location in the Indian public sphere following the country's independence from British rule. While cricket did never run short of followers, its practice continued to be opposed even half a century after the British left India as the sport retained its Englishness unlike football and hockey, which lost their foreign roots rather quickly. Naha tries to solve the conundrum by examining how journalists collectively transcribed cricket into an identifiable, transnational sport by selective translation of the game's English discourses. This had arguably pitched cricket as a game of the leisured, disciplined, moral, elite class, which could be garbed as imperialist and capitalist. This was both cricket's appeal and disgrace. The narrative of resolution, or rather the lack of it, of the transcultural dilemma apparently guided much of the mediation of Anglo-Indian rhetoric exchange, which the author analyses with reference to Bengali cricket writers.

Cultural brokering was not exclusively yoked to transfer of sport codes but could be seen in the realm of sport administration too, particularly during the massive reorganization of global sport bodies after the Second World War. The article by Philippe Vonnard and Grégory Quin analyses the role played by South America in creating a geopolitically inclusive outlook among European football administrators, leading to the reorganization of FIFA and formation of UEFA as a representative European institution. The dialogues between South Americans and Europeans about governing a game invented in Europe, in which the former gradually prevailed over the latter, indicate what can be termed as a first wave of decolonizing Western sport. Grounded in the period of building international organization and cooperation, facilitated by new technology, these dialogues, occurring for about half a century across Europe and South America, bring out vividly the emergence of a connected, cosmopolitan bureaucratic hierarchy in world politics. The production of difference was no longer a prerogative of the modern West. The 'rest' could now exercise it, with the West consigned to adopting the perceived difference within its systems, just as the European administrations ordered themselves both in opposition and according to the knowledge produced in South America.

The next article, by Felix Jimenez, discusses the emergence of sport mega-events as a site of international activism against injustice. Whereas Vonnard and Quin talk about the balance of power within sport administration, Jimenez examines the interplay of power between sport/national administration and civil society. Human rights had become a watchword for post-war generations, which had found in sport a venue for protesting violation of humanity, such as the global protest against South Africa's racial discrimination policy (Cornelissen 2011). Jimenez analyses the representation of the 1978 Football World Cup in the German media, demonstrating conflicting attitudes towards the ethical role of sport, flow of information from Argentina to Germany, international social movement's (Anmesty) mobilization of sports as part of a 'repertoire of collective action', and the nexus between international sports and the global expansion of human rights in the 1970s.

The final two articles emphasize the contentious politics of immigration in the making of sporting cultures. Sine Agergaard's article is about the impact of political opportunist coaches and journalists on immigrant East-European players in Danish women's handball. It is difficult to understand what the best interests of a team are till the policy pays off. The insistence of coaches to disengage foreign players as a measure of developing domestic talent proved to be counterproductive, and efforts were made to reinstate those foreign players. However, more important to the story is the background of growing anti-immigrant sentiment in recession-hit Europe that largely informed the policy. Any effort to integrate foreign athletes being a far cry, the compulsive reactionary behaviour of administrators and its translation into public opinion by journalists expose the persistence of sacrosanct, fiercely protected national cultures even in these transnational times.

David Rowe further complicates this interplay of the local and the global by inspecting what the symbolic bond of sport mean to culturally and linguistically diverse immigrants looking to integrate into Australian society. On the one hand, contemporary sport, even quotidian and non-competitive, is increasingly becoming cosmopolitan; on the other hand, it does not cease to articulate the nation's centrality to organizing and practising sport as part of daily life. Taking a cautionary position, Rowe delegates researchers the responsibility to read the context carefully before cantering into the tempting task of erasing borders. The interviews in his article reveal, if anything, that collective belonging is as fluid as movement and is always multi-oriented towards past and present, home and away, across tangible and intangible borders.

The nation's importance to connected history is evident in some of the contributions to this volume. Howell and Leeworthy are sceptical about the location of boundary but cannot deny its existence. The articles by Agergaard and Rowe, respectively, examine the contrasting situation of the denial of cultural similitude to migrant athletes in Denmark and the drive towards self-assimilation of migrant professionals through participation in local sport in Australia. On the contrary, the nation takes an abstract form in Naha's article. It acknowledges the transfer of cricket from England to India, but both the nations are more textual than corporeal. Geographical territory is replaced by an ideological plane in which the struggles over a cultural attribute of the contentious 'English' nation are played out. Nations are important for structuring international sport organizations, as Vonnard and Quin argue, but finally it is a global power elite which represents and bends nations to its will. Hence, placing the nation in a history of global encounters is tricky. The judgement about the superfluity or essentiality of a national scale should better be left to the context.

Actors stand perhaps ahead of the nation in the hierarchy of importance in cultural encounters. They too display agendas and characteristics which are hard to reconcile to any given theory. In contrast with the British connoisseurs whose promotion of public school sports during Swiss holidays is an example of the revolutionizing of the pattern of sport education in a non-colonial context, Germans brought football to their homeland almost without involving British personnel. Football flourished in Germany despite the country's antagonism towards the British, so did cricket in postcolonial India. Cricket was played in Switzerland nearly as widely as football till the early twentieth century before inexplicably losing its footing, and almost disappearing after the Second World War. Evidently, the polyvalent nature of sport transfers speaks against a standard explanatory model of diffusion. Hence, the constellation of methodological viewpoints in this volume – Howell and Leeworthy's borderlands approach, Adam's theory of intercultural transfer, Naha's emphasis on agents of encounters, Agergaard's adoption of the theory of landscape of practice – prioritize reading the particularized context of action, rejecting the universalizing susceptibilities that global history perspectives occasionally succumb to. Jimenez's article is a reminder of the peril of taking the global for granted while taking about international organizations and events, such as enlistment of sport mega-event as a site of resistance. Does the protest by Germans, partnered by Amnesty International, against domestic problems in Argentina, qualify as a global event? While it certainly does not in the scale of participation, the form of protest was institutionally anchored in an international media–sport–human rights discourse too deeply to be deglobalized. The ideational space of the protest was, hence, more global than the physical space.

Finally, the key features of this collection are how cultural elements are introduced to sport, how changes are perceived, how sporting practices and institutions can be defined at geopolitical and other levels, how we might conceptualize the perimeter of judging the national–transnational or the local–translocal paradigms, and how we could complicate the understanding of sport/knowledge transfer by ascribing different degrees of importance to origin, process, purpose, outcome, personnel and network. Though not too global in scale, the articles try to cover as much of the canvas it has been possible under restraints of number. The global, as has been pointed out repeatedly, can very well be seen from within the limits of a parochial commonplace.

References

Agergaard, Sine, and Nina Clara Tiesler, eds. 2014. *Women, Soccer and Transnational Migration*. London: Routledge.

Bale, John, and Joseph Maguire, eds. 1994. *The Global Sports Arena: Atheltic Talent Migration in an Interdependent World*. London: Frank Cass.

Bayly, C. A, Sven Beckert, Matthew Connelly, Isabel Hofmeyr, Wendy Kozol, and Patricia Seed. 2006. "AHR Conversation: On Transnational History." *The American Historical Review* 111 (5): 1441–1464.

Beck, Ulrich. 2002. "The Cosmopolitan Society and Its Enemies." *Theory, Culture, Society* 19 (1–2): 17–44.

Bi, Yuan. 2015. "Integration or Resistance: The Influx of Foreign Capital in British Football in the Transnational Age." *Soccer & Society* 16 (1): 17–41.

Bridge, Carl, and Kent Fedorowich. 2003. "Mapping the British World." In *The British World: Diaspora, Culture and Identity*, edited by Carl Bridge and Kent Fedorowich, 1–15. London: Frank Cass.

Carter, Thomas F. 2011. *In Foreign Fields. The Politics and Experiences of Transnational Sport Migration*. London: Pluto Press.

Clavin, Patricia. 2005. "Defining Transnationalism." *Contemporary European History* 14 (4): 421–439.

Collins, Tony. 2013. "Unexceptional Exceptionalism: The Origins of American Football in a Transnational Context." *Journal of Global History* 8 (2): 209–230.

Cooper, Frederick. 2001. "What is the Concept of Globalization Good For? An African Historian's Perspective." *African Affairs* 100: 189–213.

Cornelissen, Scarlet. 2011. "'Resolving "the South Africa Problem"': Transnational Activism, Ideology and Race in the Olympic Movement, 1960–91." *The International Journal of the History of Sport* 28 (1): 153–167.

Dyreson, Mark. 2003. "Globalizing the Nation-making Process: Modern Sport in World History." *The International Journal of the History of Sport* 20 (1): 91–106.

Giulianotti, Richard, and Francisco Klauser. 2012. "Sport Mega-events and 'Terrorism': A Critical Analysis." *International Review for the Sociology of Sport* 47 (3): 307–323.

Giulianotti, Richard, and Roland Robertson. 2007. "Sport and Globalization: Transnational Dimensions." *Global Networks* 7 (2): 107–112.

Glatz, Ferenc. 1993. "State, State-nation, Cultural Nation." *European Review* 1 (4): 385–389.

Hibbins, G. M. 1989. "The Cambridge Connection: The Origin of Australian Rules Football." *The International Journal of the History of Sport* 6 (2): 172–192.

Hognestad, Hans K. 2006. "Transnational Passions: A Statistical Study of Norwegian Football Supporters." *Soccer & Society* 7 (4): 439–462.

Huggins, Mike. 2009. "The Proto-globalisation of Horseracing 1730–1900: Anglo–American Interconnections." *Sport in History* 29 (3): 367–391.

Keys, Barbara. 2003. "Soviet Sport and Transnational Mass Culture in the 1930s." *Journal of Contemporary History* 38 (3): 413–434.

Klein, Alan. 2007. "Towards a Transnational Sports Studies." *Sport in Society* 10 (6): 885–895.

Maguire, Joseph. 1999. *Global Sport: Identities, Societies, Civilizations*. Cambridge: Polity Press.

Maguire, Joseph, ed. 2005. *Power and Global Sport: Zones of Prestige, Emulation and Resistance*. London: Routledge.

Maguire, Joseph, and Mark Falcous, eds. 2010. *Sport and Migration: Borders, Boundaries and Crossings*. London: Routledge.

Maguire, Joseph, and Robert Pearton. 2000. "The Impact of Elite Labour Migration on the Identification, Selection and Development of European Soccer Players." *Journal of Sports Sciences* 18 (9): 759–769.

Millward, Peter. 2011. *The Global Football League: Transnational Networks, Social Movements and Sport in the New Media Age*. Basingstoke: Palgrave Macmillan.

Moniz, Miguel. 2007. "Adaptive Transnational Identity and the Selling of Soccer: The New England Revolution and Lusophone Migrant Populations." *Soccer & Society* 8 (4): 459–477.

Müller, Juliane. 2014. "Local Relations and Transnational Imaginaries: Football Practices of Migrant Men and Women from Andean Countries in Spain." *Soccer & Society* 15 (4): 596–617.

Nandy, Ashis. 1989. *The Tao of Cricket: On the Destiny of Games and the Games of Destiny*. New Delhi: Viking.

Odendaal, André. 1988. "South Africa's Black Victorians: Sport and Society in South Africa in the Nineteenth Century." In *Pleasure, Profit, Proselytism: British Culture and Sport at Home and Abroad 1700–1914*, edited by J. A. Mangan, 193–214. London: Frank Cass.

Onwumechili, C., and S. Oloruntola. 2014. "Transnational Communications, Attitudes and Fan Identity: Studying Nigeria Post-media Reform." *Soccer & Society* 15 (3): 389–410.

Polley, Martin. 1998. *Moving the Goalposts: A History of Sport and Society since 1945*. London: Routledge.

Ricatti, Francesco, and Matthew Klugman. 2013. "'Connected to Something': Soccer and the Transnational Passions, Memories and Communities of Sydney's Italian Migrants." *The International Journal of the History of Sport* 30 (5): 469–483.

Rowe, David. 2003. "Sport and the Repudiation of the Global." *International Review for the Sociology of Sport* 38 (3): 281–294.

Rowe, David. 2011. *Global Media Sport: Flows, Forms and Futures*. London: Bloomsbury.

Sachsenmaier, Dominic. 2011. *Global Perspectives on Global History: Theories and Approaches in a Connected World*. Cambridge: Cambridge University Press.

Sassen, Saskia. 2000. "New Frontiers Facing Urban Sociology at the Millennium." *The British Journal of Sociology* 51 (1): 143–159.

Taylor, Matthew. 2006. "Global Players? Football, Migration and Globalization, C. 1930–2000." *Historical Social Research* 31 (1): 7–30.

Taylor, Matthew. 2013a. "Editorial – Sport, Transnationalism, and Global History." *Journal of Global History* 8 (2): 199–208.

Taylor, Matthew. 2013b. "The Global Ring? Boxing, Mobility, and Transnational Networks in the Anglophone World, 1890–1914." *Journal of Global History* 8 (2): 231–255.

Van Bottenburg, Maarten. 2001. *Global Games*. Translated by Beverley Jackson. Urbana: University of Illinois Press.

Young, Christopher, Anke Hilbrenner, and Alan Tomlinson. 2011. "European Sport Historiography: Challenges and Opportunities." *Journal of Sport History* 38 (2): 182–187.

Souvik Naha
Institute of History, ETH Zurich, Switzerland
✉ souvik.naha@gmw.gess.ethz.ch

Playing on the border: sport, borderlands and the North Atlantic, 1850–1950

Colin D. Howell and Daryl Leeworthy

ABSTRACT

In this paper, we advance a borderlands perspective to delineate and distinguish the patterns of sporting development across the North Atlantic, with a particular focus on the transmission of lacrosse and basketball from North America to the British Isles in the nineteenth and twentieth centuries. The borderlands perspective and the understanding of the Atlantic as an oceanic borderland allow for a reconsideration of traditional models of diffusion–modernization, which focus on the export of sporting cultures from the UK to the wider world. The borderlands model, with its consideration of the multidirectional character of cultural transference, enables a reorientation of analysis, from the metropolitan to the peripheral, from traditional framed 'national sports' to those that are otherwise ignored in non-native contexts by diffusion modelling, from top to down models that service the national narrative to bottom-up understandings that shed light on the activities of ordinary sportsmen and women and the communities that supported them.

Introduction

In this article, we advance a borderlands perspective to delineate and distinguish the patterns of sporting development across the North Atlantic and focus on the transmission of lacrosse and basketball from North America to the British Isles in the nineteenth and twentieth centuries. By imagining the Atlantic as an oceanic borderland, where multifaceted cultural cross-currents intersect, we address the limitations of traditional models of diffusion which focus on the export of sporting cultures from the UK to the wider world especially in the nineteenth century. A borderlands approach also offers an alternative to modernization models which, within the later twentieth century context, concentrate on the influence of big-time capital, professionalization, and the commercialization of sport. For some historians, these larger processes can be connected to discourses involving American exceptionalism, imperial expansion, and cultural hegemony (Pope 2007). We find diffusion–modernization models wanting in two regards: firstly their prioritization of metropolitan influence and concomitant rejection of the agency of those who live on the periphery – what elsewhere has been called the 'metropolitan fallacy' (Howell and Leeworthy 2010, 72–74) – and secondly their lack of regard for the multiple forms of cultural exchange that traverse both landed and oceanic borders.[1]

The borderlands perspective, with its consideration of the multidirectional character of cultural transfer, enables a reorientation of analysis, from the metropolitan to the peripheral, from top to down models that service the national narrative to bottom-up understandings that shed light on the activities of ordinary sportsmen and women and the communities that supported them. It also gives attention to the way that local communities adapted transnational sporting influences to local circumstances and needs. As an oceanic borderland, the North Atlantic in the second half of the nineteenth and first half of the twentieth centuries – and even before that – was a site of economic exchange and capitalist enterprise (Falola and Roberts 2008; Sager 1989, 1993), of international labour employment and mobility (Howell and Twomey 1991), a catalyst for industrial and commercial development (Rediker 1987), and a multi-directional highway of cultural transmission from sea to shore (Harper and Vance 1999; Steele 1986). Amid the myriad of individual interactions influenced by these larger processes, there were always imbalances of power that attended the negotiation of metropolitan and local, imperial and regional initiatives, and the social relations of capitalist production. Nevertheless, and this would also be true of other oceanic pathways in the Pacific and Indian Oceans, the North Atlantic in these years served as a handmaiden of transnational and global interconnectedness in the industrial age, rivalling in significance recent communication technologies that have shaped post-industrial cultural practices and our contemporary 'glocalized' sporting experience.[2]

Although this paper focuses on the Atlantic as a sporting borderland, it is worth noting that the borderlands model is ongoing and timeless and can be employed over time and across geographical spaces throughout the world. In addition, borders are not always physical and tangible entities, but are embedded in culturally constructed categories such as class, gender and ethnicity. Not surprisingly, the borderlands model shares the preoccupation of post-colonial scholars such as Homi Bhabha and Edward Said with liminality, and with those hybrid spaces where identities shaped by the globalizing process are continually negotiated and contested (Bhabha 1994; Said 1979). At the same time, a borderlands approach allows us to focus on multidirectional processes of cultural exchange that continue to influence the nature of sport in the modern world.

Metropolitanism, borderlands and indigeneity: imagining the process of ludic diffusion

Early discussions of the process of ludic diffusion were almost invariably interpreted as an aspect of modernization and metropolitan influence, emphasizing the sophistication of the centre versus the periphery, the city over the countryside, imperial versus colonial or indigenous life. This was in keeping with the assumptions of the old imperial history. Given that many sporting traditions had developed in the British Isles and were exported throughout the British world, it was easy to replicate this essentially top-down process of cultural diffusion – from England to New England, from Scotia to Nova Scotia, from South Wales to New South Wales, as it were. Among North American historians, metropolitanism gained increasing attention and persuasiveness as an alternative to Frederick Jackson Turner and over-zealous disciples of his 'frontier thesis' who saw the frontier as the crucible of American democracy and culture. During the 1950s, Canadian historian James Maurice Careless developed his 'metropolitan thesis' in a number of books and articles emphasizing the power of the metropolis as a cultural and economic centre that organized frontier and hinterland regions (Careless 1954, 1990). According to Careless, his American contemporary Wade (1959), and in an earlier mode Schlesinger (1940), it was the city that propelled cultural development and modernization. The turn from frontierism to metropolitanism was evident in sport history as well. Paxson's (1917) early musings about the frontier mentality and American sport culture were gradually superseded by those of modernization theorists who outlined a process of diffusion that emphasized metropolitan linkages and advances in organizational sophistication (Guttmann 1978).

Although 'mapping' metropolitan influence and the process of imperial and sportive nation-building has received considerable attention over the years (Dyreson, Mangan, and Park 2012; Guttmann 1994) – and justifiably so – there is more to the writing of (sport) history than the story of imperial, national and metropolitan power. Van Bottenburg (2010) has recently cautioned against unidirectional models that assume that Britain was always at the centre of the diffusion process. These models privilege empire and nation. In place of 'oversimplifying notions of 'trickle down' effects between centres and peripheries and dominated and dominating groups', Van Bottenburg emphasizes 'reverse diffusion' and evinces a more sensitive understanding of the making and remaking of sport in cross-cultural contexts. Our focus on the Atlantic as an oceanic borderland characterized by constant cultural exchange echoes Van Bottenburg's plea. In addition, our work builds upon that of Buckner and Douglas Francis (2006, 2007), Reid, Bowen, and Mancke (2012), Armitage and Braddick (2002), and others (Duinen 2013, 2014; Nielsen 2014), who provide new approaches to both the British and Atlantic worlds. Indeed, as the forces of contemporary globalization erode the primacy of the nation state as a subject for historical analysis, the Atlantic as a mixture of various cultural flows, networks, connections and interactions has received more critical transnational analysis. As Armitage (2002, 11) sardonically comments, 'we are all Atlanticists now'. Historians speculate on the Black, the Green (Irish), the Red (revolutionary), the criminal and the military Atlantic, not to mention the Dutch, British or French. To these characterizations, we may add the 'sporting Atlantic' as a focal point for understanding the multidirectional character of ludic cultural transference and exchange (Leeworthy 2015). What is common to the various historiographies relating to the British and Atlantic worlds and the history of borderland regions is that they focus on the history of cultural exchanges of various sorts, including sport.

Since many of those involved in Atlantic world scholarship traditionally focus on the years before 1850, it is understandable that sport often escapes serious attention (Hornsby and Reid 2005; Reid, Bowen, and Mancke 2012). It is noteworthy, then, that John Reid, a scholar deeply versed in the history of the north-east American borderlands, has recently turned his attention to the diffusion issue. In a recent article in the *Journal of Sport History* (Reid and Reid 2015), he, in association with his son Robert, compares the history of cricket and hockey in nineteenth-century Maritime Canada, the former languishing despite its early introduction to the region, the latter becoming broadly popular. While the Reids acknowledge institutional and organizational impulses that affected the trajectories of two sports that spread across the Atlantic in different directions, they do so with an eye to how the discourses that surrounded them shaped public perceptions and their acceptance. They write that hockey was 'a sport that was not only codified and public, but had a well-defined surrounding discourse. Unlike ... cricket, it was explicitly Canadian and emphasized characteristics of the way in which the sport was played'. Like Phillips (2001) study of the spread of the amateur ideal to Australia and Bloyce's (2005) analysis of the response of the British press to early American baseball tours, the Reids note the importance of the discursive dimension and of local agency in the diffusion process.

In the pages that follow, then, we build upon earlier comparative and transnational work on sports such as rugby union, baseball and ice hockey, to investigate the flow of lacrosse and basketball across the North Atlantic and their growth in the British Isles. Our approach is informed by the idea of 'glocalization', giving special attention to the way communities adapt larger cultural processes to local needs. Whereas lacrosse and basketball share North American origins – the former in Canada, the latter in the US – when translated to the British and Irish contexts they developed in distinctive ways in response to particular local needs. Lacrosse, the idealized amateur game of mid-Victorian Anglo-Canadian nationalism, found its voice amongst the liberal middle class of major industrial and commercial centres such as Manchester, Belfast and Bristol. Basketball on the other hand was primarily played by working-class young men in cities such as Birmingham and Derby and in coal mining areas such as South Wales; it also enjoyed cross-class patronage in the younger universities such as Leeds and Cardiff.

Lacrosse: glocalising the 'creator's game'

When addressing the evolution of our contemporary worldwide sporting culture, it is necessary to recognize that globalization has a lengthy history, and that oceanic borderlands were important in its development. As various sports spread across the Atlantic, they were put to use in ways that made sense to the people and communities that received them. Despite a presumption that Roland Robinson's 'glocalization' thesis pertains only to the contemporary period, we find it helpful in addressing the early history in Britain of sports with a North American origin. The history of the spread of lacrosse across the Atlantic borderlands to the British Isles is a case in point. It was taken up and modified to meet the needs of various communities and constituencies, and connected to the broader organizational framework of individual amateur sport organizations throughout the British Isles.

Of the many sports played by the peoples of the North Atlantic, lacrosse is the only mainstream game to have its origins outside of the European tradition. To grapple with its history, is thus to come to terms with its attachment on one hand to nineteenth narratives about Anglo-Canadian national identity, and on the other to Iroquois nationalism and First Nations cultural sovereignty. Indeed, while lacrosse was a sport codified in 1867 by the Montreal dentist and Anglo-Canadian nationalist George Beers to reflect presumptions about 'modern' sport, it was also a game that First Nations peoples believed was gifted to them by the Creator. As 'the creator's game' – an anglicized term which conveys this alternate lineage – lacrosse was deeply rooted in the spirituality and religion of pre-contact First Nations. Since the 1980s, lacrosse has undergone a post-colonial process of re-appropriation (Forsyth and Wamsley 2006), and continues to be contested terrain even today (Downey 2012; Fisher 2002; Robidoux 2002). The divergence lies between native culture and a sport codified in ways redolent of imperial British values and compatible with what Mckay (2000) has called the Canadian 'liberal order'.

On the whole, the scholarly literature relating to lacrosse is concerned with circumstances within Canada itself and the role of lacrosse as a sport in the service of Canadian nation-building, although Fisher (2002) work extends this into a continental framework. Even though the game originated as a First Nations cultural practice, nineteenth-century nationalists appropriated it, identifying it as a Canadian sport and emphasizing its northern character. As Gillian Poulter notes, 'the linked themes of distinctive sports, wintery climate and northern geography became distinguishing characteristics of Canadian-ness' (Poulter 2003, 293; Poulter 2009). Successful enough was this inculcation of Canadianness that in the 1860s British commentators could write of lacrosse that it was 'we presume, played on ice' (*Reading Mercury*, September 7, 1867).

Three transatlantic tours of Britain, the first in 1867, another in 1876 and a third in 1883, encouraged the development of the game throughout the British Isles and overcame such false assumptions. As Brown (1987) has noted, these lacrosse tours were intended by Anglo-Canadians as expressions of Canadian identity and imperial loyalty. 'It was', writes Brown (1987, 60), 'a sport of the Empire, a Canadian imperial sport, which perpetuated, along with cricket, soccer and rugby football, a sense of unity and commonality'. As will be seen, however, closer scrutiny of the ways in which lacrosse developed in Britain and Ireland in the aftermath of the lacrosse tours suggests that the narrative of imperial unity was largely absent in Britain. Furthermore, rather than simply replicating Beers' model of lacrosse playing, British and Irish enthusiasts sought to manipulate lacrosse to their own circumstances.

Lacrosse arrived in the British Isles in the summer of 1867, when an 18-members strong team from Akwesasne (St Regis, Quebec), sponsored by the Montreal Lacrosse Club and led by Captain William B. Johnson of the Canadian volunteers, travelled across the Atlantic to play in the UK for the first time (*Manchester Courier*, July 29, 1867).[3] The opening match of the tour took place on July 30 before an elite audience at Beaufort House in Fulham, south-west London. The *London Standard* (July 31, 1867) concluded that

> there have been very few exhibitions [...] more thoroughly well worthy of a visit [...] we believe that the game will give so much satisfaction that ere long we shall be having clubs spring up in our towns for the game.

After further two exhibitions at Beaufort House, the tourists moved on to the Crystal Palace, playing there regularly from the 8th August until early September (*London Standard*, August 6, 1867). The team then went on a brief tour around southern England (*The Era* [London], August 18, 1867), and to highlight the Canadian and aboriginal connection to lacrosse, games were often followed by a snow shoe race (*Morning Post* [London], August 9, 1867).[4] The first engagement outside London was at Brighton, where two exhibitions were played on September 1 and 2 (*Sussex Agricultural Express*, August 31, 1867). Thereafter, they travelled to Reading and played there under the patronage of the town's mayor, the commander of the town's volunteer brigade and leading members of the local cricket and rowing clubs. Spectators were again treated to a snowshoe race (*Berkshire Chronicle*, August 31, 1867).

Perhaps because the aboriginal roots of the game contradict the metropolitan and modernizing presumptions of the diffusion model, the 1867 tour has long been dismissed by Canadian nationalist historians as 'hastily organised and ineffectual'. With an entirely native composition – aside from Johnson, who did not play – the 1867 touring side introduced lacrosse to British audiences not in the 'Canadian' and imperial style as propagated by Beers but rather in the native style (*Bell's Life in London*, August 3, 1867). Indeed, the entire encounter was depicted in the British press as something out of a James Fenimore Cooper novel and evoked memories of the runner Deerfoot, who had spent nearly two years entertaining British audiences earlier in the decade (*Sporting Life*, August 10, 1861; *Fun* [London], August 31, 1867). The *West Middlesex Advertiser* (August 3, 1867) observed, for example, that 'only one of the troupe speaks good English and some of them do not even converse in Canadian French, but use their own wild language'. For all that Lacrosse was presented as Canadian, then, the first people that Britons saw playing it were First Nations.

The tour prompted a number of Londoners to take up the sport themselves in the fall of 1867, forming clubs and eventually a Lacrosse Association in January 1868. The first notice to this effect came at the end of September 1867 in the pages of the north London *Islington Gazette*. Dr John Whitehead, who described himself as the honorary secretary (pro tem), advised 'gentlemen wishing to join in the [...] New Canadian Game are requested to attend a meeting at Tufnell Park Cricket Ground [...] for the purpose of forming rules, &c' (*Islington Gazette*, September 27, October 4, 1867). Whitehead was not the only enthusiast. Proponents in Richmond, south-west London, met at the Greyhound Hotel on Friday 1 November, where they agreed to adopt the rules of the Montreal Lacrosse Club. With playing colours of orange and violet, they met each Saturday in the winter season on Richmond Green to practice (*Sporting Life*, November 6, 1867; *The Sportsman*, November 21, 1867). In Blackheath, south-east London, two teams were set up, both confusingly called Blackheath Lacrosse Club to begin with (*The Sportsman*, November 7, 16, 1867)! Finally, members of the Civil Service Cricket and Athletic Club formed their own lacrosse club, playing at Battersea Park (*Sporting Life*, November 13, 1867).[5]

Growing out of this initial interest, a National Lacrosse Association was formed at the Cathedral Hotel near St Paul's Cathedral, on 15 January 1868. The lead was taken by the Richmond club, and its secretary, E. Cobham, was elected as the founding secretary of the association (*Sporting Life*, December 28, 1867; January 11, 18, 25, 1868). Amongst its first acts was the establishment of uniform rules. It also sponsored the publication of a history of lacrosse, to which the British rules would be appended, written by Mark H. Robinson of the Civil Service Lacrosse Club. This was published in May 1868 by Frederick Warne and Co, and laid the foundations for the British development of lacrosse in a similar way to Beers's own publications in Canada (Robinson 1868; *The Sportsman*, April 11, 1868). Even at this early juncture, however, the sport was set on a different path of development to that in Canada: a situation evident in the rule book. If much of the detail is the same, there are elements which demonstrate a 'British' take: certain rules relating to the ball and the size of the field are different, and laws governing violence in the Canadian game are absent the British version.[6]

As befitting a sport adopted by the well-educated middle classes, lacrosse was supported by the range of boy's magazines and journals marketed at this class of people. Amongst the most enthusiastic proponent was Samuel Beeton, husband of the chef Mrs Beeton, whose range of publications included the *Boy's Own Magazine*, *Beeton's Journal* and *Beeton's Annual*. Launched in December 1867, *Beeton's Journal* featured lacrosse in its first issue, and match reports were regularly printed thereafter. Not to be outdone, George Routledge published a lengthy article on the game in his *Magazine for Boys* published on 1 November 1868. Here too, there were perceived differences in the 'English' approach to playing lacrosse. 'The Indians have red and blue caps and knickerbockers to distinguish them', the magazine explained, 'but our English boys are hardly likely to sport these fancy-coloured continuations, and therefore a coloured belt for the waist, or gauntlet for the arm, will probably supersede here the coloured knickerbockers'. And in keeping with the masculine self-reliance being taught to boys in these magazines, rather than advertise specialist outlets from which sporting goods could be purchased, readers were encouraged to make their own crosses using hickory bought from a fishing-rod manufacturer or a 'good stout ash sapling'.

By 1869, however, this experiment in lacrosse playing had come to an end. Although Beers's book *La Crosse: The National Game of Canada* was published in Britain in 1869 by the London publisher Sampson Low, the clubs formed in 1867 had disbanded and journals no longer reported on the game. An article in *The Sportsman* (February 6, 1869) observed that it called for 'too much hard work. Perhaps, after all, it is better suited to the wiry frames and special training of the American Indians than to our own athletes, who take far more kindly to football'. Others suggested that North American sports of any kind were too foreign to be easily adopted. Warnings issued in the mid-1870s to American entrepreneurs from Boston and Philadelphia who wished to 'naturalise baseball in this country' were equally stark. 'Englishmen', recorded the *Sporting Times* (November 14, 1874), 'prefer cricket and football […] and so the importations from the other side of the Atlantic fell still-born here'.

Such warnings were premature. Within a couple of years lacrosse playing had been revived in Britain and placed on a much surer footing than in the 1860s. Most historians have explained its re-emergence as a result of the 1876 tour led by George Beers. According to Donald Fisher, the tour 'contributed to a permanent lacrosse beachhead overseas' (Fisher 2002). This is not entirely accurate, however. In fact, lacrosse had been undergoing a revival prior to the 1876 tour, with matches and clubs started by a group of enthusiasts in London associated with the Thames Hare and Hounds – an athletics club formed by members of the Thames Rowing Club in 1868 (*Sporting Gazette*, December 26, 1874). The first of these matches was played in 1875 on Wimbledon Common (*Sporting Gazette*, April 10, 1875). Every fortnight for the next few months, members of the Thames Hare and Hounds met at Wimbledon Common to play (*Bell's Life in London*, April 24; May 8, 22, 29, 1875), one team captained by Dr T. Archer, a Canadian expat who had brought a range of lacrosse equipment with him, and the other captained by Edwin Thomas Sachs, known to later generations of lacrosse players as the 'father of lacrosse' (Melland 1909) on account of his having written the first British training manual (Sachs 1885). Players such as Sachs, his brother T. R. Sachs, and their friend C. L. Mason, provided continuities that lasted into the twentieth century, and members of the Thames Hare and Hounds dominated the English national teams of the mid-1870s (*Bell's Life in London*, September 9–23, 1876).

Beers's 1876 tour, lasting from May to July, thus arrived in a country familiar with lacrosse. Arriving at Derry, on the northern tip of Ireland, the tourists made their way first to Belfast, where they played at the North of Ireland Cricket Ground on Ormeau Road, and then on to Lansdowne Road in Dublin. In total, three matches were played in Ireland: in Belfast on May 11 and in Dublin on May 13 and 15. Thereafter, the team travelled to Glasgow where they played on the Caledonian Cricket Ground; and on to Sheffield, where they spent two days enthralling crowds at Bramall Lane; and finally to London. The last match played in England – although not strictly part of the tour, but added as an epilogue as evidence of its success – was played in Manchester on 27 June, two days before the tourists left Liverpool aboard the S. S. *Moravian* bound for Quebec City. They arrived home on 10 July. There can be little doubt that the tour was a success (Fisher 2002). In its wake clubs sprang up across Britain and Ireland, and lacrosse was played on a scale that was completely new.

The game grew rapidly in Scotland, where the senior club was Caledonian in Glasgow. They were soon joined by Glasgow St Vincent, Govan Lacrosse Club (Glasgow) Paisley Lacrosse Club, Perth Lacrosse Club, Ayr Academicals and Edinburgh University. There were efforts to form teams at elite public schools such as Merchiston School, Loretto School and Fettes College in Edinburgh, Park (Glasgow), and Glasgow Academy as well (*Bell's Life in London*, September 23; December 2, 23, 1876). In the north of England enjoyed a similar rise. There were teams in Newcastle, Sheffield, Leeds, Broughton near Preston, Manchester and Stockport by the end of 1876, a team formed in Bradford by the following year (*Newcastle Courant*, June 16, 1876; *Sheffield and Rotherham Independent*, June 2, 1876; *Manchester Courier*, July 6, 1876; *Bell's Life in London*, December 16, 1876: February 24, 1877). As with previous waves of lacrosse playing, London witnessed the birth of a number of clubs and vibrant competition. There were clubs in Croydon, Dulwich, Clapton, Blackheath, Roehampton and Clapham School. By the end of 1876, there were eighteen established lacrosse clubs in England, another eighteen in Scotland and five in Ireland. Indeed, Stockport Lacrosse Club, the oldest still in existence in the British Isles today, was formed in the months following the 1876 tour.

A third international tour took place in 1883. Less significant than either of the previous tours, it nonetheless added to the growing enthusiasm for the game across Britain and the sport maintained its growth. The most important influence was in areas that had yet to take up the game in earnest. Indeed, with matches played in South Wales for the first time, the 1883 tour enabled lacrosse to expand into new territory and make it a game played across the British Isles (*Weekly Mail* [Cardiff], June 9, 1883). At least two clubs were established in Wales by the late 1880s, at Pontypool and Barry (*Weekly Mail*, October 9, 1886; *Pontypool Free Press*, February 7, 1885: February 12, 1886: June 27, 1890), although both collapsed within a few years.

By the early twentieth century, lacrosse was a clear part of English sporting life with regional centres in Lancashire, Bristol, at universities such as Oxford and Manchester, and in London (Rawson 1898). Curiously, however, it disappeared in Scotland and Ireland despite its rapid growth there in the 1880s and struggled to gain a footing in Wales. In Scotland, lacrosse was reimagined as a women's game with different rules and regulations and first played at St Leonard's School in St Andrews in 1890. In Ireland, by contrast, the establishment of the Gaelic Athletic Association in 1884 and Irish cultural revival that followed saw cricket decline as a sport. Lacrosse which from its origins was symbiotically linked to Irish cricket clubs suffered the same fate. Only Wales seemed to offer fertile territory for the spread of lacrosse from its English heartlands. As Melland (1909, 10) wrote cautiously, 'it is satisfactory to find Wales coming to the fore, and available, it is hoped, for an annual international match'. That those efforts came to nil, however, is not surprising. An exhibition in 1899, for instance, was greeted with the view that 'lacrosse would never achieve anything like the popularity of football', and calls by the YMCA to take up the sport a few years later fell on deaf ears (*Cambrian*, September 29, 1899; Western *Daily Press*, November 18, 1905). Only in Cardiff (*Evening Express*, December 14, 1904) and Barry did clubs form (*Evening Express*, March 23, August 17, 1908).

In Bristol, by contrast, there was clear enthusiasm for the game. From the mid-1890s onwards, clubs were established across the city providing the basis for one of the liveliest leagues in Britain.[7] The clubs came together in 1902 to form a Joint Lacrosse Committee – later Gloucester County Lacrosse Club – which regulated the league and dealt with matters such as quality of refereeing and match disputes.[8] Of the clubs in existence in this period, the only detailed records that have survived pertain to the Merchant Venturers' Lacrosse Club, comprising students and former students of the Merchant Venturers' Technical College, and Wills' Staff Lacrosse Club. In the case of the former, it is clear that there was tension between those who felt support should be given entirely to 'national games' such as cricket and those interested in having a range of sports including lacrosse. As one member complained, 'cricket and football are looked upon as our national games, and a strong team in either would prove a greater credit to the club and college, than one at lacrosse'. But the success of the team won over the critics, and there was no substantial attempt to have lacrosse removed from the college's list of activities.[9] The Wills' team, based at company's headquarters in Bristol, was founded by four members of staff who had previously played for the Clifton Lacrosse Club. Enjoying the patronage of the firm – including its managing director Melville Wills – it was probably the most financially secure of the early Bristol clubs (*Wills' Works Magazine*, May, 1924, 11–13).[10]

Those involved in the Bristol Lacrosse clubs were undoubtedly well off and typify the character of lacrosse players in Victorian and Edwardian Britain. Alec Reginald Towerzey, one of the founding members of the Wills' Staff Lacrosse Club, for example, was the son of a pharmacist and had been educated at the elite Clifton College in Bristol, and by 1905 was the manager of the Wills tobacco factory on Redcliffe Street, Bristol. Ten years later, he had risen still further to become the general manager of the Wills' major tobacco factory in Swindon.[11] His teammate Gerald Tittle was also a clerk at the Wills factory: his career kept him in Bristol and he retained a love of lacrosse into the inter-war years serving on county committees and as a referee. He was elected to Portishead Urban District Council as an independent in 1949 (*Western Daily Press*, May 16, 1949). One of those in the Merchant Venturer's team in the city was Alfred James Margetson, a student and subsequently a lecturer in mechanical engineering at the college. He later moved to London where he was appointed lecturer in and subsequently professor of mechanical engineering at Finsbury College – in 1917 he became Dean (*Western Daily Press*, November 13, 1906; July 25, 1917). The leading light of the Bristol Lacrosse Club, Mervyn Oliver Pragnell, was equally middle class and spent his working life running Oliver Pragnell and Company, a paint and oil manufacturer situated in the Broadmead area of Bristol. He had been educated at Weymouth College, a minor public school on the south coast of England, and then took his degree at University College Bristol (*Western Daily Press*, May 30, 1949).

The above snapshot serves as a reminder that sports do not 'diffuse' in any particular pattern as they develop, but rather respond to local circumstances. At no period of lacrosse's development in Britain is it possible to describe the sport's growth as a *process* of diffusion – either from Canada to Britain and Ireland, or within the British Isles. In addition, there was no discernible spread of the game beyond its middle-class roots. In many ways, this echoes Nancy Bouchier's findings in small town Ontario. There, she writes, lacrosse was 'idealised middle-class sport for youth', it embodied 'the idea that games build character' and to be a member of a lacrosse club was to be one of a group of young men on the make. Lacrosse was a sport for clerks, civil servants, those working in commerce and business, and university students. We hear this exclusivity in Nova Scotia, too. As the *Herald* observed of Halifax (19 August 1909), it was baseball that had 'acquired a mass following' rather than lacrosse which had 'class followings'. In neither place was there the equivalent of the working-class Montreal Shamrocks, the professional Irish lacrosse club that so upset the traditional amateur ethos of the Ontarian elite (Fisher 2002).

Lacrosse, it seems fair to suggest, then, spoke to identifiable middle-class values on both sides of the Atlantic: such traits as respectability, liberalism and amateur athleticism. This is in keeping with studies of middle-class formation that argue the overriding importance of local circumstance. Indeed, as Andy Holman (2000, 7) has written of Ontario, the 'identifiable and self-identified middle class in Canada [...] derived their identities primarily from local contexts'. British lacrosse was notably strongest in manufacturing towns and port cities, those places in which the middle class consistently engaged with the wider Atlantic world and whose politics were traditionally liberal, and where, in an age of increasing commercial wealth, there were enough young men on the make to make the sport a viable one.

Basketball: Atlantic missionaries and the unemployed

In December 1931, Prince George, younger son of King George V, undertook a three-day tour of the South Wales Valleys to inspect relief work being undertaken to ameliorate the devastating economic and social impact of the Depression. Visiting unemployed clubs, parks and playing fields provided by miners' welfare schemes, and boys' clubs, he saw (in the words of a journalist for *The Times,* December 18, 1931) 'the splendid efforts [...] of self-help and social service'. In the Rhondda, the heart of the mining industry in South Wales, the prince was taken to a park in Ton Pentre that had been constructed by unemployed miners. What once had been a rubbish tip had been transformed into a park offering a wide variety of games ranging from soccer and rugby to bowls, tennis and quoits. Such were the typical sporting interests of the community. But on that day, the members of Ton Pentre Boys' Club decided to exhibit a new game that they had learned and were getting rather good at: basketball (*The Times,* December 19, 1931). Seven years later, Ton Pentre Boys' Club beat a team from London Polytechnic to win the inaugural National Junior Basketball Championship of England and Wales. In a period when established sports, particularly rugby union, suffered to the point of 'actual extinction' (Williams 1991), basketball expanded rapidly in blighted industrial areas providing rays of hope (and success) in communities otherwise stifled by economic torment and mass outmigration.

Traditionally, basketball has been written about in the context of sport's relationship with organized religion. With origins in the Young Men's Christian Association (YMCA), the narrative of muscular Christianity, which was popular across the English-speaking world at the turn of the century, is integral to our understanding of how basketball was invented and why it became a global success (Baker 2001; Putney 2001). But basketball was not exclusively propagated by the Protestant adherents of the YMCA; equally important, but typically forgotten, were missionaries of the Church of Latter Day Saints whose teams in 1930s and 1940s Rochdale, Leeds, Birmingham and Catford (south-east London) were especially prominent (Kimball 2008, 2009; *Gloucestershire Echo* March 28, 1938; *Yorkshire Post* September 16, 1938).[12] In 1947, for example, an LDS team won the English championship (*Dundee Evening Telegraph*, January 27, 1949). Basketball was also part of the Christian corporate welfare initiatives at Quaker-owned factories such as the J. S. Fry and Sons confectionary works at Keynsham or the Cadbury factory at Bourneville in Birmingham (*Fry's Works Magazine,* April 1922, 108–109).[13] And finally, beyond basketball's religious associations, there were

GLOBAL AND TRANSNATIONAL SPORT

other secular and reform-minded impulses, including the development of basketball as a sport for boys and girls through unemployed clubs and boys' and girls' clubs.

Basketball's origin story is well known. Invented by the McGill graduate and physical education teacher James Naismith, the game was first played at Springfield College, Massachusetts in December 1891. The game was formalized by Naismith in an article published in *The Triangle*, the college magazine which he edited at Springfield, on 15 January 1892. 'It fills the same place in the gymnasium that football does in the athletic field', he wrote, 'any number of men may play at it, and each one get plenty of exercise'. The value of basketball, Naismith insisted, was that it was free of the violence and roughness associated with other leading sports – notably rugby. 'If some of the rules seem unnecessarily severe', he continued, 'it will be remembered that the time to stop roughness is before it begins'. This was a game bound from the outset by gentlemanly conduct and a desire to train, through sport, a better type of athlete (Naismith 1892). Within a year of the game's introduction, it was being played at YMCA institutes across North America, or as Naismith put it in the 1893 reissue and revision of the rules 'from Nova Scotia to California'. In keeping with the ethos of the sport, Naismith noted with enthusiasm that 'it has been found particularly adapted to business and professional men' and women (Naismith 1893). To cement its place in the sporting canon of North America, Spalding's Athletic Library published a guide in 1894 (Naismith and Gulick 1894).

Basketball arrived in Britain in 1894 and gained immediate popularity amongst members of the YMCA, particularly in the south of England, as well as in the wider Protestant youth movement. Initially, members of a YMCA in places such as Sunderland, for example, were introduced to basketball by one of their members who had seen it played elsewhere, either in England or in the US (*Sunderland Daily Echo*, June 28, 1894). By 1895, it was being played informally across Britain, from Dundee in Scotland (*Dundee Courier*, May 4, 1895), to Walsall in the English Midlands (*Walsall Advertiser*, February 2, 1895), to Swansea in Wales (*Cambrian*, February 1, 1895). The game spread to Belfast in 1899 (*Belfast News-Letter*, March 3, 1899) and the rules had been printed several times in the popular *Boy's Own Magazine* (April 27, 1895; October 31, 1896).[14] When the YMCA's recreation ground in Sheffield was formally opened in June of that year, members gave a display of traditional sports such as cricket, tug of war, field athletics, but also, to the particular delight of the crowd, basketball (*Sheffield Independent* June 24, 1895). It was in Derby, however, that basketball found its surest footing: the first competitive league in the British Isles was established in the city in 1898 (*Sheffield Daily Telegraph*, May 20, 1898). At the Derby YMCA's annual meeting in 1901, the secretary reported on the sport's successful introduction noting that 'the game [...] continues to grow in popularity' (*Derby Daily Telegraph*, February 7, 1901). And the popularity and level of organization evident in Derby was soon to be matched by competitions in the south-west England and in Scotland.

When the *Taunton Courier* (April 2, 1902) reported that the town's YMCA gymnasium was the only place that basketball was played locally, it could little anticipate the development of the game over the next decade. Key to this was the spread of basketball from the YMCA to other Protestant youth organizations in the town such as the Church Lad's Brigade (CLB) and the Wesleyan Boys' Brigade, and the regional strength of the YMCA itself (*Taunton Courier*, January 13, February 3, 1904; February 8, 1905). Indeed, by 1905, the junior section of Taunton YMCA could boast three basketball teams of its own (*Taunton Courier* January 18, 1905). And in 1907, a full-fledged tournament was launched featuring the CLB and

YMCA teams (*Taunton Courier*, November 13, 1907). By 1914, it had expanded into a league (*Taunton Courier*, December 17, 1913). These developments were paralleled in Bristol and Weston-Super-Mare, as well: whereas the first competitive match between the YMCAs in the two places was held in Bristol in May 1902, basketball was already being described in the press as 'one of the favourite games with the youths' having been present in the city for at least a year (*Western Daily Press* [Bristol], December 18, 1901; March 11, May 8, 1902). Those involved in this early period established basketball as a sport played primarily by working-class and lower middle-class boys. Harry Pring, for example, a prominent member of the basketball scene in Taunton, was the son of a builder and worked for a bakery until his sudden death in 1913 (*Taunton Courier*, October 15, 1913).

As with lacrosse, there were attempts to forge a national basketball association, and this was eventually achieved in 1907 (*Nottingham Evening Post*, December 4, 1907). Notably, the British Basketball Association (BBA) was not connected with the YMCA or, indeed, any of the existing YMCA clubs, and thus represents the beginnings of secularization. That process would proceed apace after the First World War. The BBA was established through the efforts of American businessman Nelson P. Cook. Based in Newcastle in the north-east of England by this time, but previously resident in London, Cook was more widely known as an advocate of baseball (*Dundee Evening Telegraph*, November 20, 1906). Indeed, he was the honorary secretary of the London Baseball Association and the National Baseball Association when they were established in the mid-1890s (*London Standard*, February 26, 1895). Both organizations were, as Josh Chetwynd (2008, 91) notes, 'supported by hefty American resources', and Cook took on the role of organising secretary for the British Baseball Association founded in 1906 by representatives of leading soccer clubs such as Woolwich Arsenal, Tottenham Hotspur, and West Ham, and multi-sport clubs such as the London Athletics Club and the Civil Service Athletics Club (*The Times*, April 19, 1906; Bloyce 2006). Drawing on the networks established through baseball, Cook sought to develop basketball as a sport for soccer clubs, although this seems not to have occurred and the influence of the BBA appears to have been fairly minimal.[15]

In the aftermath of the First World War, basketball enjoyed a resurgence, particularly in areas of the country where it had been little played such as South Wales. The reason for this lies in the development of secular clubs for young men and boys designed to ameliorate the impact of economic stagnation and eventually depression. This was particularly acute in coal mining areas such as the north-east of England and South Wales, and it should not be surprising that it was here that basketball broke away from its muscular Christian roots. Writing to the *Spectator* on 9 August 1929, J. Glynn-Jones, secretary of the South Wales Federation of Boys' Clubs, reflected on the problem facing his native area. 'In a mono-industrial area – such as our mining valleys make up', he explained, 'the prospects of the average boy to-day are tragically poor'. For Glynn-Jones and others like him, the boys' clubs offered a means of training boys who had left school at 14 and entered a world of no mean-ingful employment. They were given further education to maintain their mental aptitude and physical training to maintain their fitness (Glynn-Jones 1933).

Basketball was first taken up in the region by members of Aberaman YMCA in 1923 and introduced soon after to the boys' club at Treharris set up by Glynn-Jones the previous year. Despite limited resources, the experiences at Treharris demonstrated the potential for the sport to achieve the aims of the boys' club movement and Glynn-Jones endeavoured to incorporate facilities as the network of clubs expanded in the 1920s and 1930s. Thus,

Nantymoel boys' club took up basketball soon after it opened in 1925, and in the 1930s teams were established at Pontypridd, Ton Pentre, Wattstown, Onllwyn and Treorchy. Apart from the club championship held at Aberaman YMCA in the mid-1920s (*Aberdare Leader*, July 25, 1925), all local basketball competitions before 1946 were run through the South Wales Federation of Boys' Clubs, signifying the importance of that organization to the development of basketball in Wales (Anonymous 1948). One of the few clubs to emerge not associated with the boys' clubs or the YMCA was that established at the University College of South Wales and Monmouthshire, Cardiff, in 1940. Although its activities were impacted by the Second World War, the presence of American troops in Cardiff from 1942 provided students with the opportunity to learn modern playing techniques.

After the war, having adopted an American style of play, the university came to dominate the Welsh Amateur Basketball League, displacing Ton Pentre as the leading Welsh team. They took pride in being able to compete strongly with the generally all-American varsity sides at Oxford and Cambridge, and as a consequence of the relatively high profile that basketball achieved, membership of its committee was seen as a valuable commodity when running for students' union president (*Broadsheet*, February, 1951).[16] What is apparent, however, is a different style of play amongst these 'gentleman amateurs' at the university and the coalfield clubs that they competed against in the Welsh league, prompting regular complaints from the students (*Broadsheet*, November–December, 1950). As one journalist for the student newspaper, *Broadsheet*, reflected in 1950:

> Playing up the valley, this 'no contact' game is enlivened – on one occasion one of our men found himself carrying an opponent on his back; another got tired of having his nose hit instead of the ball. Playing other universities is mild after these games (*Broadsheet*, June, 1950).

Given these comments, it is perhaps ironic that the post-war period saw a sustained 'Americanisation' of basketball in the South Wales Valleys. In an era of skiffle bands, jive clubs, and eventually rock and roll, basketball had an air of modernity and was more comfortably in keeping with the universal aspects of Anglo-American youth culture than soccer or rugby. The under-16 basketball team at Ton Pentre Boys' Club even went so far as to adopt the moniker 'comets' in honour of Bill Hailey (*Pontypridd Observer*, June 11, 1960)!

Conclusion: of diffusion, cultural exchange and glocalization

The sporting trajectories of lacrosse and basketball in the nineteenth and twentieth centuries, like those of other sports such as ice hockey, cricket, rugby, soccer and baseball, highlight the centrality of the North Atlantic borderland to the internationalization of sport in the industrial age. What we have suggested here in our two case studies of lacrosse and basketball was that there is no clear process of diffusion from a central metropolitan location outward to peripheral areas. Rather sporting traditions traversed the oceanic borderlands as part of a multidirectional process of cultural exchange. Imagined in this way, the spread of sport across oceanic pathways is a fruitful subject for inquiry, just as it is in other borderland locations. Lacrosse, for example, made its way to Australia in the last quarter of the nineteenth century and from there it found its way to South Africa. It is thus not surprising that the most energetic lacrosse promoter on Canada's Pacific coast at the turn of the twentieth century, Con Jones, had learned the game in Australia and brought an interest in developing it with him to Vancouver. There are many other instances of peripatetic lives as sporting enthusiasts traversed the oceans and contributed to the cross-fertilization of sporting culture. We need to be more attentive to biographies of this sort since they offer us an indication of how various sports were received, adapted and survived or failed owing to particular local circumstances.

If oceanic borderlands were a primary site of cultural exchange and the spread of sport from the mid-nineteenth century until the Second World War, it is also important to acknowledge how modern communication technologies have driven us towards our contemporary global sporting culture. Although we have not addressed changes that have taken place in the post-industrial age in this article, we have at least hinted at a process of transition from cultural exchange in an oceanic borderland towards the globalizing influence of our present day virtual universe. Whatever period we study, however, it is fair to say that the process of internationalization is not simply a process by which metropolitan influences determine life on the periphery. Rather ours is a 'glocalized' world where metropolitan power is shaped to meet the requirements of local experience, and where people on the ground still have agency to mediate the process of cultural exchange in ways that make sense to them.

Notes

1. The idea of 'borderlands', both as geographical spaces and as an analytical framework for studying transnational cultural and historical development, was first articulated by American historian Herbert Bolton. In an address to the American Historical Association in 1932, Bolton presented his borderland thesis as an alternative to chauvinistic histories of national 'exceptionalism'. He called (1933, 448–478) instead for a comprehensive history of the Western Hemisphere within which 'each national history is but a thread of a larger strand'. Despite a growing interest in borders and borderland relations – evident in a flourishing scholarly literature, in journals such as the *Journal of Borderland Studies*, and collaborative international research initiatives such as the Borders in Globalization project headed by Emmanuel Brunet-Jailly and Victor Konrad – it is fair to say that most borderlands scholarship has focused on the south-western American borderlands. Bolton's hope that a borderlands approach could be employed in other transnational contexts and geographical spaces and as an alternative to histories of the nation state has yet to be fully realized. Nor has its utility as an approach to sport history been seriously entertained.
2. 'Glocalization' is a hybrid term which addresses the relationship of 'local' communities to 'global' processes. Sociologist Roland Robertson employed the term in order to emphasize the agency of peoples at the local level, responding to globalizing influences in ways that reinforce local cultural traditions and possibilities (Maguire 2011a, 2011b; Robertson 1995).
3. Akwesasne is itself a borderland nation, straddling the US–Canadian border and the provincial boundaries of Ontario and Quebec along the St Lawrence River.
4. They played again at the Crystal Palace on throughout August, as well as at the Metropolitan Cricket Ground, Islington, on 12 August and Kennington Oval, Lambeth, on 15 August. They played at Lord's Cricket Ground on the 17 August (*Bell's Life in London*, August 10, 1867; *Morning Post*, August 15, 19, 1867).
5. Efforts to set up a club in Brighton, however, came to nothing (*Brighton Gazette*, November 28, 1867).
6. The Canadian rules were, however, published in Britain in 1867, and a copy is held at the British Library in London.
7. These were Bristol Lacrosse Club (1896), Clifton Lacrosse Club (1897), Fairfield Lacrosse Club (1899), Wills Staff (1901), Merchant Venturers' (1903), Eastville (1905), Durdham Down (1905) and Keynsham (1907) (*Western Daily Press*, October 8, 1896; October 21 1901; December 21, 1904; November 5, 1905).
8. Bristol Record Office, Mervyn Pragnell Papers, 42,952/PP/2/3: *Minute Book of the Joint Lacrosse Committee, 1902–1904*.

9. Bristol Record Office, Society of Merchant Venturers Records, SMV/5/5/8/2, *Old Merchant Venturers' Club, Minute Book, 1902–1906*, 41, 58.
10. A complete set of this magazine is held at Bristol Central Library.
11. These details draw on his company biography. Bristol Record Office, Wills' Tobacco Company Records, 38169/Ph/B/99: A. R. Towerzey.
12. Brigham Young University Archives, Utah, MS 10615: Brigham Spencer Young (1913–2004), *Scrapbook and Correspondence, 1935–1938*.
13. The factory's basketball league was sponsored by Claude B. Fry. A complete set of the *Fry's Works Magazine* is held at Bristol Central Library.
14. The first competitive match in Scotland took place in Dundee in February 1897, although it 'did not appeal so much to the spectators as the national pastime'. (*Dundee Courier*, February 4, 8, 1897).
15. Although after the Second World War, there was good relationship between basketball and soccer. Members of Cardiff City FC, for example, were a strong force in the Welsh Amateur Basketball League of the 1940s and 1950s (*Derby Daily Telegraph*, February 11, 1949).
16. The candidate was David Reeves, a 24-year-old arts student who had been secretary of the basketball club 1949–1950. A complete run of *Broadsheet*, the student newspaper for University College Cardiff in the 1950s is held at Cardiff University's Special Collections and Archives.

Disclosure statement

No potential conflict of interest was reported by the authors.

References

Anonymous. 1948. *Basketball in Wales*. Cardiff: Welsh Amateur Basketball Committee.
Armitage, David. 2002. "Three Concepts of Atlantic History." In *The British Atlantic World, 1500–1800*, edited by David Armitage and Michael J. Braddick, 11–27. New York: Palgrave Macmillan.
Armitage, David, and Michael J. Braddick, eds. 2002. *The British World, 1500–1800*. New York: Palgrave Macmillan.
Baker, William J. 2001. *Playing with God: Religion and Modern Sport*. Cambridge, MA: Harvard University Press.
Bhabha, Homi. 1994. *The Location of Culture*. London: Routledge.
Bloyce, Daniel. 2005. "That's Your Way of Playing Rounders Isn't it? The Response of the English Press to American Baseball Tours to England, 1874–1924." *Sporting Traditions* 22 (1): 81–98.
Bloyce, Daniel. 2006. "A Very Peculiar Practice: The London Baseball League, 1906–1911. "*Nine: A Journal of Baseball History and Culture* 14 (2): 118–128.
Bolton, Herbert E. 1933. "The Epic of Greater America." *The American Historical Review* 38 (3): 448–474.
Brown, David. 1987. "Canadian Imperialism and Sporting Exchanges: The Nineteenth-century Cultural Experience of Cricket and Lacrosse." *Canadian Journal of the History of Sport* 18: 55–66.
Buckner, Phillip, and R. Douglas Francis, eds. 2006. *Rediscovering the British World*. Calgary: University of Alberta Press.
Buckner, Phillip, and R. Douglas Francis, eds. 2007. *Canada and the British World: Culture, Migration, and Identity*. Vancouver: UBC Press.
Careless, J. M. S. 1954. "Frontierism, Metropolitanism and Canadian History." *Canadian Historical Review* 35 (1): 1–21.
Careless, J. M. S. 1990. *Careless at Work: Selected Canadian Historical Studies*. Toronto: Dundurn Press.
Chetwynd, Josh. 2008. *Baseball in Europe: A Country by Country History*. Jefferson, MO: McFarland.
Downey, Allan. 2012. "Engendering Nationality: Haudenosaunee Tradition, Sport, and the Lines of Gender." *Journal of the Canadian Historical Association* 23 (1): 319–354.

Duinen, Jared van. 2013. "Playing to the 'Imaginary Grandstand': Sport, the 'British world', and an Australian Colonial Identity." *Journal of Global History* 8 (2): 342–364.

Duinen, Jared van. 2014. "The Borderlands of the British World." *Journal of Colonialism and Colonial History* 15 (1).

Dyreson, Mark, J. A. Mangan, and Robert Park, eds. 2012. *Mapping an Empire of American Sport: Expansion, Assimilation, Adaptation and Resistance*. London: Routledge.

Falola, Toyin, and Kevin David Roberts, eds. 2008. *The Atlantic World, 1450–2000*. Bloomington, IL: Indiana University Press.

Fisher, Donald M. 2002. *Lacrosse: A History of the Game*. Baltimore, MD: Johns Hopkins University Press.

Forsyth, Janice, and Kevin B. Wamsley. 2006. "Native to Native…We'll Recapture Our Spirits: The World Indigenous Nations Games and North American Indigenous Games as Cultural Resistance." *The International Journal of the History of Sport* 23 (2): 294–314.

Glynn-Jones, John. 1933. "Boys' Clubs and Camps." *In The Welsh Outlook* 20 (8): 214–217.

Guttmann, Allen. 1978. *From Ritual to Record: The Nature of Modern Sports*. New York: Columbia University Press.

Guttmann, Allen. 1994. *Games and Empires: Modern Sports and Cultural Imperialism*. New York: Columbia University Press.

Harper, Marjory, and Michael Easton Vance, eds. 1999. *Myth, Migration and the Making of Memory, Scotia and Nova Scotia*. Halifax: Fernwood.

Holman, Andrew C. 2000. *A Sense of their Duty: Middle-class Formation in Victorian Ontario Towns*. Montreal: McGill-Queen's University Press.

Hornsby, Stephen, and John G. Reid, eds. 2005. *New England and the Maritime Provinces: Connections and Comparisons*. Montreal: McGill-Queen's University Press.

Howell, Colin, and Daryl Leeworthy. 2010. "Borderlands." In *The Routledge Companion to Sports History*, edited by S. W. Pope and John Nauright, 71–84. London: Routledge.

Howell, Colin, and Richard Twomey, eds. 1991. *Jack Tar in History: Essays in the History of Maritime Life and Labour*. Fredericton: Acadiensis Press.

Kimball, Richard. 2008. "Muscular Mormonism." *The International Journal of the History of Sport* 25 (5): 549–578.

Kimball, Richard Ian. 2009. *Sports in Zion: Mormon Recreation, 1890–1940*. Chicago: University of Illinois Press.

Leeworthy, Daryl. 2015. "Skating on the Border: Hockey, Class, and Commercialism in Interwar Britain." *Histoire Sociale/Social History* 48 (96): 193–213.

Maguire, Joseph. 2011a. "Globalization and Sport: Beyond the Boundaries." *Sociology* 45 (5): 923–929.

Maguire. Joseph. 2011b. "Globalization, sport and national identities." *Sport in Society* 14 (7–8): 978–993.

Mckay, Ian. 2000. "The Liberal Order Framework: A Prospectus for a Reconnaissance of Canadian History." *Canadian Historical Review* 81 (4): 616–678.

Melland, Norman. 1909. *How to Play Lacrosse*. Manchester, NH: Self Published.

Naismith, James. 1892. *Rules for Basket Ball*. Springfield, MA: Springfield Printing and Binding Company.

Naismith, James. 1893. *Rules for Basket Ball*. Springfield, MA: The Triangle Publishing Company.

Naismith, James, and Luther Gulick. 1894. *Basket Ball*. New York: American Sports Publishing Company.

Nielsen, Erik. 2014. *Sport and the British World, 1900–1930: Amateurism and National Identity in Australia*. New York: Palgrave Macmillan.

Paxson, Frederick L. 1917. "The Rise of Sport." *The Mississippi Valley Historical Review* 4 (2): 143–168.

Phillips, Murray G. 2001. "Diminishing Contrasts and Increasing Varieties: Globalization Theory and Amateurism in Australian Sport." *Sporting Traditions* 18 (1): 19–32.

Pope, Steven. 2007. "Rethinking Sport, Empire and American Exceptionalism." *Sport History Review* 38 (2): 92–120.

Poulter, Gillian. 2003. "Snowshoeing and Lacrosse: Canada's Nineteenth-century 'National Games.'" *Culture, Sport, Society* 6 (2–3): 293–320.

Poulter, Gillian. 2009. *Becoming Native in a Foreign Land: Sport, Visual Culture and National Identity, Montreal 1840–1885*. Vancouver: UBC Press.

Putney, Clifford. 2001. *Muscular Christianity: Manhood and Sports in Protestant America, 1880–1920*. Cambridge, MA: Harvard University Press.

Rawson, W. Stepney. 1898. "Lacrosse: How, When and Where to See It." *The Badminton Magazine of Sports and Pastimes* 6 (32): 332–345.

Rediker, Marcus. 1987. *Between the Devil and the Deep Blue Sea: Merchant Seamen, Pirates and the Anglo-American World, 1700–1750*. Cambridge: Cambridge University Press.

Reid, John, H. V. Bowen, and Elizabeth Mancke, eds. 2012. *Britain's Oceanic Empire: Atlantic and Indian Ocean Worlds, 1550–1850*. Cambridge University Press: Cambridge.

Reid, John, and Robert Reid. 2015. "Diffusion and Discursive Stablilization: Sports Historiography and Contrasting Fortunes of Cricket and Hockey in Canada's Maritime Provinces, 1869–1914." *Journal of Sport History* 42 (1): 87–113.

Robertson, Roland. 1995. "Glocalization: Time-space and Homogeneity-heterogeneity." In *Global Modernities*, edited by Mike Featherstone, Scott Lash, and Roland Robertson, 25–44. London: Sage.

Robidoux, Michael A. 2002. "Imagining a Canadian Identity Through Sport: A Historical Interpretation of Lacrosse and Hockey." *The Journal of American Folklore* 115 (456): 209–225.

Robinson, Mark H. 1868. *La'Crosse*. London: Frederick Warne.

Sachs, E. T. 1885. *Lacrosse for Beginners*. London: Wright and Company.

Sager, Eric. 1989. *Seafaring Labour: The Merchant Marine of Atlantic Canada, 1820–1914*. Montreal: McGill-Queen's University Press.

Sager, Eric. 1993. *Ships and Memories: Merchant Seafarers in Canada's Age of Steam*. Vancouver: UBC Press.

Said, Edward. 1979. *Orientalism*. New York: Random House.

Schlesinger, Arthur M. 1940. "The City in American History." *The Mississippi Valley Historical Review* 27 (1): 43–66.

Steele, Ian K. 1986. *The English Atlantic, 1675–1740: An Exploration of Communication and Community*. Oxford: Oxford University Press.

Van Bottenburg, Maarten. 2010. "Beyond Diffusion: Sport and Its Remaking in Cross-cultural Contexts." *Journal of Sport History* 37 (1): 41–54.

Wade, Richard C. 1959. *The Urban Frontier: The Rise of Western Cities, 1790–1830*. Cambridge, MA: Harvard University Press.

Williams, Gareth. 1991. *1905 and All That: Essays on Rugby Football, Sport and Welsh Society*. Llandysul: Gomer Press.

The intercultural transfer of football: the contexts of Germany and Argentina

Thomas Adam

ABSTRACT
Historians of sport have paid little attention to the ways in which modern sports such as football were transferred from its place of origin to receiving cultures around the globe. While it is recognized that this ball game emerged in nineteenth-century English public schools, little is known about the transformations this game underwent in becoming modern-day German football and modern-day Argentine football. Applying the model of intercultural transfer, my contribution will investigate the process of the transfer of this ball game from English public schools to German and Argentine high schools. The emergence of football and its transfer across the world was carried out by teachers and students and it was part of educational reform since this game offered an alternative to the traditional ways of imposing discipline. Discipline did not come from an outside force such as the teacher but from the rules of the game. This game, further, encouraged team work in order to achieve victory and offered sons of middle-class families an introduction into the mechanisms of the capitalist market. The introduction of soccer into urbanizing cultures was also part of social hygiene debates and many of the protagonists of this game were also involved in social reform debates about improving the quality of living in modern cities.

Football is undoubtedly a global phenomenon. Yet, historians have studied the emergence of football nearly exclusively within the narrow framework of nation states and with an eye on the construction of national cultures and national identities (Eisenberg 1997). While such an approach certainly enriched our understanding of the construction of national identities and the place of sports within it, it ignored the causes and the context for the global spread of football and its integration into local (but not national) cultures and social milieus across the globe.

Football was born as a modern sport at English public schools in the 1860s. While it was British and non-British teachers and students who transferred the game into high schools across continental Europe and South America, it was soldiers and a few administrators who brought the game to the British colonies in Africa and Asia (Hill, Vincent, and Curtner-Smith 2014; Eisenberg 1997). In continental Europe and in South America, the introduction of football was intended to improve education and contribute to school reform. After it was introduced as a teaching subject to make education more attractive and to create self-discipline among students, football quickly became a popular pastime for high-school students. This transfer was followed by the nationalization of the sport which was reinvented as an intrinsic element of national identities such as the Argentine and German identity. Its English roots were increasingly obscured and national narratives that constructed Argentine and German roots of football were invented. In the course of the twentieth century, international football matches pitted national teams against each other and the game often took on overtly nationalistic tones. The matches were portrayed in terms of war and national honour. This nationalistic climate stripped football of its transnational and global roots. The hiding of these transnational roots went hand in hand with the internationalization of football that resulted in international matches and even the creation of international football organizations.[1]

To force the history of football into the straitjacket of the nation state and to ignore the intercultural transfer of football in the nineteenth century that connected high schools at localities as far away as Rio de Janeiro and Buenos Aires with the public school at Eton artificially creates borders where there were none. It further removes the game of football from the transnational context of school reform and the discourse about urban hygiene in the last decades of the nineteenth century in which football was just one aspect among others. This article will tell the story of football not from a comparative point of view but from the point of transfer studies (Adam 2012; Adam 2013; Werner and Zimmerman 2006). The focus is on the intercultural transfer of football from English public schools to high schools in Buenos Aires (Argentina) and Braunschweig (Germany). It will explore the reasons which made this game so attractive to nineteenth-century educators and social reformers and it will, further, discuss the integration of football into urban subcultures that were defined by economic aspects in the case of Argentina and by politic orientations in the case of Germany. Historians of football have all too often overlooked the deep divisions in nineteenth-century societies which resulted in the creation of these subcultures. Football became part of these subcultures rather than of a national or even regional culture. In the case of Germany, a Socialist football culture emerged side by side to a Conservative football culture. This division was forcefully destroyed only in 1933 with Adolf Hitler's ascension to power and the destruction of the Socialist subculture.

The concept of transnational history and intercultural transfer studies

This article builds upon the concept of transnational history which represents a counter-model to the paradigm of national history (Adam 2013; Saunier 2013). Rather than seeing history as a function of nation states and only in its national variants, transnational history considers history as a universal and global project. The concept of intercultural transfer is based upon the fundamental belief that humans live in an interconnected world. Instead of researching and writing the history of a particular phenomenon within the confines of a given nation state, transnational history encourages historians to follow a particular phenomenon wherever it leads us. The space of our account is not determined by the imagined and constructed spaces ascribed to particular nations (Anderson 2006; Hobsbawn 1992), but rather by the transfer of the game of football which created its own space. Within this space of football, different 'provinces' emerged since the game and its rules were modified in the process of intercultural transfer (Adam 2012). These provinces were defined by particular football rules and practices. They grew over time and 'annexed' neighbouring provinces through the creation of rules and regulations that could be accepted in several places since football relied on the need to have an opposing team for a football match. The need to facilitate such matches increased the desire to create standards for the game that extended beyond a particular locality or province of football. One should not, however, infer that the necessity to stage matches automatically led to the creation of national football spaces and international matches. The example of Germany in particular will make very clear that the spaces that emerged from the standardization of football rules did not always result in national spaces, but rather in spaces that were defined by sociopolitical conditions and which did not coincide with national spaces.

Processes of the transfer of material and immaterial goods between different cultures have increasingly been studied by historians in the last three decades. However, historians have all too hastily employed a terminology of copying, influencing and modelling to label these processes. Many historians still embrace concepts of diffusion – of which the notion of Americanization is the most prominent – to conceptualize such transfers (Hill, Vincent, and Curtner-Smith 2014; Rogers 1995). Yet, neither of the terms of copying or modelling nor the idea of diffusion grasps the complexity of the processes of intercultural transfer. They mistake transfers to be one-way roads; they wrongly strip the receiving culture of all agency; and they wrongly infer that the product transferred and received in the receiving culture is identical to the product in the giving culture. Such concepts simply cannot explain the conundrum of the modern world that the world becomes more similar and more dissimilar at the same time (Kroes 2002; Rodgers 1998).

If we study intercultural transfers closely and attentively, we will see that phenomena transferred from one culture to another experienced significant mutations and transformations that occurred in the process of transfer and which were determined by the actions of the agents of transfer as well as the needs and expectations of the receiving culture. Intercultural transfers occurred because of a need to fill a perceived gap in the receiving culture. Transfers were often accompanied by a discourse in which the giving culture was described as being superior. However, the giving culture had no or a very limited role in the process of transfer beyond presenting a phenomenon for selection. Agents of transfers almost always came from the receiving culture and had some connection to the giving culture. The phenomenon selected for transfer experienced significant transformations and it was made to fit into the receiving society by members of that society. The fitting into the receiving society was often done in ways that the origins of the transferred phenomenon were almost obscured and members of the receiving culture began to believe over time that this phenomenon had always been part of their culture and history (Adam 2012).

The intercultural transfer of football and the nationalization of football

The transfer of football was closely connected with educational reform and involved the activities of teachers and students who acted on their own volition and not on the orders of governments and states. The individuals involved in the intercultural transfer of football were later stylized as founding fathers of this sport for their respective nations. These founding fathers and the introduction of football became the subject of elaborate myths, and legends were created. In the case of Argentina, it was Alexander Watson Hutton (1853–1936) who was embraced as the founding father of Argentine football. Born in Glasgow (Scotland),

Hutton graduated from the University of Edinburgh and then moved to Buenos Aires in 1882 in order to become the headmaster of St. Andrews School. This high school was an educational institution for English families living in Argentina. In 1884, he founded with the English High School his own educational institution, which served the English community of that growing capital (Archetti 1997; Blakeslee 2014; Mason 1995).

In the case of Brazil, the story of introduction is more complicated and involves English as well as German actors. However, most accounts credit two individuals – Charles Miller and Oscar Cox – with the introduction of this sport. Charles William Miller (1874–1953), who was born to Scottish–English parents living in Brazil, was sent to school in Southampton (England). When he returned to his home country to work for the Sao Paulo Railway Company in 1894, he brought a football with him to Sao Paulo. Oscar Cox (1880–1931), who was also born to English parents living in Brazil, was sent to attending a high school in Lausanne (Switzerland). It was here that he first experienced playing football. Upon his return to Rio de Janeiro, he brought the ball game with him (Caldas 1997; Mason 1995; Rispler 2012).

Traditional accounts of German football credit Konrad Koch (1846–1911) with introducing football to Germany. Koch began upon graduation from the University of Leipzig in 1868, a career as a teacher of the classic languages at the Gymnasium Martino-Katharineum in Braunschweig. Here, he has been said to have introduced the game of football into the school curriculum (Hoffmeister 2011; Oberschelp 2010). Yet the sources of Koch's knowledge of the game and its various versions are unclear. Koch never travelled to England. He did not participate in the everyday life of an English colony of which there were so many across Southern and Central Germany, such as in the cities of Stuttgart and Dresden. Little is known about his university education, which he obtained at the universities at Göttingen, Berlin and Leipzig. His major subjects were theology and Latin and Greek philology. His only contact with English culture and education was a thesis he wrote in the field of pedagogy about Thomas Arnold. It seems that this thesis caused Koch to become interested in the inclusion of sports into the high-school curriculum (Hoffmeister 2011).

Koch claimed, according to Kurt Hoffmeister, to have learned about football from reading various reports of German travellers such as J. A. Voigt, Karl Hillebrand and Ludwig Wiese who observed the English school system during their travels in England in the 1850s and the 1870s (Hillebrand 1876; Hoffmeister 2011; Voigt 1857; Wiese 1852). However, these travel reports, presumably utilized by Koch, did neither provide extensive descriptions of ball games at public schools nor did they embrace these games as a model for German education. Wiese in particular wrote with great dismay about the practice of games among English high-school students. He even suggested that engaging in these games led to a disproportional strengthening of arm muscles at the expense of muscle formation in legs. To improve the health of young students, Wiese advocated the introduction of gymnastics into English high-school curricula rather than the introduction of sports into German high school curricula (Wiese 1852).

It seems more likely that Koch who had also enjoyed reading Thomas Hughes book *Tom Brown's Schooldays* found a more favourable account of sports in this particular book. The first German translation of Hughes' book (1867) was produced by Ernst Wagner, who also authored a report about the English school system that appeared in 1864 (Wagner 1864). However, Wagner seemed to have shared Wiese's attitude with regard to the place of sports in school education. Instead of providing a favourable account of the inclusion of sport into English school curricula, Wagner cited in his book several English manufacturers and entrepreneurs who praised gymnastics and military exercises for preparing students for the industrial workforce. Gymnastics and military exercises improved, according to the cited statements made by English industrialists, the ability of individuals for collaboration and conformity. Both characteristics appeared, according to Wagner's account, highly desirable among English businessmen (Wagner 1864). In his annotated translation of *Tom Brown's Schooldays*, Wagner inserted in the chapter that provided the famous description of a football game at Rugby a lengthy footnote explaining the rules of football as it was presumably played at Rugby. In this footnote, Wagner wrongfully insisted that players were allowed to use only their feet to kick the ball. The use of hands was, according to Wagner, ruled out (Hughes 1867).

Miller and Cox were – just as Koch – born and grew up in the space to which they transferred football. They had been born in Brazil but because of their parents who had migrated from England to South America, they had a connection to England. They were also raised within English language and culture and sent to obtain education in Europe. In contrast to Koch who never travelled abroad and who obtained his education in his home country, Miller and Cox had first-hand experience of the game in a place other than their place of birth. And while Miller experienced football in its English cradle, Cox witnessed already the first wave of intercultural transfer that brought the game to the European continent. Miller's actions, thus, resulted in a primary transfer of football. Cox's advocacy for football upon his return from Lausanne to Rio de Janeiro represented a secondary transfer of football.

The story of Hutton's introduction of football to the English high schools of Buenos Aires differs markedly from the other two transfers. Hutton – in contrast to Koch, Miller and Cox – did not grow up in the place – here Buenos Aires – to which he introduced football. Instead he grew up in Scotland and migrated to Argentina after he finished his university training. Hutton made that city his new home and continuously taught at English high schools of that city. However, he did not bring the game to indigenous students but to the English enclave in Buenos Aires. His goal was not the introduction of football to Argentine society but to the English schools in Buenos Aires.

These three cases represent three different types of contact: (1) The first type of contact was established through the reading of travel reports that contained observations of the English educational system, written by non-English observers who belonged to the receiving society. In this case, the agent of intercultural transfer had no direct first-hand encounter with football in its place of origin. (2) The second type of contact was arranged through travel as part of the education of the individual who also acted as agent of intercultural transfer. In this case, the agent had a direct first-hand experience with the game at its birthplace or a secondary location to which it had already successfully been transferred. (3) The third type of contact was established through relocation of the agent of intercultural transfer, who was a member of the giving society, from the giving society to the receiving society. While such relocation and the origin of the agent in the giving society in particular prove almost always detrimental to the success of the transfer of a phenomenon from one society to another, it can in rare and exceptional cases such as this one facilitate such a transfer.

Foreign roots and the involvement in the creation of a national sport of individuals who were not members of the receiving society were either written out of history or reinvented by increasingly nationalistic accounts of this sport. The English roots of German football, to take just one prominent example, were already hidden by Konrad Koch who saw them as an obstacle to the acceptance of football in an increasingly nationalistic German culture. Over time, these agents of intercultural transfer became the subject of the formation of legends. They were turned into the founding fathers of national sports and they became the centre of stories about the beginnings of football in their respective countries. In some cases, they even were made the focus of popular movies such as the movie *Escuela de Campeones* (School of Champions), made in Peron-era Argentina in 1950 and the German movie *Der Ganz Grosse Traum* (Lessons of a Dream) made in the post-national era in 2011.

Escuela de Campeones reflects the stereotypical national re-interpretation of the birth of football in any particular nation. Made in the Peron era, it was to provide the Argentine audiences with a patriotic reading of their glorious past history and to bolster national identity and self-confidence. The story is severely tweaked in that Hutton does not appear as an English outsider but rather as an agent of the Argentine state. Instead of acting on his own, Hutton is shown asking the minister of education Domingo Sarmiento (who had previously been president of that country from 1868 to 1874) for permission to found his new high school in 1884 and to introduce football into the curriculum of that school. The deal is sealed with a handshake between Sarmiento and Hutton. This symbolic scene places the English High School within the context of the development of the Argentine school system. Rather than understanding Hutton's school as an extension of the English school system replicated in Argentina, it becomes the first successful Argentine public school.

Further, after a tragic accident – an English student is killed during a game against the team from St. Andrews (the first English high school at which Hutton taught when he moved to Buenos Aires) – the fate of Hutton's school seems to be in peril. It causes the English students to leave the school, which forced Hutton to consider closing his school. Abandoned by the English, the survival of the school is saved by Diego Brown who brings a dozen boys of Hispanic origin whom he calls 'sons of Argentina'. Not only did the admission of these boys into Hutton's school keep the school open but it was their participation in the football team that earned the English High School its decade-long dominance. The movie, thus, reinvents Hutton as an agent of the nascent Argentine nation and his school as the beginning of the national school system which is populated with Argentine rather than English pupils.

The German film *Der Ganz Grosse Traum*, made six decades later and in an environment in which nation states and national master narratives have lost some of their attraction, does neither hide the English roots of the game nor the English influence that clashed with the nationalist climate at German high schools in the Wilhelmine Empire. The story is focused exclusively on Koch who is portrayed as a rebellious teacher who refused to use corporal punishment to discipline students and instead tried to make learning fun. He is, further, reinvented as an English teacher who had just returned from his training in Great Britain and who is in charge of introducing modern languages to the high school in Braunschweig. The football was part of his luggage when he arrived in Braunschweig.

These stories about the arrival of football in any national culture were often from the beginning worked into the national (hi)stories under construction. The English origins of football were in the process increasingly written out of history. The intercultural transfer of football from English to German high schools occurred after all in the last third of the nineteenth century and, thus, at a time, when national history and identities took increasingly root within the German population. Foreign ideas were not necessarily welcomed and phenomena such as football had to be disguised as a truly German invention. Koch felt compelled to argue in his book *Die Geschichte des Fußballs im Altertum und in der Neuzeit* (1983) that football was not an English game, but that it had been played across continental Europe already in the Middle Ages. He, further, argued that no nation could claim to have invented football but that it was rather an European phenomenon, in which Germans had participated already in earlier centuries. Koch had realized that he needed to win over German nationalists to secure the success of football in German society (Damm 2007). This tendency to write out of history the English origin of that sport and instead portray the sport of football as a game that originated within the space claimed as cradle of the German nation reflects a main characteristic of the model of intercultural transfer. While the modern world is based upon intercultural transfers that reflected the interconnected nature of the human experience, these connections were often hidden by agents of transfer in order to facilitate the smooth transfer of practices such as football across hardening national borders (Adam 2012).

In order to turn the English game of football into a German game, Koch had to translate and thereby reinvent the rules of the game. He also needed to create a terminology for this new game, which initially combined the rules of rugby from the Public School at Rugby and association football from the Public School at Eton since Koch decided to adopt the rules of the Public School at Marlborough, which represented a mix of both (Koch 1983). Koch initially favoured, according to his colleague August Hermann, rules that allowed the use of hands in order to propel the ball. However, since his colleagues preferred the game that favoured kicking the ball over throwing the ball, Koch gave in and developed rules that prohibited the use of hands in the game (Hermann 1895). In 1875, Koch published his first set of rules for playing football at the high school in Braunschweig. The game was, according to these rules, created as a winter game. During the winter season, students met for bi-weekly games. The playing field had two goals on opposite sides and it was the purpose of the game for each team to hit the ball above the goal line (which was 3.5 m above the ground). The players were allowed to use only their feet to hit the ball. The ball could only be handled if it was thrown back to the goal of the defending team. Koch introduced the 'Abseits' rule according to which all players of one team had to be between their goal line and the ball. No player was allowed to be in front of the ball. And Koch insisted on fair play. All beating and tripping was banned. Games lasted for one hour with a change of sides after 30 minutes. The team with the highest number of points was declared as victor. Victory was determined by the number of points each team had reached. Twenty points were given for hitting the ball over the goal line but between the two supporting pillars. Five points were awarded for each attempted goal. The game introduced in Braunschweig represented a combination of the football played at Rugby (shape of goals) and the football played at Eton (kicking of the ball) (Hoffmeister 2010; Koch 1875; Oberschelp 2010).

In order to Germanize the game, Koch attempted to translate all technical terms from English into German. Team was translated with Gespielschaft (group of friends). The team captain was translated with Spielkaiser (game emperor), which reflected an overzealously monarchical and nationalist attitude, which might not have been received well since emperor could refer only to one person at the head of the state. Halfback was translated with Markmann, Offside with Abseits, and Tripping with Beinstellen. Some of these translations caught on quickly such as Abseits; others were translated multiple times before a term was found that appealed to a broad audience. The goal was, for instance, first translated as Mal which referred to a border marking. After a net was added to the goal posts, it was replaced with Tor (gate). And Gespielschaft which reminded too much of harmony and gymnastics was finally replaced by Mannschaft (Damm 2007; Heineken 1993; Hoffmeister 2011).

While individuals such as Koch and Hutton certainly played an important role in popularizing the sport of football in their respective countries and took key roles in establishing norms, regulations and teams, they were not solely responsible for the intercultural transfer of football. Koch acted together with other individuals who had, in contrast to him, first-hand knowledge of the game of football and both educators were not the only ones who introduced the game to a particular culture. Industrialization, trade and shipping, and travel played an important part in the intercultural transfer of football. In Germany, it was the English colonies that had sprung up in cities such as Karlsruhe, Baden-Baden, Stuttgart and Dresden where rugby and football was first played in the 1860s and 1870s (Broschkowski and Schneider 2005; Eisenberg 1997; Heineken 1993). The ball game often remained, however, an activity within these English communities and did not transfer into the surrounding society. William Cail, who became president of the Rugby Football Union in 1892, reminisced:

> My recollections then carry me to the valley of the Neckar, where many of us English lads, some from the public schools finishing education at Stuttgart, some at the schools at Cannstatt used to meet weekly and play our Rugby game,…. (Heineken 1993, 236)

Industrialization caused the mobility of many English labourers, engineers, miners and their families around the globe and games such as football travelled with them. The introduction of football from these English expatriates was limited since the representatives of the giving culture supposedly had strange rules and spoke an even stranger language. Only after these rules had been translated and thereby nationalized – as in the case of Koch – did the game of football have success in being accepted from among the members of the receiving culture. The intercultural transfer of football into a culture was, however, not the action of a single individual. It was also not a one-time event. Football was introduced several times in several places by members of the giving and receiving culture. Multiple versions of the sport – rugby and association football – were introduced and presented to a particular culture. These transfers occurred within the English diaspora that included English communities in cities such as Stuttgart and Buenos Aires and it facilitated the transfer of this game from within the spaces created by the English diaspora into their surrounding urban environments.

Even if one ignores the multiple entry points of football into German society (Hesse-Lichtenberger 2003), it can hardly be contended that Koch could claim sole responsibility for bringing football to Braunschweig. He acted in concert with a number of individuals that included his father-in-law Friedrich Reck as well as his teacher colleague August Herrmann and the owners of the firm of Dolffs & Helle. In 1874, Koch had married Margarethe Wecke whose mother remarried after the death of her first husband. Her second husband was the military physician and social reformer Friedrich Reck (1827–1878). During his service in the military from 1855 to 1868, Reck had travelled to England repeatedly and witnessed ball games (Blasius 1887; Hermann 1895; Hoffmeister 2011; Koch 1878). It was Reck who brought football to Koch's attention and encouraged him to introduce the game into the school curriculum (Hoffmeister 2011; Koch 1983). It was, further, Koch's colleague August Hermann (1835–1906) – since 1864 the instructor for gymnastics at the high school in Braunschweig – who brought the first football ball to Braunschweig. Hermann's sister-in-law Marie Tolle was the director of an exclusive girl's school in Braunschweig, which educated girls from well-off families from Germany, England and France. Tolle travelled frequently to London and Paris in order to recruit new students. Her travels to London and the students she brought to her institute seem to have facilitated the transfer of knowledge about football to Braunschweig. Hermann, further, provided a home to English students in his own house. In an article for the *Zeitschrift für Turnen und Jugendspiel*, Herrmann wrote that he received instructions in the game's rules from one of the students living in his house after the latter was sent a football from England (Hoffmeister 2011; Oberschelp 2010).

Koch also relied on the production of football and other gear needed for the game from the firm of Dolffs & Helle (founded in Braunschweig in 1865). This firm was the first enterprise in Northern Germany to import (since 1883) and later produce footballs. It advertised its services as 'German Cricket and Football Industry'. By 1887, it supplied products to 297 schools, and gymnasts' associations in the Duchy of Braunschweig and in Northern and Western Germany. A mutual relationship developed between Koch and this enterprise since his articles and books often carried its advertisements. These advertisements, published in connection with Koch's texts and independently of them, always contained references to Koch's rules and regulations of football (Hoffmeister 2011; Oberschelp 2010; Rat der Stadt Braunschweig 1921).

Koch's role in the process of intercultural transfer of football might have been rather limited since the ball was supplied by his colleague, the inspiration came from his father-in-law, and Koch had never travelled to England. Yet, he still managed to secure an important position for himself in the transfer process. Herrmann and Reck's contributions to this transfer were largely forgotten because of Koch's publishing activities. While he acknowledged Reck's importance by dedicating to him his book *Geschichte des Fußballs im Altertum und in der Neuzeit* and referring to the fact that it was Reck who had inspired the introduction of football in Braunschweig, it was Koch who had written the rules and created the technical language of football in German (Koch 1983).

In contrast to Koch, Hutton had first-hand knowledge of the game from his days as a student in public school and university. It seems that he did not rely on the participation of other individuals in the transfer process. And while Koch sought to translate and nationalize football, Hutton embarked on an opposite course of action. He did not translate the football rules into Spanish since he envisioned the game as a teaching tool for the students at his English high school. Football initially remained within the confines of the English colony of Buenos Aires. In 1893 football had spread, however, from Hutton's school to other English schools in the city. Several football teams had emerged and Hutton decided to create the Argentine Football League. This league was initially limited to students from the English schools and the clubs and the league were dominated by English speakers (Blakeslee 2014; Mason 1995).

The role of football in educational and social reform

The model of intercultural transfer suggests that transfers resulted from a perceived gap in a given society, which agents of this society sought to fill by transferring an idea from another society that was perceived and described as superior to the receiving society. Football proved to be attractive to German educators and social reformers in Wilhelmine Germany because it offered an alternative to the discipline enforced upon students with brutal force from the outside. It also provided an outlet for activities in an urbanized world in which the distance between nature and human experience steadily increased. And it offered a way to introduce students to competition and team work that was needed in a capitalist economy.

In the case of Germany it was, further, the crisis of gymnastics that provided an opening for the introduction of football. Gymnastics as it had been developed by Friedrich Ludwig Jahn at the beginning of the nineteenth century in the context of the creation of a German identity was turned into a school subject by Adolf Spiess (1810–1858) in subsequent decades. Based upon Jahn's exercises, which stressed harmony and conformity, Spiess developed what he called 'free gymnastics'. These free exercises were activities that did not require any apparatus – i.e. marching exercises. School gymnastics was strictly organized and run in a quasi-military style. There was no space for individual agency or spontaneity. Students were forced to march in formation and to exercise in formation. One might imagine that such activities were not too attractive to young students. Reck was very critical of the practice of gymnastics in Braunschweig's schools and warned that the young men should not be burdened with military exercises and discipline before they entered military service (Eisenberg 1999; Hesse-Lichtenberger 2003; Oberschelp 2010).

Since gymnastics had lost much of its appeal in the general population, Reck advocated the introduction of sport as an alternative form of physical activity. Sport games such as football had the advantage that they included competition and that they were oriented towards winning a game. Gymnastics did not know either. Victory in football was clearly established since the goals were openly counted. Games appealed to students because it gave them freedom and self-determination and at the same time encouraged collaboration between the members of a team. Football provided an option to create discipline among students that was not imposed by the teacher but a discipline that was created by the impersonal rules of the game and the necessity to work together in achieving victory over the opposing team. Students were not forced to work together to strike a goal; they decided to work together to achieve victory (Hopf 1983).

Gymnastics might have been part of the project to create a national body through the integration of individuals into the group – the national body – and by focusing on exercises in which each gymnast moved in the prescribed and identical way as the others. Games such as football, by contrast, reflected a capitalist order in which competition and winning were emphasized. This appealed especially to the entrepreneurial middle class which saw football as an opportunity to prepare their sons for their future business life.

Older interpretations of the success of football in modern society put forward by Norbert Elias and Eric Dunning stressed the significance of civilizing people but paid insufficient attention to the context of educational reform and completely ignored the context of social reform (Dunning and Sheard 2005; Elias 1998; Murphy, Sheard, and Waddington 2000).[2] This flawed interpretation emerged from narrow theoretical premises as well as from the limited framework of the nation. If one focuses on one nation only, the story of that nation's football can only be told in a vertical and, thus, chronological direction. It starts out within high schools and colleges but moves quickly to football clubs and the history of organizations and matches. The role of educators as agents of transfer and of education as the proper framework for the emergence of football is largely marginalized (Young, Hilbrenner, and Tomlinson 2011).

The horizontal approach of intercultural transfer studies, by contrast, allows us to research the introduction of football into multiple societies on a horizontal perspective and, thus, compare the context of football's introduction into various cultures and the entry points. Such an approach reveals the significance of educational reform for the acceptance of football and the key role of educators in the creation of national football cultures. From Koch to Hutton, the founding fathers of football across continental Europe and South America had either been professors or students who encountered football in their training. The introduction of football was in general closely related to education reform and it is safe to assume that educational reform was aside from Great Britain's leading economic and imperial position the precondition for football's global spread.

It all began with the reforms introduced at the Public School at Rugby by Thomas Arnold (1795–1842). English public schools had originally been founded by public benefactors for the education of poor boys. In the course of the nineteenth century, these schools turned into educational institutions for the aristocracy and gentry. Rugby stood somewhat out from these schools because it had a low proportion of children from titled families. Common to these schools was also the fagging system which allowed older students to haze younger students who were forced into serving older students. Arnold sought, after he became headmaster of Rugby in 1828, to reform the fagging system not by getting rid of it – that proved impossible – but by regulating it. He introduced a system of indirect rule in which student prefects exercised power in place of headmasters. It was this concept of self-government of the students which attracted educators in continental Europe such as Koch to become interested in Arnold's reforms and the place of games within it. Koch wrote, when he was a student at the University of Leipzig, a thesis about Arnold and his pedagogical concept, which stressed self-determination of the students as well as a balance between physical and intellectual activities (Hoffmeister 2011).

Since Arnold outlawed the traditional aristocratic pastimes of hunting, shooting and fishing, which had been firmly embedded in the leisure time activities of Rugby students and which had resulted in countless complaints from local farmers and residents, he needed to fill the void created with a new activity. Arnold found this new activity in the games of cricket and football, which had been embraced by students across the British Islands for some time. Ball games offered to Arnold and to the students a game that supported the hierarchies among students. It provided a new leisure time activity and it also introduced new learning opportunities (Dunning and Sheard 2005).

Since the Public School at Rugby was still seeking its place in the educational landscape of public schools, there was also an incentive to develop a distinguished game. Teachers and students developed a form of football that was distinct from older forms of that game played on the streets of English towns and villages for centuries. They embraced the oval ball and H-shaped goals. In 1845, *The Laws of Football as Played at Rugby School*, which emphasized carrying and handling the ball, provided the first codified rules of this new game. These rules stipulated that all students had to participate in the game. They, further, ruled out the use of bats and sticks. Players were allowed to propel the ball only with their body (*The Laws of Football as Played at Rugby* 1862). In response, the Public School at Eton developed a game with rules that stipulated that hands were allowed to touch the ball only 'to stop the ball, or touch it when behind. The ball must not be carried, thrown or struck by the hand' (Curry 2001, 12). Rugby and association football were, thus, born.

The introduction of football in England, Germany and Argentina was intrinsically linked with educational reform. It was further linked to the urban hygiene discourse that emerged because of accelerated urbanization in the Atlantic World at the end of the nineteenth century. Towns and cities in Germany and Argentina experienced significant population growth, which went hand in hand with an alienation of inhabitants from their surrounding nature. Many city dwellers did never leave the city and spent too much time in closed spaces (factories, apartments, pubs and schools). Even German gymnastics was no longer taught and practised outside but in specifically built gymnasiums.

Football emerged at the same time at which urban spaces were closed towards playful activities through the growth of the city and police ordinances limiting the activities of city dwellers. Local city ordinances increasingly banned games and play in the city's streets. In the city of Braunschweig, for instance, a Police Ordinance of 1872 outlawed throwing balls and various games on sidewalks throughout the city. Playing football on a military exercise field outside the old city provided an outlet for the desire to play a game within the urban environment (Hoffmeister 2010).

Football was foremost an urban phenomenon. The creation of football fields occurred at about the same time modern cities created public parks and provided land for urban garden plots to preserve and recreate nature within overbuild and overpopulated cities. These football fields were of course as artificial as the nature in the public parks, which were created by city planners and landscape architects and cared for by gardeners. And yet, they still offered a scenery that was different from the busy roads and places of the modern city. In the case of Germany, it was the highly urbanized regions in Northern and Western Germany that provided specifically designed public spaces for football games. Of the 117 towns with more than 2000 inhabitants in the Kingdom of Saxony, 66 (=56%) had one or more football fields in the early 1890s. In the case of Bavaria, by contrast, it was only 40 out of 144 towns (=28%) (Woikowsky-Biedau 1894).

The direct connection between the discourse about improving urban hygiene and football is made Reck's writings. Reck was an ardent urban reformer for whom the introduction of football into the curriculum of Braunschweig's high schools was part of a much larger reform project of modern life. He authored many articles about topics that included diseases caused by urban living conditions, water quality and the need to improve urban waste disposal systems (Blasius 1887).[3] His interest in football fit into the frame of his concern for the well-being of urban dwellers and in general into the improvement of the living conditions of urban populations. The introduction of sports into modern urban cultures was, thus, not only part of educational reforms but it also coincided with debates about improving the health conditions in cities and the reform of human life in modern society by the transnational lifestyle reform movement.

Football and social divisions in society

Equally absent from most stories of football within a given national context is the integration of that game into existing socio-economic and sociocultural milieus. In both countries, Argentina and Germany, the legends about the creation of football as a national pastime focus on the introduction of football into high schools that were reserved for students who came from middle- and upper-class families. This is, however, only half of the story since in both countries two different traditions of football and two different football cultures emerged: one football culture for the middle and upper classes and one football culture for the working class. In Argentina, this division was even more solidified by the language division between the English-speaking upper class of the English enclave and the Spanish-speaking labourers.

While football, because of the introduction to elite schools – the English School in Buenos Aires and the Gymnasium in Braunschweig – had the odour of being an elite phenomenon, the game also attracted young men from working-class backgrounds. Excluded from the elitist English schools, children of the poor neighbourhoods in Buenos Aires played football on the city streets. Since this occurred outside of the school setting and without adult supervision, this variant of football was rougher and virtually unregulated. Winning the game superseded ideas of fair play. Playing football focused more on the individual than on the team (Blakeslee 2014).

Football – English high-school football and Spanish street football – spread quickly throughout the city of Buenos Aires and drew in more and more young men. Hundreds of clubs emerged across the city and the country. The clubs formed at the elitist English high schools sought to dominate the emerging football culture by publishing binding football rules in Spanish in 1905 and by reviving the Argentina Football League which was Hispanicized (Asociación Argentina de Football). This association established itself as a national organization that sought to monopolize the game. It created clear rules about membership: (1) each club was required to have its own field and was not permitted to play on another club's field and (2) each club was further required to provide separate facilities for home and visiting teams including locker rooms and showers. These requirements proved to be a great challenge since space within the city was scarce and expensive. Clubs either had to move out to the suburbs or they had to expand their membership base to bring in funding for the acquisition of land with membership fees (Blakeslee 2014; Mason 1995).

The elitist football clubs' focus on fairness, amateurism and enjoyment over victory was detrimental to the broadening of its membership and fan base. Such a game did simply not appeal to the broad masses and it failed to create a spectators culture. A visitor observing a game played in one of the exclusive English clubs would be very disappointed since there was not much enthusiasm among players with regard to winning the match. The game was friendly and not confrontational, and the players appeared to be more interested in refreshments than in the game. The need to obtain funds for buying land, building stadiums and constructing club facilities forced the elitist clubs to adopt the more aggressive football style developed by working-class clubs. Spectators asked to pay entrance fees had high expectations. They wanted to see an exciting game in which two opposing teams competed for victory. Amateurism was, therefore, slowly abandoned or circumvented by providing perks such as housing and paying for groceries to football players that drew in large crowds. As a result, differences between elite and working-class football slowly disappeared and football clubs and national leagues integrated English and Argentine traditions already after the First World War (Blakeslee 2014).

While social divisions in the case of Argentina were overcome rather quickly, Germany saw the growth and expansion of two parallel football cultures: one bourgeois and one working-class that co-existed up until 1933 when Socialist football clubs fell victim to the destruction of the Socialist subculture by the Nazis. The reason for the longer endurance of these divisions in the case of Germany was the political and ideological basis of this division. It was not simply a social division but because of the attempts of the Conservatives and Monarchists to exclude the Socialists from participation in political life a Bourgeois and a

Socialist subculture was created that included societies and associations such as consumer and housing companies, mutual health insurance systems, adult education societies and all kinds of leisure activity associations that provided all essential services for its members (Adam 1999; Nitsch and Pfeiffer 1995; Wunderer 1980).

In the 1880s, bourgeois football clubs emerged in many German cities including Berlin, Bremen and Leipzig. Members and players were predominantly middle- and upper-class men. For nearly two decades, football remained a game of high school and university students who came from very wealthy families. However, even within bourgeois culture, football was at first not welcomed by the fathers of these students. The Deutsche Turnerschaft, which had been founded as a national organization in 1868 to spread gymnastics as it was created by Friedrich Ludwig Jahn, rejected the game of football because of its English roots and un-German character. The rejection of the new sport did, however, not deter young students from embracing it and, thereby, defy the norms of their fathers and grandfathers. In 1888, a football team was created within the Allgemeiner Turnverein zu Leipzig. This local gymnast association had been founded in 1845 and it belonged to the Deutsche Turnerschaft. The Leipzig football team introduced the members of the Deutsche Turnerschaft to the new game by playing a match against the London football team Orion at the annual Turnfest – a meeting of all members of the Deutsche Turnerschaft – in Munich in 1889. This early international match helped to popularize the game in Conservative circles and encouraged young gymnasts in other bourgeois gymnast associations to form football teams (Fuge 1996; Koch 1983; Oberschelp 2010; Sachse 2000).

One of the local branches of the Deutsche Turnerschaft that formed such a football team was located in Magdeburg. The Magdeburg football team managed to be included in the annual Sedan Celebrations, which were held each year on September 2 to celebrate Germany's victory over France in the Battle of Sedan in 1870. These celebrations brought together war veteran associations and the most Conservative circles of German society. The inclusion of football into these celebrations paved the way for football to be recognized as part of the bourgeois and monarchist culture. In the following years, sport teams were created as chapters of the Deutsche Turnerschaft in nearly every German city. These chapters of gymnast associations slowly transformed into independent sport associations as it happened in Leipzig in 1892. These sport associations were initially inclusive and embraced various ball games from football to tennis. The Leipzig sport association received its own playground in 1896. And from among the many sports played, football emerged quickly as the most favoured game (Hoffmeister 2011; Koch 1983).

The fact that the middle and upper classes embraced football turned this game into a bourgeois sport. Further, its focus on competition and winning increased the reluctance of Socialist leaders to accept football into the canon of physical activities appropriate for labourers young and old. The Arbeiterturnerbund, which had been founded in 1893 as a Socialist alternative to the Deutsche Turnerschaft, rejected football on ideological grounds. However, young labourers who were integrated into the Socialist subculture felt about gymnastics in the same way students from middle- and upper-class background had felt about it. Since Socialist leaders opposed football on the ground that it was foreign and elitist, young football players of working-class background were forced to create football clubs outside of the Arbeiterturnerbund. For the young sport enthusiasts involved in labour football this exclusion could come at a high price since sport injuries, which occurred quite frequently in football, were not covered by the health insurance provided to all members by the Arbeiterturnerbund. Only members of this organization were entitled to these benefits. Joining the bourgeois Deutsche Turnerschaft was an option but often not chosen because of the social and political distance between labourers and this bourgeois organization. And while bourgeois football teams had access to military drill grounds – the first games in Braunschweig were played on that city's Exerzierplatz – labour football teams were left with open grasslands outside of towns (Adam 1999).

The initial hope of the Arbeiterturnerbund leaders that its strict rejection of football would prevent the infiltration of working-class gymnastics by football eventually failed because field sports proved to be too attractive to young men of all social backgrounds. Football gained more and more ground among the young generation. The introduction and spread of football seemed to have been part of a conflict between the generation born before the founding of the German Empire and the generation that grew up in the 1880s and 1890s. The growth of labour football teams unaffiliated with the Arbeiterturnerbund seemed to endanger the future of labour gymnastics and finally forced that organization to change course. In 1912 the Arbeiterturnerbund opened its organization for football but the leadership imposed upon its teams the condition that they had to abstain from playing matches against bourgeois football teams that were affiliated with the Deutsche Turnerschaft. This ideologically motivated rule posed, of course, a significant challenge for a sport geared towards competition (Adam 1999).

The city of Leipzig, in particular, developed in the course of the 1920s into a centre of sports within Germany. In 1921, the city was the home to about 50 football associations with a combined membership of 25,000 proletarian and bourgeois men and women. About 5500 of these 25,000 football players were organized within the Arbeiterturnerbund while the remaining 19,500 players were members of the Deutsche Turnerschaft. Teams of both subcultures developed their own infrastructure complete with their own football fields, tournaments and publications. This division of German society into two opposing subcultures which also resulted in the creation of two independent football cultures ended only in 1933 with the closing and destruction of all Socialist organizations – including labour football teams – by the Nazis (Adam 1999; Adam 2004).

Both Argentina and Germany saw the creation of two parallel football cultures, which were defined by social status and in the German case also by ideology. This division continued to exist in Germany for about two decades longer than in Argentina because of the entrenched social and political divisions between labour and bourgeoisie. And yet, in Argentina this division was not just a social division but was also a language division. While two football cultures co-existed in Germany without influencing each other, the style of Buenos Aires' street football was slowly integrated into the football culture developed within the elite football clubs creating an attractive game that turned football from a leisure time activity into a public spectacle for which people were willing to pay money.

Conclusion

Historians trained in national histories often raise the question for why we should forgo the old and proven ways of national history. Why should we embrace a transnational approach which requires the historian to become fluent in at least two languages and two national historiographies? They also charge that such a historical approach is in danger of losing its grounding since transnational history does not seem to have a space in the same way national history does. Transnational history is seen by its critics as turning history into an elusive chase of ideas that cross regions and borders and can hardly be captured. Yet, few historians seem to ask what our narratives miss out by limiting ourselves to the paradigm of national history and what our narratives could gain when we would embrace transnational approaches.

The example of football provides some insight into what is to be gained if we look beyond national variations of this sport and the role of this sport for the invention and perpetuation of national identities. The focus on the transfer of football across continents and oceans in the second half of the nineteenth century opens up new horizons and contexts in which this transfer occurred. Football was not just a sport that could be studied independently of social and cultural changes; it was a part of educational and social reform projects that were to improve urban life through bringing students out of unhealthy buildings onto fresh air. Football fields provided a way for social reformers to reconnect with nature albeit a nature that was artificially created.

Following the intercultural transfer of football around the globe also provides an innovative way at mapping history. Instead of creating maps that show political borders, we could imagine a map that represents the acceptance and rejection of this sport in nineteenth- and twentieth-century societies. This map would show the extent to which football was integrated into urban societies and also highlight the borders of its influence. These borders were as real and as constructed as the borders of nation states. Within the space created by football, different colours could highlight different traditions and different degrees of integration. Transnational history is certainly not a history without space. But space – national or transnational – is always constructed. Each circulating idea created a circulatory regime that appropriated a space defined, limited, and structured by this idea and its practitioners (Saunier 2013).

Notes

1. The terms 'transnational' and 'international' should not be confused since the first term points to connections of phenomena independent of the nation state while the second is based upon the existence of the nation state, which is seen as an organizing principle of human relations and history. See Clavin (2005).
2. See also the contributions to the 'Forum *European Sport and the Challenges of Its Recent Historiography*' in number 2 and 3 of volume 38 (2011) of the *Journal of Sport History*.
3. Among his many publications are: *Bericht über die Gesundheitsverhältnisse der Stadt Braunschweig in den Jahren 1864 bis 1873 und die Cholera daselbst in den Jahren 1850 und 1855*, Braunschweig: Waisenhaus-Buchdruckerei 1877; 'Das Wasser als Nahrungsmittel und eine Vorrichtung, schlechtes Wasser zu verbessern', in: *Monatsblatt für öffentliche Gesundheitspflege* 1 (1878), pp. 30–35; 'Zur Beseitigung der Abfallstoffe', in: *Monatsblatt für öffentliche Gesundheitspflege* 1 (1878), pp. 113–118; For a complete list see: Blasius, 'Friedrich Reck', pp. 130–131.

Acknowledgements

The research for this article was inspired by Roberta Wollons, edited volume (2000). The attempt of the contributors to Wollons' volume to follow the transfer of the kindergarten idea between various cultures around the world caused me to create from fall 2011 to fall 2012 a sequence of three doctoral-level courses on the intercultural transfer of football with students from the doctoral programme in transatlantic history at the University of Texas at Arlington. I would like to thank the

GLOBAL AND TRANSNATIONAL SPORT

students – Brandon Blakeslee, Kristen Burton, Jay Goldin, Nicole Leopoldie, Isabelle Rispler, Rufki Salihi and Matthew Speight – involved in the three classes that were focused on this topic and who wrote such excellent research papers on the introduction of football into various regions and countries.

Disclosure statement

No potential conflict of interest was reported by the author.

References

Adam, Thomas. 1999. *Arbeitermilieu und Arbeiterbewegung in Leipzig, 1871–1933* [Working-Class Milieu and Working-Class Movement in Leipzig, 1871–1933], Cologne: Böhlau.

Adam, Thomas. 2004. "Sport und Politik in einer deutschen Grossstadt. Sozialdemokratischer und konservativer Fußball in Leipzig vom Kaiserreich bis zur nationalsozialistischen Machtergreifung [Sports and Politics in a German City: Socialist and Conservative Football in Leipzig from 1871–1933]." In *Kulturpolitik und Stadtkultur in Leipzig und Lyon (18. – 20. Jahrhundert)* [Cultural Policy and Urban Culture in Leipzig and Lyon in comparison from the eighteenth to the twentieth century], edited by Thomas Höpel and Steffen Sammler, 275–292. Leipzig: Leipziger Universitätsverlag.

Adam, Thomas. 2012. *Intercultural Transfers and the Making of the Modern World, 1800–2000: Sources and Context*. New York: Palgrave Macmillan.

Adam, Thomas. 2013. "New Ways to Write the History of Western Europe and the United States: The Concept of Intercultural Transfer." *History Compass* 11 (10): 880–892.

Anderson, Benedict. 2006. *Imagined Communities: Reflections on the Origin and Spread of Nationalism*. London: Verso.

Archetti, Eduardo P. 1997. "Argentinien [Argentina]." In *Fußball, soccer, calcio: Ein englischer Sport auf seinem Weg um die Welt* [Fussball, Soccer, Calcio: An English Sport on its Journey around the World], edited by Christiane Eisenberg, 149–170. Munich: Deutscher Taschenbuch Verlag.

Blakeslee, Brandon. 2014 "How to Make a Foreign Idea Your Own: Argentine Identity and the Role Soccer Played in Its Formation." MA thesis, The University of Texas at Arlington.

Blasius, Wilhelm. 1887. "Friedrich Reck. Nekrolog [Friedrich Reck Obituary]". *5. Jahresbericht des Vereins für Naturwissenschaft zu Braunschweig für das Vereinsjahr 1886 bis 1887* [Fifth Annual Report of the Association for Natural Sciences in Braunschweig for the Year of 1886 to 1887], 126–131. Braunschweig: Friedrich Vieweg und Sohn.

Broschkowski, Michael, and Thomas Schneider. 2005. "*Fußlümmelei" Als Fußball noch ein Spiel war* [Fusslummelei: When Football was Still a Game]. Berlin: Transit.

Caldas, Waldenyr. 1997. "Brasilien [Brazil]." In *Fußball, soccer, calcio: Ein englischer Sport auf seinem Weg um die Welt* [Fussball, Soccer, Calcio: An English Sport on its Journey around the World], edited by Christiane Eisenberg, 171–184. Munich: Deutscher Taschenbuch Verlag.

Clavin, Patricia. 2005. "Defining Transnationalism." *Contemporary European History* 14 (4): 421–439.

Curry, Graham. 2001. "Football: A Study in Diffusion." DPhil diss., University of Leicester.

Damm, Folko. 2007. *Auf dem Weg zum Volkssport: Einführung und Verbreitung des Fußballs in Deutschland* [On the Way to Becoming a Popular Sport: The Introduction and Dispersal of Football in Germany]. Norderstedt: GRIN Verlag.

Der Ganz Grosse Traum. 2011. Directed by Sebastian Grobler.

Dunning, Eric, and Kenneth Sheard. 2005. *Barbarians, Gentlemen, and Players, Second Edition: A Sociological Study of the Development of Rugby Football*. London: Routledge.

Eisenberg, Christiane, ed. 1997. *Fußball, soccer, calcio: Ein englischer Sport auf seinem Weg um die Welt* [Fussball, Soccer, Calcio: An English Sport on its Journey Around the World]. Munich: Deutscher Taschenbuch Verlag.

Eisenberg, Christiane. 1999. *"English Sports" und deutsche Bürger: Eine Gesellschaftsgeschichte 1800–1939*. Paderborn: Schöningh.

Elias, Norbert. 1998. "The Social Constraint towards Self-constraint." In *Norbert Elias: Civilization, Power, and Knowledge*, edited by Stephen Mennell and Johan Goudsblom, 49–66. Chicago, IL: University of Chicago Press.

GLOBAL AND TRANSNATIONAL SPORT

Escuela de Campeopnes. 1950. Directed by Ralph Pappier.

Fuge, Jens. 1996. *Ein Jahrhundert Leipziger Fußball. Die Jahre 1883–1945* [One Century of Football in Leipzig: The Years from 1883 to 1945]. Leipzig: Connewitzer Verlagsbuchhandlung.

Heineken, Ph. 1993. *Das Fußballspiel. Association und Rugby* [The Football Game: Association and Rugby]. Hannover: Th. Schäfer.

Hermann, August. 1895. "Ergänzende und berichtigende Bemerkungen [Supplemental Remarks]." *Zeitschrift für Turnen und Jugendspiel* [Journal for Gymnastics and Sports] 4: 132–133.

Hesse-Lichtenberger, Ulrich. 2003. *Tor! The Story of German Football.* London: WSC Books.

Hill, John S., John Vincent, and Matthew Curtner-Smith. 2014. "The Worldwide Diffusion of Football: Temporal and Spatial Perspectives." *Global Sport Business Journal* 2 (2): 1–27.

Hillebrand, Karl. 1876. *Aus und über England* [From and about England]. Berlin: Robert Oppenheim.

Hobsbawn, Eric J. 1992. *Nations and Nationalism since 1780: Programme, Myth, Reality.* 2nd ed. Cambridge: Cambridge University Press.

Hoffmeister, Kurt. 2010. *Zeitreise durch die Braunschweiger Sportgeschichte* [Ruminations about the History of Sports in Braunschweig]. Braunschweig: Books on Demand.

Hoffmeister, Kurt. 2011. *Der Wegbereiter des Fußballspiels in Deutschland: Prof. Dr. Konrad Koch 1846–1911. Eine Biographie.* Braunschweig: Books on Demad GmbH.

Hopf, Wilhelm. 1983. "Wie der Fußball nach Deutschland kam [How Football came to Germany]." In *Die Geschichte des Fußballs im Altertum und in der Neuzeit* [The History of Football in Antiquity and in Modern Times], edited by Konrad Koch, 49–53. Münster: LIT Verlag.

Hughes, Thomas. 1867. *Tom Brown's Schuljahre. Von einem alten Rugby-Jungen. Zur Darlegung des gegenwärtigen Standes der Erziehung in den oberen Classen Englands* [Tom Brown's Schooldays. From an Old Rugby Student. A Discussion of the Quality of the Education of the Upper Classes in England]. Nach dem Englischen des "Th. Hughes", bearbeitet von Dr. Ernst Wagner. Gotha: Justus Perthes.

Koch, Konrad. 1875. *Fußball. Regeln des Fußball-Vereins der mittleren Classen des Martino-Catharineums zu Braunschweig* [Football: Rules of the Football Association of the Martino-Catharineum at Braunschweig]. Braunschweig: D. Haering.

Koch, Konrad. 1878. "August Friedrich Reck, Dr. med." *Braunschweiger Tageblatt,* November 9.

Koch, Konrad. 1983. *Die Geschichte des Fußballs im Altertum und in der Neuzeit* [Football: Rules of the Football Association of the Martino-Catharineum at Braunschweig]. Münster: LIT Verlag.

Kroes, Rob. 2002. "American Empire and Cultural Imperialism: A View from the Receiving End." In *Rethinking American History in a Global Age,* edited by Thomas Bender, 295–313. Berkeley: University of California Press.

The Laws of Football as Played at Rugby School. 1862. Rugby: Crossley and Billington.

Mason, Tony. 1995. *Passion of the People? Football in South America.* London: Verso.

Murphy, Patrick, Ken Sheard, and Ivan Waddington. 2000. "Figurational Sociology and its Application to Sport." In *Handbook of Sports Studies,* edited by Jay Coakley and Eric Dunning, 92–105. London: Sage.

Nitsch, Franz, and Lorenz Pfeiffer, eds. 1995. *Die Roten Turnbrüder: 100 Jahre Arbeitersport* [The Red Gymnasts: 100 Years of Working-Class Sport]. Marburg: Schüren Presseverlag.

Oberschelp, Malte. 2010. *Der Fußball-Lehrer: Wie Konrad Koch im Kaiserreich den Ball ins Spiel brachte* [The Football Teacher: How Konrad Koch introduced the football game to Germany]. Göttingen: Verlag Die Werkstatt.

Rat der Stadt Braunschweig, ed. 1921. *Braunschweig.* Berlin: Deutscher Architektur- und Industrieverlag.

Rispler, Isabelle. 2012. *'Football is Our Mother': On the Intercultural Transfer of Soccer from Britain to Brazil.* Research Paper. Arlington, TX: The University of Texas at Arlington.

Rodgers, Daniel T. 1998. *Atlantic Crossings: Social Politics in a Progressive Age.* Cambridge, MA: Belknap Press of Harvard University Press.

Rogers, Everett M. 1995. *Diffusion of Innovations.* New York: Free Press.

Sachse, Horst. 2000. *Fußball in und um Leipzig. Von den Anfängen bis 1945* [Football in Leipzig: From its Beginnings until 1945]. Leipzig: Leipziger Universitätsverlag.

Saunier, Pierre-Yves. 2013. *Transnational History.* New York: Palgrave Macmillan.

Voigt, J. A. 1857. *Mittheilungen über das Unterrichtswesen Englands und Schottlands* [Report about Schooling in England and Scotland]. Halle: Eduard Anton.

Wagner, Ernst. 1864. *Das Volksschulwesen in England und seine neueste Entwicklung* [The Lower Schools in England and newer trends in education]. Verlag der J. B. Metzler'schen Buchhandlung.

Werner, Michael, and Bénédicte Zimmerman. 2006. "Beyond Comparison: Histoire Croisée and the Challenge of Reflexivity." *History and Theory* 45 (1): 30–50.

Wiese, Ludwig Adolf. 1852. *Deutsche Briefe über Englische Erziehung* [German Letters about English Education]. 2 vols. Berlin: Wiegandt und Grieben.

Woikowsky-Biedau, Viktor von. 1894. "Über den Stand des Jugend- und Volksspiels in Deutschland 1892–1893 [About the State of Ball Games in Germany, 1892-1893]." *Jahrbuch für Jugend- und Volksspiele* [Journal for Ball Games] 3: 164–206.

Wollons, Roberta, ed. 2000. *Kindergartens and Cultures: The Global Diffusion of an Idea*. New Haven, CT: Yale University Press.

Wunderer, Hartmann. 1980. *Arbeitervereine und Arbeiterparteien: Kultur- und Massenorganisationen in der Arbeiterbewegung (1890–1933)* [Working-Class Associations and Working-Class Parties: Cultural and Mass Organizations of the Working-Class Movement, 1890–1933]. Frankfurt am Main: Campus Verlag.

Young, Christopher, Anke Hilbrenner, and Alan Tomlinson. 2011. "European Sport Historiography: Challenges and Opportunities." *Journal of Sport History* 38 (2): 181–187.

Sport transfer over the channel: elitist migration and the advent of football and ice hockey in Switzerland

Christian Koller

ABSTRACT
This article analyses the early cultural transfer of British sports to Switzerland by the example of football and ice hockey. After an assessment of Anglo-Swiss political, economic and cultural relations during the Victorian period, it identifies four main channels, all of which linked to elitist migration, through which football and ice hockey were transferred to Switzerland: British student and merchant communities in Switzerland, Swiss migrants returning from Britain, boarding schools in Western and Eastern Switzerland (from which the games were also transferred to other continental European countries) and British tourism to the Swiss Alps. A final section assesses the pattern of popularization of the two games in Switzerland. Both football and ice hockey were considered national sports by the end of the interwar period at the very latest. This process of appropriation included cultural, social, economic, geographical and gender issues. Players became role models of masculine heroes – footballers rather of an urban and working-class type, ice hockey players rather of a rural and alpine type, whilst their elitist character of the pioneering period largely disappeared. Nevertheless, the two games' Anglo-Saxon roots were never forgotten, and unlike in many other countries, English sport terminology remained predominant in Switzerland.

Switzerland was one of the first countries in continental Europe to become acquainted with both football and ice hockey. This article will comparatively analyse the social and cultural preconditions and contexts of the early transfer of these two disciplines that were to become Switzerland's most popular team sports, as well as of the main actors and institutions involved. I shall argue that the early advent of the two games was due to different types of elitist migration between the United Kingdom and Switzerland, which turned the alpine republic not only into a place where British sports could assimilate and eventually modify their social contexts, but also into a bridgehead for their further spread across continental Europe. The cultural transfer thus included complex processes of social trickle-down and transnational cultural transit.

In the first section, I shall briefly outline the political, economic and cultural links that account for the early advent of British sports in Switzerland. The second section will then analyse several types of elitist migration that were instrumental in transferring football and ice hockey to Switzerland. The last section will focus on the subsequent popularization of the two games in Switzerland.

Social and political preconditions

At a first glance, small, landlocked and neutral Switzerland, whose inhabitants a British officer in the mid-nineteenth century described as 'exceedingly Republican in all their ideas'[1], and the United Kingdom, the leading political and economic power of the time, whose empire span the whole globe, had very little in common, when British sports set out to conquer the world. However, the quite early advent of football and ice hockey in Switzerland actually reflected a relatively strong presence of Britons in the alpine republic (Wraight 1987; Howald 2004; Wylie 2013). This was due to political affinities, economic exchange and cultural links.

Switzerland, as one of the few countries to experience a liberal breakthrough between 1830 and 1848, was patronized by large segments of the British political elites despite its strong republicanism. During the short civil war of 1847, which would eventually result in the liberal constitution of the modern Swiss Confederation, British diplomacy shielded the alpine republic against possible interventions from other great powers sympathizing with the defeated Swiss conservatives. This British role as a protector, which in Switzerland was seen as support for fellow liberals, actually rather resulted from British foreign policy's interest in preserving Switzerland as a neutral buffer state and securing political equilibrium in continental Europe (Imlah 1966). Nevertheless, the political relations between the two countries for the rest of the nineteenth century were characterized by mutual esteem and ideological sympathies (Wylie 2013).

Economically, Switzerland can be characterized as an early adapter in the process of industrialization. Proto-industrial structures at a relatively early point were transformed into a growing, yet decentralized industrial sector with many important impulses coming from the United Kingdom. The Swiss economy profited from the strong social and political position of the liberal bourgeoisie as well as from Switzerland's intensive entanglements with a globalizing capitalist economy (Bernegger 1990). It was this very openness of the Swiss economy that accounted for many British merchants' and engineers' presence in Switzerland and vice versa all over the Victorian era. During the second half of the nineteenth century, almost 20% of all Swiss exports went to the United Kingdom, and a large part of Swiss overseas trade was transacted via Britain (Wylie 2013).

Furthermore, many Britons of the upper social strata would visit Switzerland for cultural reasons. Traditionally, a stay in a Swiss city and the crossing over the Alps had been part of the young aristocrats' Grand Tour across Europe. William Wordsworth's 1790 trip to Switzerland, then, was followed by many more British artists (Wylie 2013). In the mid-nineteenth century, this was succeeded by two new phenomena. On the one hand, more and more wealthy British families would send their sons to the numerous boarding schools at the shore of the Lake of Geneva, which followed the educational model of English Public Schools (Chandler 1991). On the other hand, Switzerland in the late nineteenth century became one of British tourists' preferred destinations. In 1863, Thomas Cook organized the first trip to Switzerland. Travels to the alpine republic were then further popularized with the British elites by Queen Victoria's visit there in 1868. In the years immediately before the outbreak of the First World War, an annual 350.000 to 540.000 tourists from the United Kingdom would visit the alpine republic (Tissot 2000; Barton 2008). During the winter season, a direct luxury train used to connect London and Davos via Paris with the train ride lasting only 25 h (Busset 2000, 244).

The substantial presence of Britons in Switzerland was crucial for an early arrival of British sports in Central Europe. Whilst some primary sources hinting at football being played in Geneva as early as in the 1830s are rather dubious (Lieber 1832, 157 and *Journal de Genève*, January 22, 1869 as well as Koller 2011/12, 162–163), the existence of a 'British and Geneva Cricket Club' is confirmed for the year 1850 (*Journal de Genève*, November 25, 1850). Cricket was also played by British expats in Lausanne during the 1860s (*Journal de Genève*, October 3, 1866; *Liverpool Mercury*, August 6, 1869), and a few years later, an 'Anglo-American Boating Club' emerged in Zurich (*Neue Zürcher Zeitung*, August 1, 1871, May 21, 1872, June 13, 1874, July 3, 1876, September 12, 1876, June 27, 1877, June 24, 1879; *Gazette de Lausanne*, June 26, 1879). During the 1850s and 1860s, Britons also pioneered alpinism in Switzerland (Annan 1984; Hansen 1995; Meinherz 2008). From the 1870s on, British tourists imported Curling, Skeleton and Bobsleigh to Swiss mountain resorts (Müller 2013), and Arthur Conan Doyle's 1894 *Strand Magazine* article about a skiing trip from Davos to Arosa heavily contributed to the popularization of skiing as a core activity of alpine winter tourism (Doyle 1894, 2007, 106).

The transfer of British sports to Switzerland, however, was more than a simple example of cultural imperialism. It happened through different, though socially rather homogeneous channels. Once arrived in Switzerland, football and ice hockey would gradually change their characters and become an integral part of Swiss culture. Furthermore, Switzerland would also contribute to the further spread of these sports in continental Europe and beyond.

Channels over the channel

British expats, mainly merchants and students, used to play association and rugby football in the towns of Western Switzerland from at least the 1860s on (*Gazette de Lausanne*, November 2, 1866; *Journal de Genève*, January 20, 1869; Zincke 1874, 281). This became notorious in 1866, when young Englishmen played a match in Lausanne that was followed by heavy drinking in a hotel and eventually rioting at the train station and violent confrontations with the police (*Gazette de Lausanne*, November 2, 1866). Three years later, in what is the oldest match announcement in Switzerland known so far, the *Journal de Genève* (January 20, 1869) advertised another game between the English from Lausanne and their compatriots in Geneva.

Soon afterwards, the British football community in Geneva started to proselytize the natives. In 1871, they published several calls in the *Journal de Genève* asking local students to join their activities (*Journal de Genève*, October 14, 1871 and November 14, 1871). Remarkably, these calls were written in French. Their success is unknown. In the same year, regular games between several football clubs from Geneva, Lausanne, Châtelaine, Vevey and Montreux started (*Gazette de Lausanne*, December 2, 1871 and October 1, 1878; *Journal de Genève*, November 14, 1873, February 5, 1875, February 20, 1875, November 27, 1875, November 11, 1876, January 6, 1877, November 16, 1878, November 20, 1878, December 3, 1878, March 1, 1879; *Manchester Times*, February 28, 1874; *Wrexham Advertiser*, February 28, 1874). These clubs were quite as old as the French Le Havre AC, founded by British dockers in 1872, which is often seen as the first continental football club, and the Dresden English Football Club, founded in 1874, which is believed to be the first ever football club of Germany. First, apparently entirely British, those clubs step by step seem to have incorporated young local men from the same social strata as well as other foreigners.

During the following two decades, British students remained instrumental in the establishment of football clubs in other parts of Switzerland. In 1881, a short-lived 'Foot Ball Club' was created by students in Basel (Gerber 2007, 12). The founding of the Grasshopper Club at Zurich in 1886 owed a great deal to the British biology student Tom E. Griffith (Eggenberger 1986, 35–39). It was not coincidental that the Grasshoppers' first game was organized against a side from the Federal Polytechnic Institute at Zurich. This team almost completely consisted of Anglo-Saxon players. So did the Anglo-American Club Zurich, which in 1899 won the first official football championship of Switzerland and whose players were mainly students of the University of Zurich and the Federal Polytechnic Institute. In the Italian-speaking part of the country, an English student of the cantonal business school at Bellinzona would organize the first football matches in 1897.

As for ice hockey, this channel was less important. Nevertheless, the aforementioned student Tom E. Griffith is said to have played ice hockey with his fellow Grasshoppers as early as in 1887 (Schweizerischer Eishockey-Verband 1948, 14–15). Two decades later, in 1908, Canadian students of the University of Zurich and the Federal Polytechnic Institute together with some Swiss colleagues would found the Academic Ice Hockey Club of Zurich, the first and for more than two decades only Ice Hockey Club in the largest city of Switzerland. It participated in the Swiss championship from 1911 on and won the international Swiss championship, which allowed the deployment of foreign players, in 1916 (Akademischer Eishockey-Club Zürich 1983, 53).

During the First World War, about 4.000 British POWs, including members of the Canadian Expeditionary Force, spent some time as internees in Switzerland, where many of them were accommodated in vacant winter resorts (Gysin 1998). Some of their officers (who are likely to have had an academic background) organized ice hockey games among the soldiers that were watched and imitated by the locals and there were also matches between Canadian and Swiss players around 1916/17 (*Gazette de Lausanne*, January 29, 1931 and January 11, 1934; Iringer 1947, 349; Schweizerischer Eishockey-Verband 1948, 35). Thus, even the war could not entirely obstruct this channel of cultural transfer.

A second, though apparently less important channel of transferring football to Switzerland were Swiss migrants, especially students, in the United Kingdom. A prominent example is Treytorrens de Loys, later on to become a high-ranking officer of the Swiss Army during the First World War. He studied engineering at King's College London during the 1870s, where he also learnt how to play football. During his holidays in Lausanne, he organized a local football team together with some friends (Van Muyden-Baird 1943, 126). Outside the pioneering area around the Lake of Geneva, in Eastern Switzerland, for instance, a secondary school teacher at Weinfelden, who had familiarized himself with football during a stay in Liverpool, had his pupils play the game as early as in 1884 (*Thurgauer Tagblatt*, November 12, 1934 and November 13, 1934 as well as Mente 2015). Three years later, another teacher upon his return from England introduced football to the city of Winterthur (*Sport*, January 4, 1952). No such transfers are known for ice hockey activities.

A third channel, through which not only football but also ice hockey was transferred to Switzerland, were the boarding schools at the shores of the lakes of Geneva and Constance.

British ball games were played at the Institut du Château de Lancy in Geneva as early as in the 1850s (Coviello 2007, 80). In 1869, the game of football entered the Institut de la Châtelaine at Geneva, and probably followed the rules of Rugby. Other private schools located along the Lake of Geneva also adopted the game in the following years. The presence of football at these schools also impacted on the development of the aforementioned early football clubs in the area. The Lausanne Foot-ball Club, for instance, during the 1870s was chaired by Lewis Stein, who used to work as an English teacher for several boarding schools in Lausanne (*Gazette de Lausanne*, 1.10.1878; Van Muyden-Baird 1943, 126; Gilgen 2003, 17–18; Coviello 2007, 86–87).

No later than in the 1870s, football was also adopted in German-speaking Switzerland at the elitist Institut Wiget auf Schönberg in Rorschach at the Lake of Constance. In addition to Swiss students, this school also had British, Spanish, Italian and South American pupils. Sport played an important role in the school's curriculum. Former Swiss students of this institute in 1879 founded FC St. Gallen, the oldest existing football club in Switzerland (Furgler 1979, 23). Richard Butler, the captain of the Anglo-American Club Zurich when they became the first official Swiss football champions in 1899, was a former pupil of the Institut Wiget and then a student at the University of Zurich.

The establishment of the Swiss Football Association in 1895 that marked an important step in the institutionalization of football in Switzerland was a joint project of elitist boarding schools and early football clubs established by British expats. At the beginning, four of the five members of the association's leadership were British citizens (Giuliani 2001, 117). However, at the end of the 1898–9 season, following a conflict regarding playing on Sundays, which was unknown in Britain, most of the school teams from Western Switzerland left the Swiss Football Association to form the 'Ligue Romande de Football', from which they in turn would withdraw during the 1920s (Collet and Guillemin 2000). This schism marked the end of their prominent role in Swiss football.

Some of the boarding schools of the Lake of Geneva region would also pioneer the introduction of ice hockey in Switzerland. In the winter of 1894–5, the director of the Institut Auckenthaler ('La Villa') of Ouchy invited a Dutch bandy team from Haarlem for a match against a selection of his school (*Gazette de Lausanne*, December 24, 1925). Five years later, the same institution organized two matches of Lausanne school teams playing Canadian ice hockey (Killias 2007, 24–25). The Institut Auckenthaler was also a football pioneer as a founding member of the Swiss Football Association and participant at the first football championship (Coviello 2007, 89–90). Members of the Auckenthaler family that run the school were engaged with several sporting disciplines (*Nouvelliste Valaisan*, June 7, 1913). After the turn of the century, the school ice hockey team would regularly play matches against squads of the winter resorts of Les Avants and Leysin.[2] In 1909, it came second in the first Swiss ice hockey championship and in the following season, it would even win.

Another important school during this period was the Institut Bellerive in Vevey. Its director Max Sillig, who is sometimes referred to as the 'father of Swiss ice hockey', had his pupils play ice hockey from about 1900 on Gosteli (2008, 6). In 1905, he founded the Hockey Club Bellerive that in 1907 and 1908 won the championship of Western Switzerland and in 1909 became the first Swiss ice hockey champion, a triumph repeated in 1920 and 1921. Sillig also became the founding chairman of the Bandy Federation of Western Switzerland in 1904 and the Swiss Ice Hockey Federation in 1908 as well as president of the International Ice Hockey Federation in 1920. From 1909 on, the team of the very elitist boarding school

Le Rosey, which has campuses in Rolle at the Lake of Geneva and in the ski resort village of Gstaad, used to participate in the Swiss ice hockey championship. During the early 1920s, it used to be one of the strongest teams in Europe (Gosteli 2008, 54–55).

The Swiss boarding schools and other elitist educational institutions also contributed to the spread of British sports beyond the Swiss borders with some former pupils becoming sports pioneers in their own countries after the end of their schooling (Lanfranchi 1998; Koller 2006). A famous example is the German football pioneer, Walther Bensemann, who attended a school in Montreux, where in 1887 at the age of 14, he founded his first football club, before establishing numerous clubs in Germany, serving as one of the founders of the German Football Federation in 1900, organizing numerous international matches, as well as founding and acting as chief editor of the periodical *Kicker* (Beyer 2014). The Anglo-Brazilian Oscar Alfredo Sebastião Cox became familiar with football whilst studying at the Institut Auckenthaler from 1897. Upon his return to Rio de Janeiro, he organized the first ever football match there in 1901 and founded the Fluminense Football Club in the following year.

Vittorio Pozzo, a two-time football world champion in 1934 and 1938 and an Olympic champion as the coach of the Italian national team in 1936, studied language and business at Zurich and Winterthur between 1906 and 1908. It was during this period that he learned football at the Grasshopper Club. After another year abroad at Manchester, he returned to his home city of Turin where he acted in turn as a player, referee and sports journalist until he accepted the position of coach in 1929 for the 'Squadra Azzurra'. The brothers Michele and Paolo Scarfoglio, who were among the founders of the first football club in Naples, learned the game a short time before during a training course in Switzerland. The French banker, Henry Monnier, who always wrote his first name with a 'y' out of anglophilia, introduced football to Nîmes in 1898. Also a mountain climber, Monnier had discovered the game whilst studying at Geneva. So did the French football pioneers Falgueirettes and Julien. The Olympic ice hockey tournament of 1924, then, saw former pupils of Le Rosey school not only in the Swiss and British teams, but also in the Belgian selection (Gosteli 2008, 54–55).

Whilst boarding schools played an important role for the introduction of ice hockey in Switzerland, they were preceded by another elitist space: the Grand Hotel (Seger 2006). British tourists used to play ice hockey (first according to the English rules of Bandy) in Swiss winter resorts such as Davos, St. Moritz, Leysin and Les Avants from the early 1880s (Schweizerischer Eishockey-Verband 1948, 15–16; Busset 2000, 2001). In the winter of 1893, the first Bandy club was founded in St. Moritz (*Manchester Guardian*, March 25, 1894 and Lütscher 2014, 94). The opening of a large ice rink in Davos in 1894 was a further boost to ice sports in the Alps. In 1898, the first match according to the Canadian rules of ice hockey was played between teams from Davos and St. Moritz (Killias 2007, 25). After the turn of the century, several leading European ice hockey teams, including the Princes Ice Hockey Club of London as well as the squads of Oxford and Cambridge Universities, regularly stayed in places such as Davos, Les Avants, Grindelwald and Mürren (*L'Express*, January 9, 1908; *Manchester Guardian*, January 9, 1908, December 21, 1910, December 23, 1911, December 24, 1912, December 24, 1913; *Neue Zürcher Zeitung*, December 24, 1913; Benson 1913, 129; Feuz 2014, 96).

Swiss hotel directors early on realized the potential of ice hockey's commercial impact and organized ice hockey activities for their guests as well as attractive games with top teams. Starting in 1894, an annual Bandy match between select teams from Davos and

St. Moritz was convened. A 1904 tournament in Davos included a local selection, the Princes Ice Hockey Club and a Dutch team from Haarlem (Schweizerischer Eishockey-Verband 1948, 17–18; Busset 2000, 242). From 1909 on, an annual Bandy cup would take place at Grindelwald. In January 1910, Les Avants hosted the first Ice Hockey European Championship, won by Britain that was represented by the Princes Ice Hockey Club. A team made up of Canadian students from the University of Oxford also participated in the tournament without their games counting towards the final standings. Three years later, the first (and so far only) Bandy European Championship took place in Davos and was also won by Britain. At the same time, hotel directors from the Vaudois pre-alps together with representatives of the boarding schools established an ice hockey federation first in Western Switzerland in 1904 and then on a national level in 1908. Louis Dufour, a co-owner of the luxurious 'Grand Hôtel des Avants', was deputy chairman of the national federation from 1908 to 1916 and then its treasurer from 1916 to 1920, and Ernest Mellor from the 'Hôtel des Chamois' at Leysin acted as the Federation's secretary from 1908 to 1916 (Schweizerischer Eishockey-Verband 1933, 7).

Ice hockey activities were indeed an attraction to winter tourists – notably to both male and female ones. Several sources confirm games between male and female tourists and among women players (*Gazette de Lausanne*, February 20, 1905; Furrer 1910, 64; Killias 2007, 280; Busset 2000, 243). Tourists' ice hockey activities in the Swiss Alps were even followed by the British public at home. In January 1913, for instance, the *Times* of London published a lengthy article by its St. Moritz correspondent discussing the question whether Bandy or rather Canadian ice hockey was more suitable to be played at Swiss winter resorts (*The Times*, January 24, 1913).

After the First World War, the close connection between ice hockey and the promotion of winter sport resorts continued. Starting with the Spengler Cup in Davos, whose premiere in 1923 was won by Oxford University, several resorts established their own annual tournaments (Brunner 1994, 29–42). Furthermore, both St. Moritz (European Championship 1922, Olympic Tournaments 1928 and 1948, International University Games 1935) and Davos (European Championship 1926, International University Games 1930, and World Championship 1935) would host high-profile international competitions.

Popularization and cultural transit

Once established in Switzerland through the aforementioned channels, football and ice hockey still needed to become domestic games. The modes of popularization again show similarities and differences between the two games that were to become Switzerland's most popular team sports. As far as football is concerned, the educational system played an important role for both its popularization and its further gendering. Due to the Swiss army's militia system, gymnastic lessons for boys had been made compulsory at all schools in the late nineteenth century. Many gymnastic teachers were attracted to British sports and would familiarize their pupils with football. A number of secondary and grammar schools officially introduced football into their physical education programmes during the 1880s and 1890s.[3] However, as a parallel to English academics' switch from Association to Rugby Union football, once the former had become the 'people's game' (Dunning and Sheard 1979), some Swiss grammar schools with elitist attitudes in view of football's ongoing popularization and fading social distinctiveness[4] would abandon it again and in the early

GLOBAL AND TRANSNATIONAL SPORT

1920s adopt handball instead. Sometimes pupils with working-class background would then press for football's reintroduction during the interwar period (Hofer 1998, 43–44). Ice hockey, on the other hand, hardly entered physical education at schools on a large scale, both because of the equipment needed and because of the scarcity of ice rinks in the Swiss Plateau. Notably, Davos, which became the stronghold of Swiss ice hockey between the 20s and the 50s, introduced ice hockey at primary schools during the interwar period (*Gazette de Lausanne*, January 11, 1934).

As far as clubs are concerned, football's expansion was quicker as well, however ice hockey's delay was only partially accounted for by the need of equipment and ice rinks. By the time the First World War broke out, football clubs had become an indispensable element of the rich Helvetic community of associations. Upon its foundation in 1895, the Swiss Football Association had only counted 11 member clubs. In 1914, it would muster no less than 115 clubs with 15,000 members that were dispersed all over the country (Giuliani 2001, 120). This was clearly a result of football's naturalization through the educational system.

Another result of this early popularization was the fact that Swiss expatriates, mainly merchants and teachers, would become football pioneers around the turn of the century in many places. The most famous of them is Hans 'Joan' Gamper, who was born in Winterthur in 1877 (Eberle 2013). Acquainted with football and other British sports as a student, he was among the founders of FC Zurich. As an official in the textile industry in Lyon, he then played for FC Lyon. A short time later, he settled in Catalonia and founded FC Barcelona in 1899, which numbered many Swiss, Britons, Germans and Austrians among its members. Until 1925, Gamper held office as president of Barça. One of the most successful teams in the pioneering phase of French football was called 'Stade Helvétique de Marseille'. The gymnastic and sporting club, which was founded by the Swiss colony in the southern French commercial city of Marseilles in 1884 with the name 'La Suisse Marseille', added a football section in 1904. In 1909, this team, which comprised 10 Swiss and 1 Briton, won one of the several competing French championships and repeated this success in 1911 and 1913.

The Swiss also played a role in establishing football clubs in Italy (Lanfranchi 1998). FC Bari was founded in 1908 by the grain merchant Gustav Kuhn along with his German, French, Swiss, Spanish and Italian friends. Internazionale Milano was established that same year, and the majority of its founding members were Swiss. A year later, the Swiss dentist Louis Rauch became the first president of FC Bologna. The Winterthur native Walter Aemissegger introduced football to Venice in 1912. The Swiss also were among the founders of football clubs in Palermo and Bergamo. In 1906, there were four players from St. Gallen on the championship team from Milan as well as a former player from Grasshopper. Third place Genoa had a player from Lausanne, and the previous year's champion, Juventus from Turin, had both a Swiss president and two players from Basel. When the Turin 11 travelled to Winterthur for a friendly match in 1910, their ranks included no fewer than 5 former players from FC Winterthur (*Neues Winterthurer Tagblatt*, May 14, 1910).

Swiss sporting pioneers also introduced football into various regions of Eastern Europe and North Africa. At the turn of the century, a number of Swiss merchants played leading roles in the most prominent athletic club in the Russian capital of St. Petersburg, the multi-sport St. Petersburg Circle of Amateur Athletes, which was founded in 1888 (Emeliantseva 2008a, 20–21, 2008b, 31–32). The wealthy clothier Eduard Vollenweider, who was personally involved in a wide variety of sports, served as secretary in 1896, and then later as treasurer, and finally as chairman of the club from 1905 onwards. His brother-in-law, Konrad Schinz, who played football for the club for many years, followed Vollenweider as treasurer and then as president of the club. In contrast to the football teams founded by British engineers and merchants in the metropolitan centres of the Czarist Empire, which excluded participation by the locals, in the Circle, Swiss, German and other foreigners interacted with upper-class Russians around the round leather.

In the 1890s, Swiss gymnastic instructors, who had been appointed by the Bulgarian minister of education during a trip to Western Europe, introduced football into Bulgaria (Ghanbarian-Baleva 2006, 155–157). One of them, Georges de Regibus, moved further to become a sport teacher in Egypt. In 1901, the Jewish student Hugo Buli, who had learned the game in Germany, brought a real football – apparently just the second one in Serbian sporting history – as well as a full set of football equipment from Switzerland to Belgrade, thereby causing quite a stir (Stojanović 1953, 5). And shortly before the outbreak of the First World War, a Swiss coal merchant acted as a football pioneer in the Algerian garrison town of Sidi-bel-Abbès (Hunziker 1935, 26).

The early interwar period would then witness Swiss football's take-off. Boosted by the national team's silver medal at the 1924 Olympics, the number of organized players in the Swiss Football Association during the 1920s trebled to 67,000 people in 328 clubs (Brändle and Koller 2014, 42 and 74–78). Additionally, football organized by the socialist gymnastic and sport federation SATUS, by the communist red sport circle as well as in the framework of corporation sports further increased the number of male workers playing the game (Koller 2002, 2008; Brändle and Koller 2014, 109–125).

Women, on the other hand, remained outsiders in the universe of Swiss football. In the early 1920s, Florida Pianzola, the poly-sportive daughter of a wealthy Geneva merchant, tried to organize female football activities. In 1921, she created a female team named 'Academia-Sport' that joined the Football Club Urania Geneva but soon converted to Basketball and Gymnastics (*Journal de Genève*, December 25, 1921). In the following year, Pianzola participated at the first Women's World Games in Paris in track and field. In 1923, she organized a female sport team named 'Les Sportives' that also engaged with football training (Meier 2004, 107–11), partly ridiculed by the local press (*Gazette de Lausanne*, November 30, 1923). Furthermore, the existence of a girls' team affiliated to the Zurich Young Fellows is confirmed for the year 1927 (*Club Organ des FC Young Fellows* 5/12, September 1927). After that, no more female football activities are known in Switzerland till the mid-60s.

High-profile football games from the early 1920s attracted thousands, rather than hundreds of spectators and a process of professionalization started. In the early 1930s, the National League was founded. Football's reputation as a national game was further boosted by the spectacular Swiss victory over 'Greater Germany' at the 1938 World Cup, which was celebrated as a triumph of democratic little Switzerland over their seemingly predominant fascist neighbours (Koller and Brändle 1999). However, the football business never became really profitable in Switzerland. Professionalism was attacked for ideological reasons both from the right and the left and was abolished again by the end of the 1930s, to return only step by step several decades later (Vonnard and Quin 2012; Brändle and Koller 2014, 33–72).

Ice hockey clubs were initially strongly concentrated at the francophone part of Switzerland, including clubs in the pre-alpine winter resorts as well as in the major cities (*L'Impartial*, November 29, 1908). At the founding meeting of the Swiss Ice Hockey Federation, only three people representing four clubs (Bellerive, Les Avants, Leysin, and Lausanne) had been present (Schweizerischer Eishockey-Verband 1954, 17), and by 1918, the Federation still only mustered 23 member clubs (as compared to 126 in the Football Association). Whilst tourists' Bandy clubs in St. Moritz and Davos had emerged as early as in the 1890s (*Manchester Guardian*, March 25, 1894; *Neue Zürcher Zeitung*, January 13, 1905 and January 7, 1911; *The Times*, February 6, 1909; Schwizerischer 1948, 15; Lütscher 2014, 94), permanent domestic ice hockey clubs in the Grison winter resorts were only founded after the First World War, despite the local youth having embraced ice hockey at least one decade earlier. It is notable that in Arosa, it was the local football club that in 1924 created a permanent ice hockey team (Brunner 1994, 21). Almost immediately after their creation, however, these clubs started exerting a nearly absolute domination in Swiss ice hockey, which would last until the late 50s. The Swiss ice hockey championship during this period was won 23 times by Davos, 7 times by Arosa and 3 times by St. Moritz. Whilst at the first Olympic ice hockey tournament in 1920, the Swiss goalkeeper had played wearing a white shirt and a tie (*Sport*, March 24, 1971), ice hockey now became an embodiment of lusty Alpine masculinity that hardly reminded the winter sport activities of elegant British tourists of both genders during the *Belle Epoque*.

Female ice hockey almost completely disappeared. During the early thirties, the Paris-based female ice sport club 'Droit au But', that won all but one French women's ice hockey championships from 1930 to 1937, often resided at the Swiss winter sport resort of Villars and played several games against English women's teams there (*Manchester Guardian*, January 13, 1931, February 5, 1931, January 19, 1932, and April 12, 1932). In 1935, they also played against an Austrian male team at Villars as well as against the local male squad at Lausanne (Wiener Athletiksport Club, wienwiki.wienerzeitung.at/WIENWIKI/Wiener_Athletiksport_Club; *Gazette de Lausanne*, January 26, 1935). However, domestic female ice hockey activities in Switzerland would only start around 1980.

In the Swiss Plateau, only very few ice hockey clubs emerged before the end of the 1920s, mainly due to the lack of permanent ice rinks (Killias 2007, 32–33). This would change after the first artificial ice rink had been opened in Zurich in 1930, which immediately triggered the creation of two new ice hockey clubs in the largest Swiss city (Eggenberger 1986, 533–535; Marquart 2010). Other places would follow suit soon (*Gazette de Lausanne*, April 18, 1935), and the number of members of the Swiss Ice Hockey Federation skyrocketed from 23 clubs in 1918 to 43 in 1939 and 96 in 1945 (Schweizerischer Eishockey-Verband 1948, 67). This process was boosted by the successes of the national team that, playing in front of a home crowd, won gold at the European championship 1926, silver at the World championship 1935 and bronze at the 1928 Olympics. Yet, the ice hockey National League founded in 1937 first was quite small and the Swiss Ice Hockey Federation would continue their stubborn anti-professionalism policy well into the 1960s.

Unorganized sport activities as both the basis of popularization and a mirror of its success followed a similar pattern. As early as in 1908, a socialist newspaper complained about workers doing nothing else than drinking, chanting patriotic and religious songs and playing football (*Volksrecht*, December 7, 1908). Juvenile street football can be traced back to the turn of the century. For Zurich's workers' suburb Aussersihl, it is confirmed even for the early 1890s (Gysler 1964, 175). Unorganized ice hockey first was restricted mainly to the male youth of winter resorts that quite early had started copying British tourists and after the First World War was instrumental in the creation of domestic ice hockey clubs. In the Swiss Plateau, ice sport was boosted by the very cold winter of 1928–9, which for the first time in three decades resulted in the freezing up of the Lake of Zurich. This not only triggered the creation of an artificial ice rink, but also the male youth starting to play ice hockey, which they would continue during the following winters on improvised ice fields (Läser 1993, 73). Juvenile ice hockey players' problems can best be demonstrated by the example of the village of Ambrì, which after the Second World War would become a stronghold of ice hockey in the Canton of Ticino: Already in 1910, some teenagers had asked local authorities to create an ice rink, however only 15 years later, this project materialized. Juvenile ice hockey eventually resulted in the foundation of HC Ambrì-Piotta in 1937 as the first ice hockey club in the Italian-speaking part of Switzerland (Killias 2007, 34).

Something unorganized juvenile football and ice hockey activities had in common was a remarkable awareness of the two games' Anglo-Saxon roots. The autobiographical novel by the lawyer and journalist Paul Wehrli, who grew up in Zurich around the turn of the century, mentions street football players using chunks of English like 'eiredy' (Wehrli 1942, 16), and youth memoirs referring to the interwar period confirm the continued usage of sometimes mispronounced and only half-understood English football terminology (Stamm 1986, 18; Bietenhader 2013, 102 as well as Brändle 2007; Brändle and Koller 2014, 99–108). And according to the memoirs of Hans Dürst, who in 1948 would become Olympic bronze medal winner, boys in Davos during the 1930s played ice hockey with frozen horse droppings and nearly all of the teams claimed to be some sort of 'Canadians' (Scherrer 2010, 143). The former sport transfer over the Channel or even the Atlantic Ocean had thus become an integral part of young Swiss sport amateurs' communicative memory.[5]

Conclusion

On balance, the introduction of football and ice hockey in Switzerland was a complex process including manifold cultural, social, economic, geographical and gender issues. Driven by close links between social elites of the United Kingdom and Switzerland, the two games reached the alpine republic through different and partly overlapping channels at a relatively early point. All of these channels – academic and professional mobility as well as tourism – were closely linked to elitist migration. Institutionalization in clubs then happened comparatively early, also thanks to Switzerland's liberal constitution fully granting freedom of association.

The early arrival of football and ice hockey in Switzerland had crucial consequences:

First, it created a bridgehead for the further spread of these games across continental Europe. This again was mainly the by-product of elitist migration (though migrating workers might potentially have had a role as well, for which, however, no evidence is known (Koller 2011–12, 162–163). Switzerland then would also play a remarkable role in establishing the International Federation of Association Football in 1904 and the International Ice Hockey Federation in 1908.[6]

Second, the early presence of football and ice hockey also allowed for a quick popularization that would change the character of the two games considerably. Whilst their Anglo-Saxon roots weren't forgotten and actually even added to their attractiveness, they nevertheless mutated to national games that completely lost their formerly elitist character. Players became role models of masculine heroes – footballers rather of an urban and working-class type, ice hockey players rather of a rural and alpine type. The two games thus had become an integral part of Swiss culture by the end of the interwar period at the very

GLOBAL AND TRANSNATIONAL SPORT

latest – ironically less than two decades before Switzerland's position on the international level started to decline for both games.

Notes

1. The National Archives (Kew), WO 32/10,674 British Swiss Legion, Central Depot Schlestadt, to War Department, April 1856.
2. See *Journal de Genève*, 8.1.1904 and 2.2.1905; *Gazette de Lausanne*, 5.1.1904 and 11.1.1904, *Feuille d'avis de Lausanne*, 6.1.1904 and 2.2.1905.
3. See, for instance, *Neue Zürcher Zeitung*, 17.8.1888; *Geschäftsbericht der Stadtschulpflege von Zürich über das Schulwesen der Stadt Zürich im Schuljahr 1891/92*. Zurich: Ulrich, 36; *Geschäftsbericht der Stadtschulpflege von Zürich über das Schulwesen der Stadt Zürich im Schuljahr 1892/93 (Mai bis Dezember) nebst einer Übersicht über die Organisation und Entwicklung desselben von 1877 bis 1892*. Zurich: Ulrich, 8 as well as Gerber 2007, 12–13; Hadorn 2015, 87 and 106.
4. See on the concept of 'distinction' Bourdieu 1979.
5. See on the concept of 'communicative memory' Assmann 1995.
6. On the establishment of international sport federations around 1900 and its contexts, see Eisenberg 2001.

References

Akademischer Eishockey-Club Zürich. 1983. *75 Jahre AECZ: Jubiläumsschrift* [75 years of AECZ]. w. p.

Annan, Noel. 1984. *Leslie Stephen: The Godless Victorian*. London: Weidenfeld and Nicolson.

Assmann, Jan. 1995. "Collective Memory and Cultural Identity." *New German Critique* 65: 125–133.

Barton, Susan. 2008. *Healthy Living in the Alps: The Origins of Winter Tourism in Switzerland, 1860–1914*. Manchester, NH: Manchester University Press.

Benson, Edward Frederic. 1913. *Winter Sports in Switzerland*. London: G. Allen.

Bernegger, Michael. 1990. "Die Schweiz und die Weltwirtschaft." [Switzerland and the Global Economy], In *Die Schweiz in der Weltwirtschaft (15.-20. Jahrhundert)*, edited by Paul Bairoch and Martin Körner, 429–464. Zurich: Chronos.

Beyer, Bernd-M. 2014. *Der Mann, der den Fussball nach Deutschland brachte: Das Leben des Walther Bensemann: Ein biografischer Roman* [The Man Who Brought Football to Germany: The Life of Walther Benseman: A Biographical Novel]. Göttingen: Werkstatt Verlag.

Bietenhader, Ueli. 2013. *Mollmoll: Moll, da sänd no Lüüt: Gschichte, verzellt i de Altstätter Mundart* [Yes, These Are People: Stories Narrated in the Dialect of Altstätten]. Herisau: Appenzeller Verlag.

Bourdieu, Pierre. 1979. *La Distinction: Critique Sociale du Jugement* [Distinction: A Social Critique of the Judgement of Taste]. Paris: Les Éditions de Minuit.

Brändle, Fabian. 2007. "Tennisbälle, Dolen und zerbrochene Scheiben: Zur Geschichte des Schweizer Strassenfussballs vor dem Zeitalter des Automobils (1920–1945)." [Tenis Balls, Drains, and Broken Windows: The History of Swiss Street Soccer before the Age of the Automobile, 1920–1945]. *SportZeiten* 7 (3): 7–20.

Brändle, Fabian, and Christian Koller. 2014. *4 zu 2: Die goldene Zeit des Schweizer Fussballs 1918–1939* [4–2: The Golden Age of Swiss Football, 1918–1939]. Göttingen: Werkstatt Verlag.

Brunner, Elmar. 1994. *70 Jahre EHC Arosa: Ein Dorf schreibt Schweizer Sportgeschichte* [70 Years of ECH Arosa: A Village Writes Swiss Sport History]. Chur: Eigenverlag F&L-Planungen AG.

Busset, Thomas. 2000. "'… Quelque joie au milieu de la nature maussade et froide de l'hiver': Les relations ville/montagne vues à travers les débuts du hockey sur glace en Suisse." [The Relationship between the City and the Mountains and the Beginnings of Ice Hockey in Switzerland] *Histoire des Alpes* 5: 241–250.

Busset, Thomas. 2001. "De la sociabilité mondaine à la competition: Les débuts du hockey sur glace en Suisse." [From Mondaine Sociability to Competitive Sport: The Beginnings of Ice Hockey in

GLOBAL AND TRANSNATIONAL SPORT

Switzerland]. In *Sports en formes: Acteurs, contextes et dynamiques d'institutionnalisation*, edited by Thomas Busset and Christophe Jaccout, 127–136. Lausanne: Antipodes.

Chandler, Timothy J. L. 1991. "Games at Oxbridge and the Public Schools, 1830–80: The Diffusion of an Innovation." *The International Journal of the History of Sport* 8: 171–204.

Collet, Ernest, and Daniel Guillemin, eds. 2000. *Ligue romande de football (LRF): 100 ans de joli jeu* [The Football Legaue of the Romandie: 100 Years of Beautiful Game]. Lausanne: Ligue Romande de Football.

Coviello, Michele. 2007. "Die Macht der Disziplin: Ursprünge des modernen Fussballs in Grossbritannien und der Schweiz." [The Power of Discipline: Beginnings of Modern Footbal in Great Britain and Switzerland]. MA thesis, University of Zurich.

Doyle, Arthur Conan. 1894. "An Alpine Pass on 'Ski." *The Strand Magazine*, Vol. 8, December.

Doyle, Arthur Conan. 2007. *Memories and Adventures*. London: Wordsworth Editions.

Dunning, Eric, and Kenneth Sheard. 1979. *Barbarians, Gentlemen and Players: A Sociological Study of the Development of Rugby Football*. Oxford: Martin Robertson.

Eberle, Christian. 2013. "Protestant – Katalane – Ikone: Joan Gamper: Gründervater des FC Barcelona." [Protestand, Catalan, Icon: Joan Gamper: The Fouding Father of FC Barcelona]. In *Memorialkultur im Fussballsport: Medien, Rituale und Praktiken des Erinnerns, Gedenkens und Vergessens*, edited by Markwart Herzog, 113–132. Stuttgart: Kohlhammer Verlag.

Eggenberger, Yves. 1986. *100 Jahre Grasshopper-Club Zürich* [100 Years of Grasshopper-Club Zurich]. Zurich: Grasshopper-Club.

Eisenberg, Christiane. 2001. "The Rise of Internationalism in Sport." In *The Mechanics of Internationalism: Culture, Society, and Politics from the 1840s to World War I*, edited by Martin H. Geyer and Johannes Paulmann, 375–403. Oxford: Oxford University Press.

Emeliantseva, Ekaterina. 2008a. "Ein Fussballmatch ist kein Symphoniekonzert!' Die Fussballspiele und ihr Publikum im spätzarischen Russland (1901–1913)." [Football Games and Their Audience in Late Imperial Russia, 1901–1913]. In *Überall ist der Ball rund – Die Zweite Halbzeit: Zur Geschichte und Gegenwart des Fussballs in Ost- und Südosteuropa*, edited by Dittmar Dahlmann, Anke Hillbrenner, and Britta Lenz, 13–43. Essen: Klartext.

Emeliantseva, Ekaterina. 2008b. "Sport und urbane Lebenswelten im spätzarischen St. Petersburg (1860–1914)" [Sport and Urban Live Worlds in Late Imperial Saint Petersburg, 1860–1914]. In *Sport als städtisches Ereignis*, edited by Christian Koller, 31–76. Ostfildern: Thorbecke.

Feuz, Patrick. 2014. "Herzogin auf Ski, Lord auf Kufen: Hoteliers erzwingen die Wintersaison." [Duchess in Ski, Lord on Skids: Hotel Directors Create the Winter Season]. In *Kronleuchter vor der Jungfrau: Mürren – eine Tourismusgeschichte*, edited by Patrick Feuz. 89–113. Baden: Hier und Jetzt.

Furgler, Martin. 1979. *1879–1979: Ein Jahrhundert FC St. Gallen: Offizielles Jubiläumsbuch zum 100. Geburtstag des ältesten Fussballclubs der Schweiz*. [1879–1979: A Century of FC Saint-Gall: The Official Jubilee Book fo the 100th Anniversary of the Oldest Football Club in Switzerland]. Herisau: FC St. Gallen.

Furrer, Edwin. 1910. *Winter in der Schweiz: Wintersport und Winterkuren* [Winter in Switzerland: Winter Sports and Winter Holidays]. Zurich: Bürgi.

Gerber, Hans-Dieter. 2007. "Fussball in Basel: Von den Anfängen bis zum Zweiten Weltkrieg." [Football in Basle: From the Beginnings Till World War II]. *Basler Zeitschrift Für Geschichte und Altertumskunde* 107: 9–33.

Ghanbarian-Baleva, Gergana. 2006. "Ein 'Englischer Sport' aus der Schweiz: Der bulgarische Fussball von seiner Entstehung bis zum Beginn der 1970er Jahre." [An 'English Sport' from Switzerland: Bulgarian Football from its Beginnings till the early 70s] In *Überall ist der Ball rund: Zur Geschichte und Gegenwart des Fussballs in Ost- und Südosteuropa*, edited by Dittmar Dahlmann, Anke Hillbrenner, and Britta Lenz, 155–182. Essen: Klartext.

Gilgen, Alexandre. 2003. "Implantation et Développement du Football à Lausanne et dans le Canton de Vaud: De la fin du XIXe siècle à la Seconde Guerre Mondiale." [Import and Development of Football in Lausanne and in the Canton of Vaud: From the End of the 19th Century till World War II]. MA thesis, University of Lausanne.

GLOBAL AND TRANSNATIONAL SPORT

Giuliani, Markus. 2001. *"Starke Jugend – Freies Volk": Bundestaatliche Körpererziehung und gesellschaftliche Funktion von Sport in der Schweiz (1918–1947)* [Physical Education by the Federal State and the Social Functions of Sport in Switzerland, 1918–1947]. Bern: Peter Lang.

Gosteli, Mike. 2008. *100 Gesichter – 100 Geschichten: 100 Jahre Schweizer Eishockey* [100 Faces - 100 Stories: 100 Years of Swiss Ice Hockey]. Zurich: Orell Füssli.

Gysin, Roland. 1998. "Die Internierung fremder Militärpersonen im 1. Weltkrieg. Vom Nutzen der Humanität und den Mühen in der Asylpolitik." [The Internment of Foreign Military Persons in World War I: The Usefulness of Humanity and the Troubles of Refugee Policy]. In *Krisen und Stabilisierung. Die Schweiz in der Zwischenkriegszeit*, edited by Sebastien Guex, Brigitte Studer, Bernard Degen, Markus Kübler, Edzard Schade, Béatrice Ziegler, 33–46. Zurich: Chronos.

Gysler, Heiri. 1964. *Damals in Zürich: Erinnerungen an Zürich vor der ersten Stadtvereinigung* [Once Upon a Time in Zurich: Memoirs of Zurich Before the First City Unification]. Zurich: Eigenverlag.

Hadorn, Christian, ed. 2015. *"Die Welt Riss Mich": Aus der Jugend eines feinsinnigen Rebellen (1876–1929)* [The Youth of a Sensible Rebel]. Zurich: Chronos.

Hansen, P. H. 1995. "Albert Smith, the Alpine Club, and the Invention of Mountaineering in mid-Victorian Britain." *The Journal of British Studies* 34: 300–324.

Hofer, Hansjörg. 1998. *"Völker, Hört Die Signale ...": Erinnerungen eines Basler Kommunisten* [Memoirs of a Communist From Basle]. Basle: Pharos-Verlag H. R. Schwabe.

Howald, Stefan. 2004. *Insular Denken: Grossbritannien und die Schweiz: Facetten einer Beziehung* [Insular Thinking: Great Britain and Switzerland: Aspects of a Relationship]. Zurich: Neue Zürcher Zeitung.

Hunziker, Adolf. 1935. *Erlebnisse und Schilderungen aus der Französischen Fremdenlegion* [Adventures and Narrations from the French Foreign Legion]. Olten: Selbstverlag.

Imlah, Ann Gordon. 1966. *Britain and Switzerland 1846–1860: A Study of Anglo Swiss Relations during Some Critical Years for Swiss Neutrality*. London: Longmans.

Iringer, Rolf. 1947. "Eishockey." [Ice Hockey]. In *Stadion Schweiz: Turnen, Sport und Spiele*, Vol. 1, 346–362. Zurich: Metz.

Killias, Rudolf, ed. 2007. *Powerplay: 100 Jahre Schweizer Eishockey* [Powerplay: 100 Years of Swiss Ice Hockey]. Worb: Killi's Consulting Company.

Koller, Christian. 2002. "Zur Entwicklung des schweizerischen Firmenfussballs 1920–1955." [The Development of Swiss Corporation Football, 1920–1955]. *Stadion* 28: 249–266.

Koller, Christian. 2006. "Prolog: 'Little England': Die avantgardistische Rolle der Schweiz in der Pionierphase des Fussballs." [Prologue: 'Little Englan': Switzerland's Avantgardistic Role in Football's Pioneering Phase]. In *Die Nati: Die Geschichte der Schweizer Fussball-Nationalmannschaft*, edited by Beat Jung, 11–22. Göttingen: Werkstatt Verlag.

Koller, Christian. 2008. "Kicken unter Hammer und Sichel – Die vergessene Geschichte des Schweizerischen Arbeiterfussball-Verbandes (1930–1936)." [Kicking Under Hammer and Sickle - The Forgotten Story of the Swiss Workers Football Federation, 1930–1936]. In *Überall ist der Ball rund – Die Zweite Halbzeit: Zur Geschichte und Gegenwart des Fussballs in Ost- und Südosteuropa*, edited by Dittmar Dahlmann, Anke Hilbrenner, and Britta Lenz, 241–267. Essen: Klartext.

Koller, Christian. 2011–12. "Transnationalität und Popularisierung – Thesen und Fragen zur Frühgeschichte des Schweizer Fussballs." [Transnationality and Popularisation - Theses and Questions Regarding the Early History of Swiss Football]. *Ludica* 17–18: 151–166.

Koller, Christian, and Fabian Brändle. 1999. "'Man fühlte, Dass die Eidgenossen eine Grosstat vollbracht hatten': Fussball und Geistige Landesverteidigung in der Schweiz." [Football and Spiritual National Defense in Switzerland]. *Stadion* 25: 177–214.

Lanfranchi, Pierre. 1998. "Football et Modernité: La Suisse et la Pénétration du Football sur le Continent." [Football and Modernity: Switzerland and the Spread of Football over the Continent]. *Traverse* 5 (3): 76–88.

Läser, Edwin. 1993. *Läsi: Erinnerungen aus meiner Bubenzeit* [Läsi: Memoirs of My Youth]. Wallisellen: Selbstverlag.

Lieber, Francis, ed. 1832. *Encyclopaedia Americana: A Popular Dictionary of Arts, Sciences, Literature, History, Politics and Biography*. Vol. 11. Philadelphia, PA: Carey, Lea & Carey.

Lütscher, Michael. 2014. *Schnee, Sonne und Stars: Wie der Wintertourismus von St. Moritz aus die Alpen erobert hat* [Snow, Sun, and Stars: How Winter Tourism Conquered the Alps Departing from Saint Moritz]. Zurich: Neue Zürcher Zeitung.

Marquart, Denise. 2010. "Die älteste Kunsteisbahn der Schweiz." [The Oldest Artificial Ice Rink of Switzerland]. *Züritpp Online*, October 18.

Meier, Marianne. 2004. *"Zarte Füsschen am harten Leder...": Frauenfussball in der Schweiz 1970–1999* [Women's Footbal in Switzerland, 1970–1999]. Frauenfeld: Huber.

Meinherz, Paul. 2008. "Alpinismus." [Alpinism]. In *Historisches Lexikon der Schweiz* (electronic publication), March 11.

Mente, Michael. 2015. "Wie Die 'Mordiokugel' nach Weinfelden kam." [How the 'Deadly Ball' Came to Weinfelden]. *Unser Thurgau*, Vol. 11, 88–89.

Müller, Reto. 2013. "Wintersport." [Winter Sports]. In *Historisches Lexikon Der Schweiz (electronic publication)*, November 5

Scherrer, Claudia, ed. 2010. *Damals in Davos: Kindheitserinnerungen* [Once Upon A Time in Davos: Childhood Memoirs]. Oberengstringen: Claudia Wartmann Natürlich.

Schweizerischer Eishockey-Verband. 1933. *Jahrbuch 1933/34.* [Year Book 1933-34] w. p.

Schweizerischer Eishockey-Verband, ed. 1948. *Le Hockey sur Glace en Suisse – Eishockey in der Schweiz* [Ice Hockey in Switzerland]. w. p.

Schweizerischer Eishockey-Verband. 1954. *Offizielles Jahrbuch 1954/1955* [Official Yearbook 1954–55]. w. p.

Seger, Cordula. 2006. "Wintersport im Grand Hotel: Strategien einer Inszenierung – Das Oberengadin zwischen 1886–1914." [Winter Sports at the Grand Hotel - Strategies of Staging - The Upper Engadine 1886 to 1914]. In *Pour une Histoire des Sports d'hiver – Zur Geschichte des Wintersports: Actes du Colloque De Lugano 20 Et 21 Février 2004*, edited by Thomas Busset and Marco Marcacci, 35–49. Neuchâtel: Editions CIES.

Stamm, Alfred. 1986. *Die Stadt am Nabel der Welt: Winterthur rund um die Zwanziger Jahre* [The City at the Navel of the World: Winterthur during the Twenties]. Winterthur: Vogel.

Stojanović, Danilo. 1953. *Čika Dačine Uspomene* [The Memoirs of Čika Dača]. Belgrade: S. D. Crvena zvezda.

Tissot, Laurent. 2000. *Naissance d'une industrie touristique: Les Anglais et la Suisse au XIXe siècle* [The Birth of a Tourism Industry: The English and Switzerland during the 19th Century]. Lausanne: Payot.

Van Muyden-Baird, Anne. 1943. *Ouchy, mon Village … Souvenirs de l'autre siècle 1855–1880* [Ouchy, My Village... Memoirs of the Last Century 1855–1880]. Lausanne: Editions Spes.

Vonnard, Philippe, and Grégory Quin. 2012. "Eléments pour une Histoire de la Mise en Place du Professionalisme dans le Football Suisse durant l'entre-deux-guerres: Processus, Résistances et Ambiguïtés." [Elements of a History of the Establishment of Professionalisme in Swiss Football during the Interwar Period: Processes, Resistance, and Ambiguities]. *Schweizerische Zeitschrift Für Geschichte* 62: 70–85.

Wehrli, Paul. 1942. *Martin Wendel: Roman Einer Kindheit* [Martin Wendel: Novel of a Childhood]. Zurich: Büchergilde Gutenberg.

Wraight, John. 1987. *The Swiss and the British*. Salisbury: Russell.

Wylie, Neville. 2013. "Grossbritannien: Vom 19. Jahrhundert bis zum 2. Weltkrieg." [Great Britain: 19th Century till World War II]. In *Historisches Lexikon Der Schweiz (electronic publication)*, July 18.

Zincke, Forster Barham. 1874. *Swiss Allmends and a Walk to See them being a Second Month in Switzerland*. London: Smith, Elder.

With or without cricket? The two lives of the English game in a decolonizing India

Souvik Naha

ABSTRACT

This article explores the contradictory responses to cricket in India from the perspective of transcultural encounters. Football and hockey lost their foreign character by the time of India's independence in the mid-twentieth century, but cricket was not indigenized the same way and retained its Englishness. As a result, it was often considered as inimical to nation-building in the age of decolonization, leading to periodic calls for its boycott. Although cricket grew in popularity and gradually emerged as India's favourite sport, its English origin and discourses are still criticized in the mass media and public sphere. The historiography of cricket in India has analysed the proliferation of cricket in India as an accomplishment of the state, corporate and private patronage networks, and the 'games ethic' as cultivated by cross-cultural interactions. It has focused on the diffusion and resistance models but has overlooked the complex entanglements of the bridges of transfer, the conflicts in the ideational space mediated by agents of transfer, and the hypertexts of transferred culture across social strata. This article offers a corrective to this methodological problem by analyzing the dilemma of cricket's appropriation in the light of the ambiguities of cultural transfer. By linking the debates about cricket's legitimacy as an Indian sport to the operations of political ideologies, it maps the history of cultural transfers in a postcolonial setting.

Introduction

On a Sunday morning, sometime in 1960, a debate took place in a house on Khurut Road in Howrah, a town across the river Ganges from Calcutta. A group of friends – including three professors, two authors, two clerks, one schoolteacher, one lawyer, one businessman, one government officer and one engineer – aged from 20 to 45, vociferously argued if cricket was really worth spending time on. In the opinion of Sankar, a popular author, cricket was an 'illegitimate, immoral, ill-conceived, illogical' English pursuit. The sight of two batsmen dominating 11 fielders reflected an obscene bureaucracy and 11 fielders closing in on two batsmen resembled a slaughter. Cricket was a dreadful remnant of the British rule in India (Basu 1961). Sibnarayan Ray, a Marxist philosopher, who taught at Calcutta University and was friends with Bertrand Russell, said that no progressive country in the world played cricket. He cited the examples of Germany, the land of the greatest scientists and philosophers, France, the leader of pursuits of intellect and luxury, Russia, the rebellious redeemer of humanity, America, the champion of fast and consumerist living, and China, which was full of diligent, 'yellow-skinned' people (Basu 1961, 5). The critics declared that cricket was merely a passive recreation suitable for people of wealth and leisure. At this point, Sankariprasad Basu, a professor of Bengali language at Calcutta University, launched a long polemic in cricket's favour.

Basu made an a priori assumption that though lack of a blemish could lead to a country's positive development, lack of a certain excellence could not be considered a merit – its absence was not something to be praised. England was no less civilized or developed than the nations Ray had mentioned. Among the virtues to have contributed to England's superiority, the three most important were parliamentary democracy, drama and cricket.[1] It was shameful that other countries did not play cricket (Basu 1961). The sport-loving public of Calcutta would have largely agreed with him. They made any Test match at Eden Gardens the highlight of the annual sporting calendar for years to come. Yet, the debate whether it was ethically right for Indians to play and watch an English sport after independence never really disappeared.

Cricket in the nineteenth century promised social mobility, but also buttressed the division of class and ethnicity. The situation did not radically differ even in the 1960s. In 1968, English cricket administrators dropped a non-white player from the squad because South Africa refused to play against a mixed-race national team (Murray 2001). Marylebone Cricket Club (MCC) was one of the last sport authorities in the world to sever ties with the Apartheid regime. It underestimated for years the potential of former colonies. It used to send second-string teams to the Indian subcontinent for decades, and started sending full-strength squads only after a number of defeats, most memorably on its home turf in 1971. It even terminated the county contract of an Indian cricketer in 1977 after the latter had questioned the morality of a certain English cricketer (Naha 2013). In spite of the wide publicity of these instances in India, 'English cricket' was only moderately dislodged from its high pedestal, so successful was the inculcation of the game's moral lessons. In 1972 Shibdas Bandopadhyay wrote to the editor of the leftist newspaper *Dainik Basumati* (30 December 1972, 6): 'Cricket is not simply a game for the English; it is a symbol of principle and discipline, the life-force of the English character. Cricket runs in the blood of English cricketers'. This testifies how deep the love for cricket's moral values and connection with Englishness ran in the public's mind. The newspaper which by principle detested the gentry, thought it appropriate to publish a letter which unconditionally admired cricket and the very bourgeois philosophy the game typified. In a decade when revolutionary upheavals swept through the Third World, does such respect for England's national game in a former colony, with a long history of anti-colonial struggle, seem regular? It was not. Cricket's detractors materialized just as a team trooped into Calcutta for a Test match.

This chapter explores these contradictory responses from the perspective of transcultural encounters. It draws together the three fields which historians consider the most important in the context of Anglo-Indian cultural synthesis – politics, language and cricket (Ahmed 2004). Previous scholarship, which will be discussed in detail later, has analysed the proliferation of cricket in India as an accomplishment of the state, corporate and private patronage networks. This historiography mentions introduction of the 'games ethic' through schools and colleges (Mangan 1985) and cross-cultural interactions such as migration of foreign cricket professionals to the physically defined space of the nation (Ponsford 2015). The diffusion and resistance models barely consider the more complex processes of perception and translation of cultural codes. A major pitfall of these histories is their preoccupation with studying the production of an indigenous brand of cricket among the upper middle classes of colonial Bombay and Calcutta, eliding from their accounts the bridges of transfer, the conflicts in the ideational space mediated by agents of transfer, and the hypertexts of transferred culture across social strata. Hence, these studies advocate the logic of fixed group identities and nearly identical mechanisms of appropriation across the nation. This chapter offers a corrective to this methodological problem by analyzing the dilemma of cricket's appropriation in the light of the ambiguities of cultural transfer.

Cricket's Englishness and its discontents

In 1968, a rather infuriated D.M. Brittain from Aberdeen wrote to the editor of *The Times* (25 June 1968, 11), 'Now I know that this country is finished. On Saturday, with Australia playing, I asked a London cabby to take me to Lord's, and had to show him the way'. His tone conveys the sense that unfamiliarity with the location of the country's premier cricket ground was a crime and England's place in the world depended on how seriously its residents took cricket. Once upon a time, corresponding to the period wedged between the mid-nineteenth century and the beginning of the Second World War, cricket had a special place in the English educational institutions and political fields. Cricket's origin can be traced variously to Ancient Scotland (Bowen 1970) and Early Modern France, but its modern form was developed in nineteenth-century England (Brookes 1978). Cricket was for the Victorians the ultimate lesson in 'ethics, morals, justice, religion and life itself' (Sandiford 1983, 310). It was invested with ideals of sporting spirit and fair play, and promoted as an ideological template to strengthen a player's moral and physical character, thereby producing exemplary citizens and subjects (Williams 1999). The ethos of amateurism, fair play and rusticity so intricately woven into cricket's history was gradually invented in mid-to-late-nineteenth-century England. To apply Hobsbawm's (1983) concept of the invention of tradition, this formal invention which cumulatively 'anglicised' cricket was ritualized by a group of white men – administrators, authors, or both. Many of them resisted any chance of its mutation, trying to project cricket not as new and vague but as a time-honoured, binding social practice that should be embraced without question. The rich literature on English cricket, authored by a disparate group that included several Nobel and Poet Laureates, established a cult of cricket which was emblematic of what the idea of 'England' symbolized, almost without exception (Birley 1995).

The game's 'golden age' was cruelly curtailed by the First World War but the romanticization did not wane in the inter-war years. Cricket's moral vocabulary and pastoral nostalgia became more popular, and more people and regions came into its fold (Holt 1996). A cartoon published in *The Star* (20 December 1920) days before Christmas, entitled 'The Relative Importance of Things', shows cricket, even in its off-season, to tower above Christmas, the weather, the latest divorce, politics and other people's trouble in the pecking order. The global economic and political trends in the inter-war years and particularly after the Second World War, along with the surge of football fandom, increasingly trapped the dwindling constituency of 'English' cricket followers in a dungeon of history. In a world that kept pushing Test cricket to the brink of irrelevance, cricket needed to be preserved, shielded from modern encroachments. The people who mediated the space between the sport and its followers came to the rescue. Cricket's audience were constantly reminded of the sport's nineteenth-century tradition which has been variously called 'England's lifeblood' (Lucas 1989, 215) and 'old imperial propaganda' (Marqusee 2005, 41). Cardus (1984, 142) wanted his readers to believe that the world of ideas, politics and strife was alien to cricket; the game was a world in itself. He made a sweeping claim that:

> If everything else in this nation of ours was lost but cricket – her constitution and the laws of England of Lord Halsbury – it would be possible to reconstruct from the theory and practice of cricket all the eternal Englishness which has gone to the establishment of that Constitution and the laws aforesaid. (Birley 1979, 11)

A similar effort was undertaken by the Test Match Special commentators on BBC Radio. As Marqusee (2005, 22) found out in the 1970s, they reiterated the part cricket played in the lost, imperial 'world of deference and hierarchy, ruled by benevolent white men'. It was a world in which professional players, who played cricket for a livelihood, were compelled to address those who played for fun, the amateurs, as 'Mister' or 'Sir'. The professionals relaxed in segregated changing rooms, ate on separate tables, entered the ground through different gates, or risk termination of contract for breach of etiquette. The team captain had to be an amateur even if he was the worst player in the team. The system was so stringent as late as in 1937 that Wally Hammond was converted after 17 years of playing as a professional to an amateur by a monetary grant from Marsham Tyres, a subsidiary of the Dunlop Tyres, so that he could lead the MCC in 1938 (Wagg 2000). It was only in 1963 that the annual Gentlemen v Players match was scrapped and all first-class cricketers declared profession-als. It has been noted that there was very little dissent towards this class division, which indicates that social inequality in the English society was far outweighed by consent to harmony (Williams 1999). Radio commentators were no exception to the band who con-ceived cricket as a game above such mundane predicaments. They tried to make Marqusee (2005, 22) realize, without success, that cricket did not belong to the world of the welfare state, feminism, trade unions, sex, drugs and rock and roll. The suggested epitomization of England's *Belle Époque* by cricket was largely incompatible with the 1970s, yet self-appointed custodians of the game's tradition continued to refer to its Englishness at every opportunity.

Englishness is a loaded term, which for the sake of simplicity can be introduced, as Gikandi (1996, xii–xiii) wrote, as a 'cultural and literary phenomenon produced in the ambivalent space that separated, but also conjoined, metropole and colony'. It was undoubt-edly established as a boundary separating the people of England from Britain and the rest of the world. As Colley (1994) argues, the idea of a British identity was created on the back of the Act of Union of 1707 that combined England, Scotland, Wales and Ireland into a single geopolitical entity which was ruptured along the lines of locality and social class. Britain was thus a nation invented by politicians and appended by the monarchy and participa-tion of its various communities in the imperial project as soldiers and civilians. Although there was a tendency to conflate Englishness with Britishness due to England's position of power, the fault lines of the overarching civic identity were manifested time and again by the Irish or Scottish declarations of their own distinctiveness, namely, rejection of cricket (Kumar 2012). Hence, on the one hand, Englishness was at the heart of the empire, by giving the colonizers from England a homogenous identity; on the other hand, the empire and migration threatened to corrupt this ethno-linguistic similitude (Webster 2005). National cultural homogeneity as a group identity is an impossible dream as cultures do not germinate in isolation, and hence contain transcultural traces. Likewise, an 'empirical Englishman', contends Žižek (1991, 110), invariably takes in something non-English. Popular narratives of Englishness from the inter-war years sought to protect the idealized English behaviour and landscape from incursion of foreign culture. Cricket featured prominently in the list of endangered institutions.

One of the methods of preservation was invocation of amateurism, which was the great rhetoric of nineteenth-century sport. In England as in the United States, it was apparently an ideology of demarcating class identities and instilling in the middle and upper class the sense of a disciplined, systematic life ordained by playing sport the 'proper' way (Holt 1989; Mangan and Walvin 1991; Lowerson 1995; Pope 1996). Fry (1939, 223) wrote in his autobiography that W.G. Grace was the quintessential Victorian personage not because he was a brilliant cricketer, but as he played in 'the Grand Manner'. In an eagerness to present Grace as the paradigmatic amateur sportsman, a simple, rotund, middle-class country doctor with an exceptional talent for sport, his supporters glossed over his penchant for betting or habitual refusal to obey the rules (Rae 1998). In order to be considered an authentic English hero, a cricketer had to comply with this amateur ideal. As Holt (1989, 266–267) shows, it was not just great batting performances that made the professional cricketer Jack Hobbs 'The Master'. His behaviour – 'the reserve, the modesty, the shy humour, the very "gentlemanliness", sobriety, religiosity and acceptance of the status quo – made him 'a true aristocrat of labour'. Holt (1989, 268–269) further observes that the ideal of respecting superiors and fairness became particularly important in the inter-war years when political and public life were being reorganized in keeping with the changing times. Unchallenged faith in the constitution would have made the working and middle-class public self-disciplined, and curb the emergent radicalism represented by left-wing politics. Hence, the umpire or referee became a metaphor for the state, who sustained the national tradition of justice. This was supposed to be an integral segment of cricket's Englishness. The extent to which these ideals were standardized is, however, open to question.

Appadurai (1996, 90) calls cricket a hard cultural form which alters its participants more readily than it itself is amenable to change. By hardness of form he probably meant that the sport required its followers to appreciate its external codes as they were. The codes could be challenged and changed but the result would be a sport with a different essence, not 'cricket'. Cricket literature is abounding with stories of actors clinging unwaveringly to their perception of cricket. Some of the early members of the Captain Scott XI, a village team put together by Thompson (2006), understood amateur to mean nonserious. They thought that serious play was against the spirit of cricket. More often than not they deliberately underperformed and prevented their teammates from doing well too. Thompson himself understood amateurism as a principle of playing hard and fair and enjoying doing so. His antithetical code, insistence on putting up a good fight, annoyed many of his teammates who left, paving the way for more competitive players to join and ultimately make the club a respectable cricket team. The concept of hard form is thus individually determined, undercutting Appadurai's characterization of cricket's form as innate and inflexible. He (1996, 90) recognizes the process of cricket's indigenization despite it being a hard cultural form, and justifies the change saying that the sport resonated well with Indian cultural values and the emergent Indian nationhood. Nevertheless, this theory is inconsistent with the fact that cricket represented to one section of Indians a metaphor of virtue while simultaneously being criticized by another section as cultural imperialism. Unlike other sports, cricket was synonymous with England and Englishness.

Cricket in the colonies assumed characters informed by 'indigenous epistemological and ontological codes' (MacLean 2010, 100). In the nineteenth century, cricket was an important, unofficial element of the colonial 'civilising mission' (Dimeo 2004). It travelled to the colonies and dominions, nested within the everyday activities of displaced, white Europeans. This transnational passage of cricket was not a triumphant March. It did not necessarily conform to the sport's characterization as ideally amateurish and bucolic, and was often resisted. Americans disconnected the flow by favouring baseball over cricket to articulate their dislike for everything British (Majumdar and Brown 2007). In South Asia, elite public and missionary schools had better success in propagating cricket as 'moral training', though the extent of their influence is dubious (Mangan 1985). Many Indians embraced cricket enthusiastically, but not necessarily accepting uncritically the social relations spawned by cricket in England. As one anonymous reviewer of J. M. Framjee Patel's *Stray Thoughts on Indian Cricket* wrote in 1905, 'in this country of sport indifferentism such a distinctly Anglo-Saxon pastime as cricket has secured the amazingly strong position that it holds today' (*The Times of India*, 12 June 1905, 8). However, they transformed cricket into an instrument of at once imitating and interrogating imperial institutions.

The central theme in the historiography of Indian cricket has been the way in which colonial subjects appropriated cricket, recasting its role from a 'civilising mission' to a powerful mechanism for subverting imperial hegemony. Holt (1989, 221–222) briefly touches upon the 'political meanings' carried by cricket and the 'new national confidence' it generated in the colonies. Taking this argument further, Guttmann (1994, 179) suggests that cricket offered the colonial subject the space for emulation, an opportunity to boost their self-esteem, 'for nothing can be more delightful than "beating [the British] at their own game"'. This act has been often endowed with a nationalist/anti-colonial agency in which subversion of the colonial regime was enacted through 'apparent' imitation. In the context of the Caribbean Islands, James (1963) has foregrounded the discursive functions of sport as a cultural form which alternately upheld and sabotaged colonial hegemony. The circulation of cricket was more uneven than historians such as Guttmann (1994, 33) believe, who claims that the British governors such as Lord Harris and Lord Brabourne patronized cricket hoping that the sport might 'bond together India's religiously, linguistically and ethnically diverse population'. Nevertheless, pedagogic measures did not travel beyond the premises of a minuscule number of educational institutions and clubs. Indians generally learnt the game by observing the English play, and then set up their own clubs.

Nandy (2000, 1) has rather uniquely interpreted this obligation of emulation. He argues that Victorian discourses of cricket were coextensive with conventional Indian temperament and philosophy. The idea of moral masculinity embedded in cricket dovetailed particularly well with the 'rather classical Brahminic concept' which stressed 'control over [one's] impulsive self', 'superiority of form over substance, mind over body, culture over nature' and 'serenity in the face of the vagaries of fate' (xx). Cricket's 'posture of moral superiority', suggests Nandy, empowered Indians to question the post-utilitarian colonial government for not living up to their own standards of morality (7). Cricket was not indigenized the same way as other western sports such as football and hockey. While the latter lost the English connection long ago, cricket retained its Englishness. Sandiford (1994, 156) reckons this paradox to be the 'ultimate triumph of Victorian imperialism', but his approach fails to take sufficient notice to the emergence of cricket as a site of contesting imperialist hegemony in the colonies.

Guha's (2002) critical exploration of this aspect shows how imperatives of colonial politics often resulted in the sport's unique appropriation, with cricket gradually emerged as an arena on which was inscribed an indigenous brand of nationalism. Contradiction of colonial ideology through symbolic resistance, he argues, was the dominant feature of colonial sports, especially cricket and football, from the early twentieth century. For instance, when the Hindus defeated a European representative team in 1906, the news quickly spread all over the country and was celebrated as a feat comparable to the military victory of Japan over Russia in 1905 (Guha 1998). Cricket in the 1930s came to be associated so much with Indian national identity that even the otherwise loyalist princes were not left untouched. Hamidulla Khan, Nawab of Bhopal who served as the BCCI president too, asked the All-India team to 'keep India's flag flying' at a farewell dinner given prior to its departure for England in 1936 (Ali 1976). Despite such political overtures, cricket was not explicitly part of the struggle for independence, but rather an outlet of self-identities at various levels.

In his work on cricket in colonial India, Majumdar (2004) emphasizes the complexities of these self-identities as borne out by acts of patronage. In the Bengal Presidency, the *bhad-ralok* (educated middle class) adopted the game in the 1870s as a means to challenge the Raj and counter the European allegation that Indians were physically and hence intellectually incapable of keeping up with the strides of modern civilization. From the mid-nineteenth century, groups of Indians strove to dispel this humiliating myth of the physical downfall of a once proud culture. Numerous *akharas* (gymnasiums) sprang up across India, mostly in modern-day Bengal and Uttar Pradesh. Quite a few political leaders and associations espoused the cause of cultivating strong physique in retaliation to European criticism of fragile Indian body and mentality (Rosselli 1980). A strong body started carrying nationalist connotation. The physical culture movement grew strong in the late nineteenth century, but as its political overtone started waning in the twentieth century – failing to motivate the masses – Indians started using cricket and football as non-violent means of challenging the Raj (Majumdar 2004). Texts played a critical role in this element of subversion. The cultural investments in C.K. Nayudu's body, for instance, made him appear to be a colossus whose function was to defeat the English on the field of play. His ancestral connection with the Telengana region was appropriated by Andhra nationalists to carve a cultural niche for the state. His real-life nationalist activities were rather modest (Naha 2012). Hence, cricket was not so much an English game as it was a colonial game before India's independence in 1947.

However, people were known to have been smitten by the English game. Kiranlal Roy, a High Court Judge and cousin of Pankaj Roy, played f or East Bengal and then Edgware Club while he studied law in London. He was what the English meant by the perfect sportsperson. He would not dispute the umpire's call. If he was certain that the umpire was wrong to judge him not out, he would walk or sacrifice his wicket. In 1938, he was at the crease with his team Town Club nine wickets down against Mohun Bagan and staring at defeat. Birendra Kishore Ray Choudhury, the Dhrupad style classical musician, not one to accept defeat, signalled the end of play by ringing bells. When Roy found out about this trick, he led the teams back to the field so that the opposition was not denied the deserved victory. He later said that cricketers from the colonial times respected elder cricketers like elder brothers, the captain as a leader, and complied with orders without complaint. Cricket was bliss; the arena a lesson in etiquette. He stopped watching Test cricket in the 1960s, the reason for which, as one of his relatives said, 'was not difficult to understand'. Cricket was not cricket anymore (Mukul 1970b).

Merely a week after independence, Marathi newspapers from Poona were full of articles and letters on the pros and cons of continued patronage of cricket. One group argued that cricket should follow the departing British back to its country of origin. Another camp, led by Capt. S.V. Damle from the Maharashtriya Physical Culture Institute, criticized the practice of educational institutes of allocating maximum funds to cricket, and wanted equal distribution of resources to every sport. The students' organizations in some colleges were provoked to launch campaigns to abolish cricket from their institutions. The authorities of some schools were approached to consider reducing their cricket budget. The former cricketer D.B. Deodhar chastized this 'wanton vandalism'. He admitted that cricket was more expensive to organize than other sports, but if India were to continue playing international cricket, grassroots level cricket could not be discontinued as cricketers were reared through schools, colleges and Gymkhanas. He said, 'There is no other game as spectacular, as dignified, as glamourous as cricket, where even the best player can be turned into a nonentity by one single piece of bowling or fielding'. He considered cricket to be an important connection to the Commonwealth of Nations (*The Times of India*, 31 August 1947, 13).

There were people who despised India's effort to emulate the English. Saladin Chamcha, one of the two protagonists in Rushdie's The Satanic Verses (1988), is contemptuous of everything Indian, including the national team's attempt to beat England in cricket. In a fundamental fit of alienation, probably owing to his location among the minority which he sought to resolve by growing out of his Indianness, a barely teenaged Saladin cheered for the English cricketers when they played at the Brabourne Stadium in Bombay. He wanted England to defeat 'the local upstarts, for the proper order of things to be maintained' (37). A fragmentation of identity haunted Saladin throughout his life, the inception of which started early in his childhood as he resisted his congenital identities and grafted himself onto a culture which ultimately did not accept him. Some lived with a dual identity. Even if not so converted to Anglomania, their thinking would be organised around an uncertain cultural fidelity engineered by upbringing. England lived in their everyday life.

Critics rarely complained against football and hockey, two other mass sports introduced by the English.[2] In their cynical judgment, praise for cricket amounted to a perverted version of Anglophilia. They pointed out that as a foreign imposition cricket was quite pestilential because of its Englishness. Giving too much importance to cricket could be detrimental to the independent nation. The former colonizer's signature sport was suspected to have the potential to assimilate decolonized citizens into the now officially defunct colonial project, thus alienating the latter from the group context, in a Fanonian (1968) sense, and undermining the national drive towards self-determination. The definition of Englishness and Anglophilia was not fixed at any moment of this debate. Cricket still flourished, and within decades of independence it strikingly became the most popular sport even in Calcutta, the capital of football. Literary mediation of Englishness arguably played a significant role in the rise of cricket.

The empire without colony and the agents of transfer

Cricket lovers needed to justify their fascination with cricket in order for it to survive opposition. They found the instrument in cricket's Englishness, which they reproduced in the vernacular, forming successfully a large indigenous subculture with an English imprint. In many ways cricket writing in Bengali was a belated project, and the delay arguably afforded authors a beneficial critical distance. It began in earnest in the 1960s, more than half a century after a similar process had begun in England. The Bengali output was a big leap forward from the English writings in terms of subjects and style of writing, if not volume. It was the first time that Indian authors went beyond instructional writings, match reports and praise for fair play, and engaged with complex cultural issues. They imbibed Anglo-Australian cricket writings, recognized the value system written into it, and adapted those concepts to the local context. Hence, they acted as intermediaries who, according to Middell (2014, 146), 'select, translate, transport, and integrate seemingly foreign cultural elements'. Some of these writings moved beyond the traditional ideas of gentlemanly behaviour etc. but did not displace them. Episodes from Victorian, inter-war and post-war cricket cohabited in this emerging literature in the same imaginary time. Invocation of cricket's past was not an exercise undertaken by Bengali writers alone, but as Bateman (2009, 23) argues, past was a popular trope among writers even as cricket began to be framed as a 'product of modernity' in the late-nineteenth century. The history of cricket's appropriation in a postcolonial state was thus marked by both denunciation of and a return to the colonial times.

The gap between the inherited and the practiced soldered Homi Bhabha's (1994) notion of colonial mimicry to postcolonial tricks of creating intermediate identities. The identity of West Bengal in the 1950s conforms to Mbembe's (1992, 3) conceptualization of a postcolony as a recently decolonized society, pluralistic but trying to design a distinctive character. The colonial institutions of culture were still so deeply ingrained in public life that negotiations with a new identity were still floundering in the stream of delinking. Although several political parties demanded outright rejection of colonial traditions, so componential had they become in the society that separation of the hybrid from the original was a moot question. Cricket as a practice was neither hybrid nor indistinct; its extrinsic codes remained intact. However, the translation it went through at various levels of appropriation transformed the domain of its moral codes, characterized by simultaneous acceptance and opposition. Hence, identity politics around cricket was always in flux, underlining the creation during transcultural encounters of what Roy (1998, 2) calls 'philosophical or epistemic secondariness'. Roy means by this the paradoxical situation in which a standardized code transferred from a different culture, such as nationalism, inhabits a threshold zone between the original and the derived. A map of code-translation-and-sharing in Bengali cricket writings illustrates this transcultural arbitration.

P. Chowdhury, whose first name is not given by his chronicler Sankariprasad Basu, was a pure-bred Indian follower of the English game. He was a freedom-fighter, had probably clashed with the colonial police too, and held strong nationalist opinions even after leaving politics (S. Basu 1976b). He did not belong to the anglicized, transplanted and cosmopolitan classes of Indians which had absorbed European sport more eagerly. When asked why cricket was the only English thing he liked, he seldom had an answer to offer. He spoke in a state of reverie about having 'dream-like visions' every time he watched cricket since his childhood. He had seen himself 'standing on the cerulean ground of the sky, watching radiant figures play cricket' (255). Evidently for him cricket was played on an existential plane in which he was a changed person, detached from reality. Chowdhury started an annual fixture which had a very local folk culture woven around it.

Rusticity was an essential part of cricket's Englishness. The game's literature perpetually evoked nostalgia among city dwellers for a village green untarnished by modern civilization (Westall 2007). Cardus (1997, 10) considered cricket a mirror of English nature, so did Edmund Blunden, and Lucas (1989), for whom cricket was 'the backyard, the garden, the playground, the school field, the club and college ground, and, above all, the village green'. Stories from village cricket, mostly fictitious, involved a set of colourful characters who defied conventions and produced unforgettable, rollicking incidents. In a story about Rabindranath Tagore, winner of the Nobel Prize in literature in 1913, playing cricket, the authors chose the village of Gomoh as the site of action (Brahmanyabhusan and Bandopadhyay 1976). It was a direct tribute to the country meadows in pre-industrial England. Since Gomoh was the junction of three railway zones, there was a hint of the advent of modernity in the hinterland. Additionally, Gomoh was the place from which the great Bengali freedom-fighter Subhas Chandra Bose took the train to Delhi on the way to his great escape from house arrest.

The matches organized by Chowdhury inscribed onto an imaginary geography of modern West Bengal a vanishing folk culture, which engaged in a foreign game and yet was authentically Bengali. In this transcultural world of selective mutation, the old Sanyal takes the field with his hookah (tobacco pipe) in one hand and bat in the other. The umpire holds his hookah while he takes stance. The decrepit Ghosh is helped to the crease by his grandson while spectators taunt him to ask his old wife for assistance. People play in local apparels like *vidyasagari choti* and *namaboli*; Chakraborty goes to bowl wearing a combination of *fatua* and full pants. Batsmen take wrong stances, which English cricket critics would have called Oriental informality (S. Basu 1976b). Although these incidents matched episodes from English village cricket in oddity, the purpose of these stories was to portray the field of cricket as a democratic space that equalized social ranks. Basu's intention was replicated later by Shibdas Bandopadhyay (*Dainik Basumati*, 30 December 1972, 6) who wrote about how everybody were drawn to the 'verdant field of gold, bathed in the shining winter sun' that did not distinguish between the rich and the poor, the ruler and the subject, and made people forget all agony. The public were shown to be linked with cricket in an organic relationship. The journalist and commentator A. Basu (1976a, 134–135) wrote an explicitly detailed account of this rapport:

> The people of Calcutta are quite sensitive about Eden. Nowhere else would one find a playground so charmingly adorned by a carpet of green grass. Once upon a time people went there just to inhale fresh air. The soaring pines encircling the ground swayed with the wind, and shades cast by the late afternoon sun produced a stunning, unforgettable light and shadow play … Nature reigned supreme in the ground, beyond the boundary ropes, before repulsive brick and cement structure was raised … The pavilion was a marvellous ode to British architecture. It dovetailed harmoniously with the calm surroundings. It still exists, hidden behind the tall, unspectacular galleries. There was a straw structure that the British called 'the hut', open on all sides with only a roof cover. Cricketers and other important persons used to watch play from under the 'hut'. Cricket is an English game. The English played in the suburbs, villages and sometimes in towns, with the intention to spend a few hours close to the nature. This is why they chose the 'village green' as the theatre of cricket. They built the straw hut here in Calcutta just to replicate the idyllic ambience of playing cricket … Those were the days of bullock carts, peace of mind, abundant leisure and opportunities of amusement. We spent many a winter afternoon basking in the mild sun, sitting on the green carpet rolled out at Eden.

By remembering, resituating, reconstituting and re-instantiating an experience in the public press, authors established the personal as the communal (Rineart 2013, 280). Such coupling of people, an environment tamed by cricket, and nostalgia for a lost better past was homologous with the descriptions by English authors. Another frequently evoked aspect was moral masculinity. According to Keith Sandiford (1994, 2), the social and cultural leaders of the Victorian age found in cricket the answer to every psycho-social problem, including illness and illiteracy. The conviction that cricket was essential for health and character-building was expressed skilfully by the headmaster Dr. George Ridding, who said: 'Give me a boy who is a cricketer and I can make something of him'. The notion of the chivalrous cricketer was important for proponents of Muscular Christianity, aimed at reforming the middle class. Cricket was afforded a social and nation-building mission, with the image of the vigorous body signifying a healthy body politic and social cohesion. The mission statement came from the novel *Tom Brown's Schooldays* (Hughes 1989, 354–355), in which the teacher emphasized the discipline and interdependence among the team that merges the individual in the collective, so that one does not 'play so that he might win, but that his side may'.

In addition to being a symbol of social cohesion and harmony, the sport theoretically performed a humanizing function as an antidote to many social evils. Bengali authors added to it the contrasting possibility of cricket provoking crime. The person who had gifted Basu a ticket to watch the Test against Australia in 1960 had issued a warning that no one should know about that ticket. Any ticket-holder could be murdered for possessing what the rest of the city craved fanatically (Basu 1960). That year, the crime rate in Calcutta was 446.6 crimes committed per 100,000 people, the third highest among Indian cities after Bangalore (448.0) and Bombay (446.8), with a 50% increase in the number of murders from the previous triennial (*Crime in India* 1960, 2–4). The story thus makes a double gesture towards unsafety in the city and the absurdity of overestimating cricket's moral lessons on the vast number of moderately educated, unemployed youth. The crunch of urban space caused by unregulated influx and settlement of refugees was imaginatively cast in the altercation among seven spectators over seating space. One of them considered it physically impossible, but others maintained that the problem could be solved spiritually, by willingness to share (Basu 1960). Implied in the story was an ad hoc solution to the problem of habitation in the city – by shared empathy. When Ramakant Desai hit Ken Mackay on the chest, the gallery erupted in jubilation, in which Basu read a rejection of India's pacifist policy in world politics (150). Contemporary conflicts of values frequently appeared in his writings, planted within discussions about good versus bad, amateurism versus professionalism, style versus efficiency in matters of cricket-playing. Not all of his readers agreed with his philosophy of cricket.

Fractured Englishness, challenged pursuit

Cricket began to be opposed even before it became popular. In a religious tract named *Terra Pacis*, published in Amsterdam in 1575, the author Hendrick Niclaes, a Westphalian Protestant monk who lived in England during Queen Mary's rule, criticized a foolish pastime called 'Kricket-Staves'. This was later proved to have been a mistranslation into English of the original Base-Almayn word *kolven*, meaning clubs, and hence not an accurate description of any malice against cricket (Major 2007). The Anglican Church, however, objected to people skipping church prayers on Sabbath for playing cricket. A number of court records from since the early seventeenth century reveals people to have been accused of 'playing at cricket in tyme of divine service' (25). The Church has come a long way since. In the nineteenth century, schools and churches were the primary channels of propagating cricket in the colonies (Stoddart 1988). In the twentieth century, David Sheppard, Bishop of Liverpool, played 22 Tests for MCC after he was ordained into priesthood. In 1966, the Vicar of Bognor, Dr. William Snow, went a step further by receiving money from a local bookmaker, for a bet placed on the batting performance of his son John Snow, and donating it to church fund (Hoult 2009). Temples and mosques in India did not quite perceive cricket as a threat. They rather encouraged fans to pray for their team to their respective gods, and often joined in the prayer by organizing rituals. Arya Pratinidhi Sabha of Punjab wanted cricket to be banned, using the familiar trope of the waste of time and money. Swami Agnivesh, secretary of the Arya Pratinidhi Sabha, cut a lone figure as a somewhat religious figure to have criticized the imperialist character of cricket. He proposed its ban in a letter to the central government (*Jugantar*, 17 January 1979, 3). Probably cricket was inconsistent with the idea of social spirituality that he counterposed against the off-balance worlds of capitalism and communism (Chakrabarti 2009). His action was more informed by his anti-West political stance than religious conviction. He was certainly not a singular voice of political dissent against cricket.

Socialist parties in India were very much against cricket as a bourgeois sport, in ways the Labour Party in England probably never thought of. Mention of cricket apparently made the reticent Clement Attlee 'positively garrulous' (Jago 2014, 6). Harold Wilson played cricket behind the Iron Curtain on a visit as the President of the Board of Trade, watched over by two mounted Soviet riflemen (Preston 2013). C. L. R. James, the Marxist postcolonial thinker dubbed as 'cricket's philosopher king', put cricket, life and aesthetics in the same social space (Renton 2007). Indian leaders followed a different path. Nehru, for all his socialist inclination, took the initiative in establishing the Test stadium in Delhi and attended every match played there (Bose 2006). Sengupta (1965, 126–127) lifts his stature as an exemplary person in a story about a charity match between the Prime Minister's XI and the Vice-President's XI for the flood relief fund in 1953. Nehru formed a good batting partnership with the Communist leader A. K. Gopalan, surprising spectators with their understanding while going for runs. Nehru was nearly run out trying to score briskly, but the wicketkeeper did not break the stumps, thinking about the people who had gathered to see their prime minister play well. W. G. Grace, the doyen of 'English' cricket, occasionally refused to walk when dismissed cheaply. Nehru, on the contrary, considered himself 'morally out' and threatened to declare the innings unless the umpires gave him out. The umpires did not and he declared (*The Guardian*, 14 September 1953, 1). This was cricket in its glorious moral fortitude. Sengupta concludes: 'despise the sin but not the sinner, abolish empire but love the English'. In 1954, speaking at a gathering organised to celebrate the BCCI's 25 years, the vice-president Dr Sarvepalli Radhakrishnan admitted that cricket symbolised the British civilisation, imbued the player with moral qualities, helping them to overcome race and colour bars, and developed 'national unity and international comity' (*The Guardian*, 12 February 1954, 1). These messages barely registered with a section of people who had somehow developed the idea that cricket was a capitalist sport and hence should be discarded.

The universal principles of workers' sport, contrary to bourgeois sport, were inclusivity and altruism. It was to serve as an alternative to commercialized, chauvinistic, statistically obsessed sport culture bred by capitalist societies (Jones 1988; Riordan 1991; Krüger and Riordan 1996). Sport was not supposed to play more than a recreational role in workers' movements, but was to develop its own anti-bourgeois character. The proletariat was to guard against a possible corruption of their sport by bourgeois tantalization (Rigauer 2002). There is no evidence to show for Indian politicians to have grasped the significance of any of these theories or the structural similarity or work/labour and modern sport. England's national game was their object of hatred as part of a larger campaign to replace everything colonial with 'Indian' institutions – such as substitution of English by Hindi as the state's official language, removal of colonial statues, rebranding roads named after colonial administrators etc. Dr. Ram Manohar Lohia, leader of the Socialist Party, an avid cricket follower himself, wanted the game to be banned as it created a 'tremendous cultural link within the Commonwealth', an organization he wanted India to avoid (*The Guardian*, 8 May 1957, 9). The categorization of cricket as a capitalist game baffled many, including the editor of *The Times of India* (23 August 1959, 8) who sardonically compared Indian communists to hockey players as hockey combined the 'symbolism of pushing towards a goal with the added symbolism of doing so while waving sticks in their hands'. The anti-bourgeois and anti-English movement took a major turn in West Bengal in 1967 as the United Front, consisting of several communist and socialist parties, came to power, with Jyoti Basu as the deputy chief minister.

English was for the majority of politicians a former language of dominance and elitism (Dasgupta 1993). It was irreplaceable as a common thread in the multilingual country. Hence, after several protests and riots over the relative merits of giving weightage to various languages as the medium of learning and governance, the Official Languages Act of 1967 made English a permanent official language. All matters of administration were to be recorded in English alongside Hindi (Sedlatschek 2009). The usefulness of choosing English as the main foreign language to learn continued to come under scrutiny in West Bengal. The famous author and polyglot Mujtaba Ali (1967a) wrote in an article that learning English was not too essential. His opinion was supported by a few, and countered by some, such as Amita Roy and Rudrajit Dasgupta, who wrote back saying that learning two or more languages was always helpful. Academics in particular ought to learn more than one language, and compulsorily English, to remain up to date with latest research. Moreover, in a multilingual country like India, learning exclusively one's mother tongue would make people more provincial and hinder opportunities of occupational migration to others states (*Desh*, 18 November 1967, 293–295). Mujtaba Ali (1967b), in an effort to salvage his pride, responded with a piece trying to substantiate that English was not the best language in the world and hence its knowledge was not mandatory. Arguments against cricket were tied up with this very question of the lingering traces of England. These often referred to English language and culture as corollary infestations by a regime of absurdity. On the occasion of the India–England Test in 1977, anti-cricket arguments were expressed the most precisely by Pranabesh Chakraborty in a letter to the editor of *Dainik Basumati* (8 January 1977, 4):

> The exploitative British imperialists and the local princes have historically indulged in extravagances such as playing cricket, which we continue to watch stupidly and burp with satisfaction. The British gifted cricket to the class of opportunist stooges, princes in the context of India, in each of their colonies ... No socialist country has adopted this lazy and passive game that takes places over five days, four or five times in a complete series. How can we aim to be socialist unless we stop clinging to cricket ... It is like opium, with which people are poisoning themselves willingly. Such level of dedication can hardly be seen in other activities ... We should

not tolerate this farce that has bewitched a group of consumers ... By watching cricket, people waste hours of productive labour. Test matches encourage dishonest social behaviour such as giving one's superior in office a ticket as a form of bribe. Again, who other than hoarders of black money are able to purchase a 70-rupee ticket for 300? It has become necessary to flaunt tickets as a statement of one's social prestige. Cricket is as toxic as horseracing. World cricket operates under the logic that there should be a number of weak national teams in order for England to play and win.

Chakraborty's letter was preceded by a number of similar letters. For Subroto Mukhopadhyay, cricket meant a million people wasting time after a nonsense sport. Three football matches could have been organized at Eden Gardens instead of hosting a Test match. That legacy left by the English should be legally abolished. Pradeep Bhattacharya was unhappy with the lack of action and intensity in cricket. He had found the previous week's national volleyball championship livelier (*Dainik Basumati*, 4 January 1977, 7). Sanghamitra Das calculated using some unimaginable mathematics that a total of 18,000,000 h were misused when a foreign team played a Test series in India (*Khelar Asar*, 20 October 1978, 15).

The India-MCC Test in 1973, which resulted in an Indian victory, had drawn a flurry of exchanges too. Basanta Kumar Mukhopadhyay called cricket a virus. He suspected that the game might not qualify as a sport since not more than three–four countries played it. The principle governing the contest was grudge and hatred between the opponents; the fear of being upstaged by the other guided the play (*Anandabazar Patrika*, 16 January 1973, 4). Ranjan Kumar Das contradicted him arguing that should cricket be banned on account of its foreignness, every other competitive national sport would have to be stopped too since all of them were transmitted from abroad. He was in favour of the country's half billion people being given the freedom to decide whether they would like cricket to continue. Progressive countries spent fortunes on sport as it was an essential part of nation-building, and India should follow a similar course (*Anandabazar Patrika*, 16 January 1973, 4). In a retort against A. F. Qamruddin's letter which pitched the view that there is no need to be inebriated with cricket, Ashok Mukhopadhyay suggested the need of remedial action for those who had not yet learnt to appreciate cricket. He wanted bigger stadiums to be built and new grounds opened across the state in order to increase cricket literacy (*Anandabazar Patrika*, 16 January 1973, 4). No consensus was in sight. A few people tried to synthesize what they perceived as the good and bad aspects of cricket. Pratapchandra Jana wrote in a letter to the editor of *Jugantar* (29 December 1978, 3) that language and cricket were the only positive legacies of the British Empire. However, just as sport was considered in conventional Marxist thinking a tool of entertainment that masks everyday realities, he speculated if cricket was introduced as a plot to keep the colonial youth away from the freedom struggle (Allison 1986). The same barrage of opinions has subsequently appeared during every Test match at Eden Gardens.

In 1977 a Left Front led by the Communist Party of India (M) came to power having won the state assembly elections. Jyoti Basu, now the chief minister, was a competent footballer in his student days in Calcutta and London. He believed that sports floated on an ethical level far removed from that of politics. During the tumultuous days in the late-1960s, when asked if the conflict of interest within the United Front could be resolved by approaching the problem with a sporting spirit, Basu had responded that so many interests intersected in politics that the spirit of fair play could not be used here (Mukul 1970a). Not many of his comrades shared his perspective, evident in the resumption of critiques in 1980 as the

Pakistani team arrived in Calcutta. Nandalal Mukhopadhyay saw no reason for organizing cricket in a poor country. He cited examples of socialist countries that did not play cricket because the sport reduced industrial production and hampered learning (*Jugantar*, 31 January 1980, 4). Kumar Chattopadhyay and Samar Chakraborty provided solidarity, complaining against so much interest in matters of bat and ball when millions of young people were unemployed and insufficient healthcare claimed innumerable lives (*Jugantar*, 7 February 1980, 4). A predictable counter-letter, from Bibhutibhusan Dutta, attacked this judgement as irrational, asking why the criticism would not be extended to similar forms of entertainment such as Rabindranath Tagore's birth anniversary, the Olympic Games and film festivals (*Jugantar*, 7 February 1980, 4).

CPI (M) in its first 20 years of rule subscribed to the left's historical antipathy to capitalism, liberal democracy, globalization and the like, except Western professional sport (Edelman 1993). In the 1980s, when South-East Asia realized the importance of technology and services sector, West Bengal conceded its advantage of a significantly longer history of Western education, middle class and industrialization. It resisted development of industry and computers, and abolishing English in government primary school, depriving the locals a critical advantage (Malik 2010). Cricket not just escaped the state's list of proscriptions; it commanded a pride of place among the party's achievements. The top brass of CPI (M) leaders was peopled by an educated middle class which Chaudhuri (2013) aptly terms 'orphans of bhadralok history', bhadralok being the Bengali equivalent for gentleman. The intellectual strain circling round the party's leadership and publications distinguished it from its competitors. Cricket with all its cerebral pastiches was consistent with what the party thought of leisure. It was heard through the grapevine that it bribed the 1996 World Cup's convener-secretary Jagmohan Dalmiya to have the opening ceremony in Calcutta. Without state support, detractors of cricket could not really bare their fangs. The periodical display of animosity was too repetitive and devoid of content to have any real effect on cricket following.

Instances of contempt for a foreign game could be seen in other national contexts too, and some of it was even directed to football, 'the world's game'.[3] As an American correspondent found out during his travel to the subcontinent during the 2003 World Cup (played in South Africa), the few Indians who disliked cricket did so with the grit of a fanatic. One of them told him that poor people waste valuable hours watching cricket every day, thus reinforcing poverty upon themselves. He did not think the same happened in America, obviously unaware of the fandom for NFL and MLB (*New York Times*, 23 March 2003, 19). More importantly, even after several decades since cricket in India began to be ideologically opposed to and trumped its critics, the outlook of some people remained unchanged. Cricket was still held responsible for whatever was wrong with the country. A winning streak mutes the criticism; a string of defeats invites the rapier. The cycle of drifts was condensed into four lines by the poet K. V. V. Subrahmanyan (2004, 143):

Despite all the multitudes that throng the cricket field

Some do run down the game with comments veiled,

Talking of ennui and waste of time the spectacle does yield

But on the might of the game their lips are sealed.

Conclusion

In the years following independence cricket was India's intimate enemy. Unlike many other colonial contexts, such as the American colony of Philippines (Gems 2016), there was no tendency to return to indigenous games once the colonizers left. Resistance to colonial institutions provided a critical impetus to visions of nation-building, but so did the Enlightenment values and Universalist dreams entrenched in sections of the civil society. The early history of the nation-state is thus one of indecision and hybridity. Indian cricket was no exception. The struggle between highly effective myths and tyrannical political theory, featured in newspapers and political rallies, deterritorialized cricket from the station of its origin. Its incomplete integration into Indian society and consequent reinscription highlight the relevance of perception in transnational encounters. The constant negotiation is what gives cricket its formative role in public culture. It ceases to be just another sport as soon as the public starts responding to the question of what cricket is. Answers are more important than questions in postmodern criticism, as they have the ability to reconstruct and shift the meaning of the question. Texts facilitate this negotiation by writing into concrete historical forms the answers given by a plethora of actors, and hence producing a visible, long-term account of similarity or difference.

This dilemma of appropriation was not exceptionally Indian. Australian Aboriginals were never assimilated into the white pastime of cricket, for which the racist attitudes of white settlers were to be held responsible. Cricket did not afford the Aboriginals any social mobility and selection in the national or state teams, so averse were the settlers to share power or encourage advancement of the other (Gemmell 2008). Indians were more in control of their political self. Although in the minority, critics have been accorded an extraordinary liberty to voice their dissent. A reason could be that these criticisms were never considered subversive enough to destabilize cricket's popular position. Moreover, critics provided the context within which cricket's ideologues could resolve the prejudices against the sport's alleged imperialist and capitalist substructure. The questions of ethics and economy, so frequently asked of them, left cricket hanging in an antithetical balance that continues to provide content for newspapers.

Notes

1. In a book that came out nearly half a century after Basu's, Ferguson (2004, 14) mentions 'the English language', 'team sports', and 'representative assemblies' as three of the eight cornerstones of the British Empire.
2. Gangopadhyay (1969, 227–228) asked in his column why should hockey be India's national sport instead of football or cricket? Why does the public's concern with cricket's Englishness not extend to hockey?
3. Ghosh (1992, 27) found out during his fieldwork in a remote Egyptian village that at least one village elder loathed football. Abu-Ali would scream in anger from time to time, 'Isn't there work to do? Allah! Is the world going to live on soccer? What's going to become of …'.

Disclosure statement

No potential conflict of interest was reported by the author.

References

Ahmed, Akbar S. 2004. *Postmodernism and Islam: Predicament and Promise*. London: Routledge.

Ali, Mushtaq. 1976. *Cricket Delightful*. 2nd ed. New Delhi: Rupa.

Allison, Lincoln. 1986. "Sport and Politics." In *The Politics of Sport*, edited by Lincoln Allison, 1–26. Manchester: Manchester University Press.

Appadurai, Arjun. 1996. "Playing with Modernity: The Decolonization of Cricket". In *Modernity at Large: Cultural Dimensions of Globalization*, 89–113. Minneapolis: University of Minnesota Press.

Basu, Ajay. 1976a. "Smritituku Shona Hoye Thak." *Amrita Krira Binodon Sankhya*: 135–136.

Basu, Sankariprasad. 1960. *Eden-e Shiter Dupur*. Calcutta: Bookland.

Basu, Sankariprasad. 1961. *Ramaniya Cricket*. Calcutta: Karuna Prakashani.

Basu, Sankariprasad. 1976b. "Not out." In *Sankariprasad Basu, Cricket Omnibus II*. Calcutta: Mandal Book House.

Bateman, Anthony. 2009. *Cricket, Literature and Culture: Symbolising the Nation, Destabilising Empire*. Farnham: Ashgate.

Bhabha, Homi. 1994. *The Location of Culture*. London: Routledge.

Birley, Derek. 1979. *The Willow Wand*. London: Simon & Schuster.

Birley, Derek. 1995. *Land of Sport and Glory: Sport and British Society 1887–1910*. Manchester: Manchester University Press.

Bose, Mihir. 2006. *The Magic of Indian Cricket: Cricket and Society in India*. London: Routledge.

Bowen, Rowland. 1970. *Cricket: A History of Its Growth and Development throughout the World*. London: Eyre and Spottiswoode.

Brahmanyabhusan, and Kshama Bandopadhyay. 1976. "Kabigurur Cricket Khela." In *Cricket Omnibus II*, edited by Sankariprasad Basu, 370–375. Calcutta: Mandal Book House.

Brookes, Christopher. 1978. *English Cricket: The Game and Its Players through the Ages*. London: Weidenfeld and Nicolson.

Cardus, Neville. 1984. *Autobiography*. London: Hamish Hamilton.

Cardus, Neville. 1997. *English Cricket*. London: Prion.

Chakrabarti, Rajesh, ed. 2009. *The Other India: Realities of an Emerging Power*. New Delhi: Sage.

Chaudhuri, Amit. 2013. *Calcutta: Two Years in the City*. New York: Knopf Doubleday.

Colley, Linda. 1994. *Britons: Forging the Nation 1707–1837*. London: Pimlico.

Dasgupta, Probal. 1993. *The Otherness of English: India's Auntie's Tongue Syndrome*. New Delhi: Sage.

Dimeo, Paul. 2004. "Sporting and the 'Civilizing Mission' in India." In *Colonialism and Civilising Mission: Cultural Ideology in British India*, edited by Harald Fischer-Tiné and Michael Mann, 165–178. London: Anthem.

Edelman, Robert. 1993. *Serious Fun: A History of Spectator Sports in the USSR*. New York: Oxford University Press.

Fanon, Frantz. 1968. *Black Skin, White Masks*. New York: Grove Press.

Ferguson, Niall. 2004. *Empire: How Britain Made the Modern World*. New York: Penguin.

Fry, C. B. 1939. *A Life worth Living: Some Phases of an Englishman*. London: Eyre & Spottiswoode.

Gangopadhyay, Narayan. 1969. "Cricket, Hockey, Ityadi." *Desh* 37 (3): 227–228.

Gemmell, Jon. 2008. "All White Male? Cricket and Race in Oz." In *Cricket, Race and the 2007 World Cup*, edited by Jon Gemmell and Boria Majumdar, 23–39. London: Routledge.

Gems, Gerald. 2016. *Sport and the American Occupation of the Philippines: Bats, Balls, and Bayonets*. Lanham: Lexington Books.

Ghosh, Amitav. 1992. *In an Antique Land*. London: Granta Books.

Gikandi, Simon. 1996. *Maps of Englishness: Writing Identity in the Culture of Colonialism*. New York: Columbia University Press.

Guha, Ramachandra. 1998. "Cricket and Politics in Colonial India." *Past and Present* 161: 155–190.

Guha, Ramachandra. 2002. *A Corner of a Foreign Field: The Indian History of a British Sport*. London: Picador.

Guttmann, Allen. 1994. *Games and Empires: Modern Sports and Cultural Imperialism*. New York: Columbia University Press.

Hobsbawm, Eric. 1983. "Introduction." In *Invention of Tradition*, edited by Eric Hobsbawm and Terence Ranger, 1–14. Cambridge: Cambridge University Press.

Holt, Richard. 1989. *Sport and the British: A Modern History*. Oxford: Clarendon.

Holt, Richard. 1996. "Cricket and Englishness: The Batsman as Hero." *International Journal of the History of Sport* 13 (1): 48–70.

Hoult, Nick, ed. 2009. *The Daily Telegraph Book of Cricket*. London: Aurum Press.

Hughes, Thomas. 1989. *Tom Brown's Schooldays*. Oxford: Oxford University Press.

Jago, Michael. 2014. *Clement Attlee: The Inevitable Prime Minister*. London: Biteback.

James, C. L. R. 1963. *Beyond a Boundary*. London: Stanley Paul.

Jones, Stephen G. 1988. *Sports, Politics and the Working Class: Organised Labour and Sport in Inter-War Britain*. Manchester: Manchester University Press.

Krüger, Arnd, and James Riordan, eds. 1996. *The Story of Worker Sport*. Champaign, IL: Human Kinetics.

Kumar, Krishan. 2012. "Varieties of Nationalism." In *The Victorian World*, edited by Martin Hewitt, 160–174. London: Routledge.

Lowerson, John. 1995. *Sport and the English Middle Classes, 1870–1914*. Manchester: Manchester University Press.

Lucas, E. V. 1989. "The English Game." In *Cricket All His Life*, 213–215. London: Pavilion Library.

MacLean, Malcolm. 2010. "Ambiguity within the Boundary: Re-Reading C.L.R. James's *beyond a Boundary*." *Journal of Sport History* 37 (1): 99–117.

Major, John. 2007. *More than a Game: The Story of Cricket's Early Years*. London: Harper.

Majumdar, Boria. 2004. *Twenty-two Yards to Freedom: A Social History of Indian Cricket*. New Delhi: Penguin.

Majumdar, Boria, and Sean F. Brown. 2007. "Why Baseball, Why Cricket? Differing Nationalisms, Differing Challenges." *The International Journal of the History of Sport* 24 (2): 139–156.

Malik, Ashok. 2010. "A Place Time Forgot." *The Times of India*, January 20: 6.

Mangan, J. A. 1985. *The Games Ethic and Imperialism: Aspects of the Diffusion of an Ideal*. Harmondsworth: Viking.

Mangan, J. A., and James Walvin, eds. 1991. *Manliness and Morality: Middle-class Masculinity in Britain and America, 1800–1940*. Manchester: Manchester University Press.

Marqusee, Mike. 2005. *Anyone but England: An Outsider Looks at English Cricket*. 3rd ed. London: Aurum Press.

Mbembe, Achille. 1992. "Provisional Notes on the Postcolony". *Africa: Journal of the International African Institute* 62 (1): 3–37.

Middell, Matthias. 2014. "Is There a Timetable When Concepts Travel? On Synchronicity in the Emergence of New Concepts Dealing with Border-crossing Phenomena." In *The Trans/National Study of Culture: A Transnational Perspective*, edited by Doris Bachmann-Medick, 137–154. Berlin: De Gruyter.

Mujtaba Ali, Syed. 1967a. "Panchatantra." *Desh* 35 (1): 35–36.

Mujtaba Ali, Syed. 1967b. "Panchatantra." *Desh* 35 (4): 347–348.

Mukul. 1970a. "Kritir Krirabhumika [Famous People and Sport]." *Desh* 37 (16): 296.

Mukul. 1970b. "Kritir Krirabhumika [Famous People and Sport]." *Desh* 37 (25): 1233.

Murray, Bruce. 2001. "Politics and Cricket: The D'Oliveira Affair of 1968." *Journal of Southern African Studies* 27 (4): 667–684.

Naha, Souvik. 2012. "Producing the First Indian Cricketing Superhero: Nationalism, Body Culture, Consumption and the C.K. Nayudu Phenomenon." *The International Journal of the History of Sport* 29 (4): 562–582.

Naha, Souvik. 2013. "Sport Controversy, the Media and Anglo-Indian Cricket Relations: The 1977 'Vaseline Incident' in Retrospect." *Sport in Society* 16 (10): 1375–1385.

Nandy, Ashis. 2000. *The Tao of Cricket: On Games of Destiny and the Destiny of Games*. 2nd ed. New Delhi: Oxford University Press.

Ponsford, Megan. 2015. "Frank and Bhupinder: The Odd Couple of Indian Cricket." *Sport in Society* 18 (5): 565–576.

Pope, Steven W. 1996. "Amateurism and American Sports Culture: The Invention of an Athletic Tradition in the United States, 1870–1900." *International Journal of the History of Sport* 13 (3): 290–309.

Preston, Hubert. 2013. "From Russia with a Dropped Catch". In *The Essential Wisden: An Anthology of 150 Years of Wisden Cricketers' Almanack*, edited by John Stern and Marcus Williams, 40. London: Bloomsbury.

Rae, Simon. 1998. *W G Grace: A Life*. London: Faber & Faber.

Renton, Dave. 2007. *C.L.R. James: Cricket's Philosopher King*. London: Haus.

Rigauer, Bero. 2002. "Marxist Theories." In *Handbook of Sports Studies*, edited by Jay Coakley and Eric Dunning. London: Sage.

Rineart, Robert. 2013. "Poetic Sensibilities and the Use of Fiction for Sport History: Map-making in Representation of the Past." In *Examining Sport Histories: Power, Paradigms, and Reflexivity*, edited by Richard Pringle and Murray Phillips, 273–294. Morgantown, WV: Fitness Information Technology.

Riordan, James. 1991. *Sport, Politics and Communism*. Manchester: Manchester University Press.

Rosselli, John. 1980. "The Self-image Of Effeteness: Physical Education and Nationalism in Nineteenth-century Bengal." *Past and Present* 86: 121–148.

Roy, Parama. 1998. *Indian Traffic: Identities in Question in Colonial and Postcolonial India*. Berkeley: University of California Press.

Rushdie, Salman. 1988. *The Satanic Verses*. London: Vintage.

Sandiford, Keith. 1983. "Cricket and the Victorian Society." *Journal of Social History* 17 (2): 303–317.

Sandiford, Keith. 1994. *Cricket and the Victorians*. Aldershot: Scholar Press.

Sedlatschek, Andreas. 2009. *Contemporary Indian English: Variation and Change*. Amsterdam: John Benjamins.

Sengupta, Achintya Kumar. 1965. *Mriga Nei Mrigaya* [Hunt without Deer]. Calcutta: Anandadhara.

Stoddart, Brian. 1988. "Sport, Cultural Imperialism, and Colonial Response in the British Empire." *Comparative Studies in Society and History* 30 (4): 649–673.

Subrahmanyan, K. V. V. 2004. "In Defence of Cricket". In *'A Breathless Hush ...': The MCC Anthology of Cricket Verse*, edited by David Rayvern Allen, 143–144. London: Methuen.

Thompson, Harry. 2006. *Penguins Stopped Play: Eleven Village Cricketers Take on the World*. London: John Murray.

Wagg, Stephen. 2000. "'Time Gentlemen Please': The Decline of Amateur Captaincy in English County Cricket." In *Amateurs and Professionals in Post-War British Sport*, edited by Adrian Smith and Dilwyn Porter, 31–49. London: Routledge.

Webster, Wendy. 2005. *English and Empire 1939–1965*. Oxford: Oxford University Press.

Westall, Claire. 2007. "What Should We Know of Cricket Who Only England Know? Cricket and Its Heroes in English and Caribbean Literature". PhD thesis, Warwick University.

Williams, Jack. 1999. *Cricket and England: A Cultural and Social History of the Inter-War Years*. London: Frank Cass.

Žižek, Slavoj. 1991. *For They Know Not What They Do: Enjoyment as a Political Factor*. London: Verso.

Did South America foster European football?: transnational influences on the continentalization of FIFA and the creation of UEFA, 1926–1959

Philippe Vonnard and Grégory Quin

ABSTRACT

UEFA was formed in Basel in June 1954, and began to take control of European football soon after its inception. It was an exceptional Pan-European organization in the context of the ongoing cold war since it almost exclusively granted memberships to football associations from Eastern Europe and the Iberian Peninsula, managing to tower above divisive ideological antagonisms. This article approaches the history of UEFA's establishment from a global history perspective. It highlights the hitherto overlooked impact of FIFA's dialogues with the South American football confederation and national associations on the creation of UEFA as a representative European institution. Firstly, it traces the South American demand for more influence on the governance of world football (especially within FIFA's committees) in the inte-rwar years, a situation that created a rift between South American and European representatives in FIFA. This confrontation arguably 'helped' the European associations to self-integrate, leaving behind their internal differences, in order to restore the hegemony they used to exercise inside FIFA before the South American dissent. Secondly, it emphasizes the role played by the South American confederation in the reorganization of FIFA in the early 1950s. Thirdly, it briefly focuses on how the South American confederation initially served as a model for the activities of UEFA.

Introduction

In June 1954, 28 national football associations from across Europe gathered in Basel to create a continental organization. This was a direct response to the change in the statutes of the Fédération Internationale de Football Association (FIFA) in 1953 which required member associations to form continental organizations, each of which would in turn elect one representative to the FIFA Executive Committee (FIFA, FIFA Statutes, edition of 1954). Thus, and contrary to prevalent ideas, the organization's first goal was not to start new European competitions but rather to create an interest group within FIFA. In October 1954, the 'Groupement' was named as the Union of European Football Associations (UEFA). Its first official General Assembly was held in Vienna in March 1955. From 1955 to 1960, UEFA increased its prerogatives, created a number of competitions (Vonnard 2014), and began to control broadcasting (Mittag and Nieland 2013) and other aspects of European football, for example youth football (Marston 2015). At the end of the decade, the organization had successfully connected most of the European football associations and established itself as one of the foremost powerbrokers of football's politics.

Taking into consideration the context of the process of European integration post-Second World War, UEFA's creation was not an isolated occurrence. Since the beginning of the 1950s, Pan-European political, economic, scientific and cultural initiatives as diverse as the Council of Europe, the European Economic Community, the European Free Trade Association, the European Broadcasting Union, the European Community of Writers (Racine 2008) and the European Confederation of Post Office (Laborie 2010) came up. The French historian concept of 'Europe-organisation' describes perfectly the development of a 'European' way in the creation of organizations. UEFA's structure was nevertheless an exception because contrary to most other continental organizations it did not exclude East European countries, somehow rising above cold war antagonisms (Loth 2004). Moreover, it included also the Iberian countries, Spain and Portugal, which were then blacklisted from international competitions due to their dictatorial governance (Cavallaro 2009). In 1955, it accepted Turkey's request for membership, though formal admission was granted only in the beginning of 1960s (Senyuva and Tunç 2015). Therefore, from a geographical point of view (Péchoux 2004), UEFA constituted the most pervasive European organization in the 1950s. This built-in internationalist outlook was arguably a result of long-term negotiations among football associations from Europe and South America, leading to UEFA's formation.

Influenced by the application of global history methods in sport studies (Collins 2015; Gleaves and Hunt 2015; Klein 2007; Singaravélou and Sorez 2010; Taylor 2013), especially in football (Giulianotti and Roberston 2009; Grainey 2012; Tiesler and Coelho 2008), this article analyses the global context of UEFA's creation, highlighting South American influence on this European organization. None of the studies on the early years of UEFA (Archambault 2012; Barcelo 2004; Mittag 2015) mention this connection, and only two contributions have so far focused on the influence of non-European administrators on the structural hierarchy of UEFA. Sudgen and Tomlinson (1997) wrote briefly about the 'continentalization' of FIFA but lack of documents (particularly at the FIFA archives) limited their understanding of the connection between South American and European football administrators. Dietschy's (2013) article on FIFA's globalization from 1920 to 1970 offers interesting insights into the intercontinental development of FIFA, but mentions only peripherally the establishment of UEFA.

The article is structured around three connected developments in world football administration in the first half of the twentieth century. Firstly, it traces the South American demand for more influence on the governance of world football (especially within FIFA's committees) in the inter-war years, a situation that created a rift between South American and European representatives in FIFA. This confrontation arguably 'helped' the European associations to self-integrate, leaving behind their internal differences, in order to restore the hegemony they used to exercise inside FIFA before the South American dissent. Secondly, it emphasizes the role played by the South American confederation in the reorganization of FIFA in the early 1950s. Thirdly, it briefly focuses on how the South American confederation initially served as a model for the activities of UEFA.

Our research is primarily based on documents from the FIFA archives, in particular the minutes of the Executive and Emergency Committees and the Congresses, as well as correspondences (of the presidents and between FIFA and UEFA, the South American and confederation and other national associations) and documents about the reorganization of FIFA between 1950 and 1953. Archives of the East German football federation (GDR) yielded documents of the creation of UEFA. Moreover, it is possible to find in the FIFA–CONMEBOL correspondences documents from the former South American confederation (mostly minutes of ordinary and extraordinary congresses, some minutes of the Executive Committee, and annual reports). Furthermore, materials drawn from the French journals *L'Equipe, Football, France Football* have helped to fill up the gaps.

This article is a first step towards more in-depth future research on this topic. In this sense, it could be really interesting to use materials from the archives of the South American confederation that would complement the European documents about the connections among the new generation of FIFA/UEFA administrators in the beginning of 1950s. A more exhaustive work at the CONMEBOL's archives (in our knowledge, no academic research in English, French, German, Portuguese or Spanish have used this material) could help broaden our understanding, an effort we plan to undertake in the future.

South American intervention and internationalization of FIFA in the inter-war period

Football developed rapidly across Europe during the first quarter of the twentieth century, supported by the newly established FIFA (Eisenberg et al. 2004). The game spread across South America around the same time (Archambault 2014; L'Hoeste, McKee Irwin, and Poblete 2015). Started largely by the upper middle classes in Brazil (Davies 2000; Fontes and de Hollandia 2014), Argentina (Alabarces 2002) and Uruguay (Armus and Rinke 2014), it was transmitted to people from the other countries, and around 1910–1920 underwent a crucial democratization process (Mason 1995). A national football association was founded in Argentina in the late nineteenth century (Hémeury 2014), which was remarkably one of the first to have been established outside Great Britain. In the following decades came up other national associations, notably in Brazil and Uruguay, and in 1915 a confederation of South American associations was established by these three countries. During the 1920s, countries such as Chile, Bolivia and Peru joined the organization, following possibly a broader contemporary effort of continental cooperation built around culture and science (Dumont 2009).

The Confederation started a competition for South American nations in 1916 – the Copa America – which was the first football tournament organized on a continental scale. So, while European teams played in regional competitions such as the International Cup (Quin 2013) or the Balkan Cup (Breuil and Pompiliu-Nicolae 2015), South America had taken the sport's globalization a step forward. Moreover, the skill level of South American players created an excellent impression on the Europeans, which was strengthened by Uruguay winning the Olympic titles in 1924 and 1928, which was considered the most important global football competition before the World Cup began in 1930. The play of the 'Celeste' startled European journalists, who began portraying South American football as other-worldly from around this time.

During the 1920s, countries such as Bolivia, Ecuador and Paraguay joined FIFA. At the same time, associations from Asia and Africa started appealing for FIFA membership (Dietschy 2010; Goldblatt 2006). However, membership to the FIFA Executive Committee remained a privilege of Europeans. In 1924, Wali Pasha from Egypt unsuccessfully tried to be elected to the Executive Committee (FIFA, Congress, May 26–28, 1924). Thereafter, FIFA started to consider granting more privilege to extra-European federations. At the 1927 Congress in Helsinki, an American delegate jokingly proposed that in 50 years, which meant the 1976 Congress, the conference should be held in his country (FIFA, Congress, June 3–5, 1927). Beyond the joke and the little laughter it might have generated, the statement indicates the feeling of marginalization among non-European members.

The pressure from non-European countries increased with every passing year, prompting some of the Executive Committee members to ponder their demand for inclusion, which is documented in FIFA statutes from the late-1920s. A new position of the councillor – one for each continent – was created to facilitate the Secretariat's contact with national bodies (FIFA, FIFA Statutes, edition of 1929). This hardly increased participation of the non-European members as the councillors were not selected from the region they represented but from Europe, who were often too busy with their day jobs to manage football governance.

In 1927, a new step was taken towards globalizing the administration of international football as Enrique Buero from Uruguay was appointed as the first non-European member of the Executive Committee. Similar to the case of councillors, the choice of Buero too was a ploy for Europeans to maintain control. Buero was not a football administrator, but a diplomat posted in Belgium, and later in England. He came from a highly Westernized family; spoke fluently several European languages, and his brother worked as a jurist in the League of Nations in the inter-war years. Initially he found it difficult to communicate with the South American confederation since he was to them an outsider. But putting the contacts made through diplomatic career to good use, he campaigned for organizing the World cup in his country and succeeded.

The European football associations were in full control of FIFA at the end of the 1920s, which began to change following the 1930 World Cup. Members of FIFA's Executive Committee, such as Rodolphe Seeldrayers or Jules Rimet, were very impressed with the tournament's organization, the architecture of huge stadiums such as the Centenarios in Montevideo, the enthusiasm of local fans, and of course the quality of football in the region. Football was no longer a decidedly European game. The South American federation was not too happy with the lack of interest among European countries to travel to the other hemisphere. Even as a majority of FIFA members had voted at the 1929 Congress for Uruguay to host the first World Cup (FIFA, Congress, May 17–18, 1929), only four European countries (Belgium, France, Romania, Yugoslavia) decided to participate in the tournament. The strongest teams – except for the British associations, which had withdrawn from FIFA in 1928 (Beck 2000) – from Central Europe (Austria, Hungary, Czechoslovakia) and Italy decided not to go, practically 'boycotting' the event. A number of football administrators saw no sense in travelling so far as Uruguay. A few among them such as Hugo Meisl or Giovanni Mauro preferred to develop a European championship (Quin 2013). Ironically, two weeks before the World Cup, the main Central European countries played in Geneva an international tournament called 'La Coupe des nations' which was widely covered by the European press.

This apathy and counter-event caused tension between South America and Europe. Some months before the tournament, the French newspaper *Football* had indicated a potential South American boycott against European teams which declined to travel (*Football*, May 30, 1930). This was a likely threat given the concurrent efforts of South American governments to create close diplomatic ties with one another (Dumont 2012), helped by a favourable economic context (Diaz Alejandro 1984; Thorp 1994). This context allowed progressively the emancipation of South American countries, both politically and economically, from Europe (Compagnon 2013). But the proponents of South American cooperation failed to notice the potential of the football field. Following the dramatic jingoism on display at the 1930 World Cup final, Argentina and Uruguay refused to face off for five years (Dietschy, Gastaud, and Mourlane 2006). No Copa America event was organized in the meantime. This friction also delayed the development of a South American stronghold within FIFA. In the 1930s they demanded more recognition and campaigned for a quota within the Executive Committee, leading to a confrontation with European countries. Only Brazil and Argentina participated in the second World Cup in Italy in 1934, which revealed the intercontinental tension. However, internal troubles weakened their collective voice.

The South America–Europe conflict reached a peak during the second round of the Olympics football event in 1936, when the Jury of the tournament overturned Peru's victory over Austria. The officials awarded the match to Austria on the pretext of the presence of Peruvian fans on the field during the second half of the extra time, some of whom reportedly injured Austrian players (Dietschy 2013). At the 1936 FIFA Congress, the South American associations demanded a replay of the game. The Executive Committee did not relent, which raised a storm of protests from the South American delegates (FIFA, Congress, August 13–14, 1936). The decision to give the third World Cup to France despite the candidacy of Argentina was seen as another Eurocentric imposition. South American members thought it was logical for the next tournament to be held on their continent. The next Extraordinary Congress of the South American confederation decided to increase group cooperation to creatively posit itself as a pressure group inside FIFA, but their internal differences once again proved to be inimical. Countries such as Chile and Peru suggested withdrawal from FIFA, but no unanimity could be reached (FIFA, Letter from I. Schricker to the Executive Committee, November 21, 1936). Other countries differed, and Argentina and Brazil felt that withdrawing from FIFA would be too extreme a step. Finally it was proposed, in terms of the Santiago Agreement, that they would push for a non-European member to be appointed in the future Jury of Tournaments. Furthermore, they wanted a fixed place for South America inside FIFA's Executive Committee. A year later, revealing this lack of unity, Argentina left the Confederation. At the 1938 FIFA Congress, the Brazilian delegate indicated that even though his country was a member of the Confederation he 'did not recognize any restriction and any intervention from the South American Confederation on his own affair and that he wanted to maintain his direct relations with FIFA' (FIFA, Congress, March 5–6, 1938).

Despite the conflict that threatened to pull the South American confederation apart, European football administrators considered their demands. The changed attitude was fostered by the increasing importance of non-European countries inside FIFA. Moreover, a confederation in Central America was created in the late-1930s by Hector Beeche (Dietschy 2013), which sided with South America. FIFA acceded to both of the demands for a fixed place on the Committee and a reserved place in the Jury of the Tournament. In 1939, the president Jules Rimet travelled to South America, met football administrators and tried to ease the tension. The trip was deemed to be successful as the South American members decided to cancel the Santiago Agreement (FIFA, Letter from I. Schricker to the Executive Committee, April 21, 1939). Although this step was nothing more than short-term appeasement, FIFA's structure underwent significant changes in the next decade, under the influence of the Second World War and the strengthening of a South American continental voice in football.

FIFA's continentalization as a new step in the internationalization of football

FIFA functioned in a reduced capacity through the Second World War, especially after 1942 (Dietschy 2006). Wartime emergencies and restrictions made it difficult for the secretary, Ivo Schricker, to maintain correspondence with South American federations. Additionally, the South American member of the Executive Committee, Luis Dupuy, had to return to his country in 1943 (FIFA, Letter from I. Schricker to E. Borrero, March 17, 1943). It was an important loss for Schricker because Dupuy was his link with South America and also a trusted companion. Furthermore, Dupuy was an enterprising administrator, always on the lookout for initiating meaningful discussions rather than just differing with FIFA's opinion. At the same time, the South American Confederation took some crucial measures to consolidate understanding among members and also to create a common voice inside FIFA. Luis Valenzuela, the new president appointed in 1939, was apparently a strong advocate of South American football. He defended his position inside FIFA for 15 years and tried to give more power to his Confederation. Under his influence, new connections between associations of the continent seemed to be created. An important step was taken when Argentina returned to the organization in 1941. Then, in 1942, they discussed the idea to celebrate a 'day for South American football', to symbolically reinforce fraternity among the associations. These actions corresponded to the emerging Pan-Americanism that helped to interconnect countries in the region, especially within South America (Compagnon 2015).

Moreover, the Confederation decided to demand more autonomy within FIFA. Firstly, in 1941, it expressed interest to host the next World cup. Secondly, it decided to send to Zurich only half of the amount of financial benefit from the international matches played in South America (Homburg 2008). At a time when football war-torn Europe hardly yielded profit, the FIFA secretary Ivo Schricker did not take kindly to this decision. Thirdly, in 1945, a letter undersigned by Augustin Matienzo, the new delegate of the South American Confederation in FIFA's Executive Committee, proposed to organize the next FIFA Congress in 1946 in Montevideo. He wrote that the Executive Committee was now illegitimate, after its mandate was finished in 1942 (FIFA, Letter from A. Matienzo to I. Schricker, July 23, 1945). This action shows that South America now directly challenged FIFA's singular control over football's international governance. The Executive Committee transferred to the delegates of the next Congress the responsibility to take a decision about these demands. In the absence of a Congress since 1938, the mandate remained inconclusive. Probably to fight against this takeover attempt, the Executive Committee decided to organize the next Congress in Luxembourg, the city chosen in 1938. Situated in the middle of Europe, it was not a favourable location for South American delegates, who wanted Lisbon to be the venue. The choice of Luxembourg, however, did not deter them from sending delegates to the meeting.

Tension between Europe and South America increased as in the following years South American members asked for more legitimacy inside FIFA. The latter wanted to decentralize FIFA's solitary authority over world football by giving more power and influence to each continental segment of the governing body. This reflected a paradigm shift in global cooperation post-Second World War, characterized by, as Eric Helleiner (2014) has showed, alliance among non-European countries, and new international organizations involving the United States and countries in Asia or South America. The European colonial powers lost their political superiority after the War; maximum global influence was now commanded by the United States of America and the Soviet Union. Even if the political bipolarity mattered little to football governance (Kowalski and Porter 2007), as football was not a major interest for the two superpowers, this situation impinged the European dominance over football.

To be more effective inside FIFA, South America went about implementing an idea discussed in the 1930s: that of creating a Pan-American organization. Included for the first time in the new statutes of the South American Confederation in 1941, the idea took a concrete shape in 1946. In 1948, the Pan-American organization had 19 members (FIFA, 'Associations members of the [new] Pan-American confederation', March 30, 1948). Now, had all of the members decided to pursue the same goal in the inter-war years, it could have created a powerful bloc inside FIFA, putting Europeans countries under unprecedented pressure. Now was an even better time. The geopolitical consequences of the War, particularly the dispute over the status of Germany (Dichter 2013; Wahlig 2010) and Italy (Sbetti 2016), were disquieting. Moreover, Communist expansion in Central Europe created a rift between the Eastern and the Western European football associations. Between the 1946 and the 1948 Congresses, a Soviet-influenced bloc emerged inside FIFA. In the context of strong East–West confrontations, participation in sporting organizations was crucial for the Soviet Union (Parks 2007) and the United States (Gygax 2012; Rider 2011), as sport was considered by both as an arena of symbolic battle between capitalism and communism and later also as a site of the sort of diplomatic exchange not possible at political or economic summits (Dichter and Johns 2014; Malz, Rohdewald, and Wiederkehr 2007). The cold war furthered the separation, so much so that from mid-1949 to mid-1952, no games were played among European countries across the Iron Curtain and competitions such as the International Cup were stopped (*France Football*, April 19, 1949).

Additionally, to operationalize FIFA's decentralization, reorganization of its structure regarding the development of football itself was considered necessary. In fact, many of newly independent countries from Central America and Asia received FIFA affiliation during the 1940s and 1950s, which marked expansion of the football world. Membership grew from approximately 30 in the middle of the 1930s to more than 70 in the early 1950s, to 88 in 1955 (FIFA, Secretary Report, 1954–1955). Football reached far and wide as air travel escalated the number of international exchanges, including the organization of matches between national teams and clubs and inter-continental tournaments (such as the Copa Rio which started in 1951), and increased circulation of players and coaches (Taylor 2006).

The increase in the number of members can also be explained in terms of the ongoing decolonization of nations. Football – and more broadly sports – represented to the emergent nation-states a means to inspire national cohesion, to affirm independent national identities and also to be taken seriously internationally (Charitas 2015). That is why the countries that were still colonized, like Gold Coast, or were resisting colonial dominance, like Vietnam, asked at the beginning of the 1950s for a FIFA membership. These newcomers wanted more than just membership; they wanted a place within FIFA's management. For example, during an Executive Committee meeting in June 1950, Gold Coast asked FIFA to support the constitution of a new 'United African Football Association', consisting of the associations of South Africa, Ivory Coast, Gold Coast, Nigeria, Sierra Leone and Togo. The objective of this union was 'to create a closer liaison amongst the African associations, to exchange their views, to organise the payment of members' contributions, to organise regular inter-colony matches and to establish an annual inter-colony competition' (FIFA, Congress, June 22–23, 1950).

Technically Great Britain, having returned to FIFA under the leadership of the Football Association (recommended by a special commission in 1944) after the Second World War, made the first attempt to decentralize football governance (Taylor 2016). The Soviet Union, which entered the Federation in 1948, wanted the same, and received in two months a fixed position in the Executive Committee. Such expedited decision-making corresponded to a change in FIFA's organization. It also empowered the promoters of decentralization, as the two new members could be seen to have spoken for the four British associations and all the associations potentially included in the Soviet Bloc. It was argued that managing a sport so globally distributed was too difficult to be undertaken by one administrative organization, which was justified by the problems arising from the 1950's 'World Cup qualifications' in South America. Some of the groups encountered difficulties as countries such as Ecuador, Paraguay, Peru and Uruguay failed to fix dates of fixtures due to a breakdown of communication for geographical distance and political problems. As the Uruguayan government did not recognize the Peruvian one, it did not even try to negotiate dates and simply rejected every proposal. Intervention of the South American confederation proved to be futile. The FIFA secretary too was located too far to mediate. Moreover, failure to fathom the ground reality made Schricker propose unrealistic solutions which were not accepted by South American administrators. The distance between the headquarters and numerous members of the Federation – literally and figuratively – nourished the idea of the necessity of an imperative decentralization of FIFA in order to improve the management and practice of football worldwide.

All these incidents further authenticated the South American demands. At the 21st Ordinary Congress of the South American confederation held in Rio de Janeiro in May 1949, the delegates discussed a possible recast of the FIFA statutes. They talked about the Argentine association's proposal to have a more equitable distribution of continental representation within the FIFA Executive Committee. Essentially, they wanted FIFA to recognize South America by assigning it additional places within the Executive committee (FIFA, South American Confederation Congress, March–May, 1949). The one place they had negotiated seemed to be under threat as the number of FIFA members kept increasing. Indeed, since the Executive Committee members were elected by voting at the Congresses, the attendance at which had nearly doubled in the last few years, the South American confederation feared more global distribution of power and reduction of the authority it claimed. Finally, the South American members sent two proposals that were discussed during the 1950 FIFA Congress, the first to be organized outside Europe, in Rio de Janeiro during the World Cup. A change in FIFA's organization seemed necessary and a few European football administrators began to contemplate revision of its constitution.

The impact of South America on restructuring FIFA and the network of European associations after 1950

The South American agenda was clear: divide FIFA in continental groups that would control and manage their own football spheres, instead of just electing representatives to the main FIFA committees (FIFA, Annexe to the Agenda of the 1950's FIFA Congress). The Congress commissioned a special inquiry to analyse the situation and propose possible measures. Despite the overt presence of European delegates in this new commission (only two out of seven delegates came from the South American associations), there was hope for a change. In fact, the idea to reorganize FIFA was supported by a new generation of European football administrators who were probably influenced by the organization and success of football in South America. They were Ottorino Barassi (Italy), Stanley Rous (England) and Ernst Thommen (Switzerland), who became the most important people in FIFA at the beginning of the 1950s following Schricker's retirement. The new general secretary, Kurt Gassmann, was a colleague of Thommen since the late-1930s as the former secretary of the Swiss federation (Berthoud, Quin, and Vonnard 2016), and was considered extremely reliable. Barassi and Rous were appointed as joint secretaries in the reorganization commission, a role that revealed their importance in international football. In their opinion, it was time to consider the possibility of creating continental organizations within FIFA, following the South American confederation model. In 1952, Barassi took a step forward and communicated in letters addressed to several European associations the idea to create a European organization (FIFA, Annexe of a Letter from O. Barassi to R. Seeldrayers, undated). These actors detached themselves from the old elite which was gradually phasing out of FIFA. They received a fillip when Jules Rimet retired in 1954, whose vision limited the application of the proposed changes.

However, the new elite did not aim for a quick reorganization of the Federation, but rather for a smooth transition. In this sense they agreed with a new version of FIFA, divided into continental groups with moderate power. Taking into account the Copa America tournament started by the South American Confederation, they expected to launch a Pan-European tournament, an idea already discussed during the inter-war period, under the aegis of the proposed European continental federation. Barassi, having travelled many times to South America for work, probably had the opportunity to witness the organization of football first-hand and to converse with the presidents and secretaries of football associations, which deeply influenced his will to copy the South American model.

Yet, all European administrators did not share these ideas. That is why, during the meetings of the European associations in Zurich and Paris held in May and June 1952 respectively under the presidency of Barassi (*L'Equipe*, March 29, 1952), the idea of creating a European group was quickly buried. These sessions served to discuss other proposals for the reorganization of FIFA, matters which would have to be debated at the next FIFA Congress, to be organized in Helsinki a few weeks later (FIFA, FIFA Congress, July 20–23, 1952). It is important to notice that no Eastern European countries, not even Yugoslavia which was a non-aligned country and buffered Western Europe from the Soviet Bloc (Svetozar 2011), took part in the meetings. Nonparticipation had without doubt prevented the inclusion of the Soviet Union and its satellites within this new organization. The cold war still restricted exchanges in continental football.

The decentralization debate continued in Helsinki. Several South American administrators started long discussions regarding regulatory issues (official language, correspondence), which seemed secondary to the Europeans. For the first time both the European and South American delegates showed interest in negotiating the same mandate, in contrast with the previous instances of the latter forcing the former to cede ground. It was decided to report the final decision to an Extraordinary Congress to be held in 1953. As a matter of fact, European members rejected the South American proposal about the method of electing vice-presidents. So far, vice-presidents had been elected by acclamation (without votes). That year, the South American members pitted Domingo Peluffo, an Argentinian delegate, against the current vice-president Seeldrayers, who had occupied the post for more than twenty years. This contest provoked an outcry among the European members, even though Seeldrayers was finally re-elected with a vast majority (FIFA, FIFA Congress, July 20–23, 1952).

Regarding the discussion at the Congress, José Crahay – another new-generation delegate and one of the first promoters of the idea of UEFA – wrote in the 1979 UEFA commemorative book that they 'realized that every single item in the agenda [had] been thoroughly studied and that the [South American] delegates [had] been truly appointed to defend positions frequently different from the ones supported by the Executive Committee of the FIFA' (Rothenbühler 1979). The formation of a 'South American bloc' in Helsinki impressed several European delegates and persuaded them to put up a similar pressure group in Europe as a countermeasure. In the middle of 1952, the idea to create a European 'Groupement' began to materialize, in which the attitude of the South American football members had played an important role.

In the following months, the idea to create a European organization was discussed at several levels. For example, Yugoslavia and Germany sent to the FIFA secretary a project to this direction and the Football Association proposed to 'continentalize' the Federation again (FIFA, '"Reorganisation". Proposal presented at the FIFA Congress of Helsinki', October 30, 1952). These projects were obviously influenced by the cold war, as the 'Europe of football' consisted of merely 21 associations from the western part of the continent. A game between Hungary and Switzerland played in September in Bern showed perhaps a little moderation of attitude. Thus, the creation of an organization comprising all European countries was still doubtful at this stage. A number of problems needed to be resolved for the unified organization to come into being. However, certain actions taken by the South American members in early 1953 forced the European associations to change their strategy. Now, South America advocated reservations for Europeans in the future Executive Committees. This proposal might have looked paradoxical at first sight but it was an excellent tactic to reinforce the idea of a continentalization within FIFA, and finally help South America to secure places in the Executive Committee alongside Europe. At the same time, it allowed them to improve their relations with the European members after the bitter exchanges at the 1952 Congress.

Regarding the new modification of the statutes proposed by the Commission, the Uruguayan association expressed concern about the continents to the east and south of Europe being overlooked for positions in the Executive Committee (FIFA, Letter from A. Ramirez to K. Gassmann, January 30, 1953). This issue came up at the session of the Commission held on 6 and 7 March 1953, and it was there that two South American members formally asked for reservation of places for Europe, 'once and for all', in the Executive

Committee. However, the proposal was not unanimously accepted; Seeldrayers and the vice-president Arthur Drewry rejected it. The opposite views 'could not be smoothed out' even after several rounds of discussions (FIFA, FIFA Study Commission, March 7, 1953). Nevertheless, the new situation was a step forward in favour of FIFA's continentalization. In fact, it nearly convinced European football administrators that creation of a continental 'Groupement' was not far off.

In June, Barassi and Rous met at Thommen's house in Basel to discuss this question. Ebbe Schwartz, the delegate of the Scandinavian associations was present too. The presence of these four important figures of European football reveals that the idea of a European organization was now afloat. No decision was reached in Basel but a new meeting with all the European associations was fixed before the next Congress. The meeting was held two days before the Extraordinary Congress (*L'Equipe*, November 15, 1953). Despite initial difficulties of conceptualizing a united front for European footballing nations, an agreement was seemed to be forthcoming. In fact, the European associations anticipated a big change in FIFA's structure and were ready to adapt to it. For the first time in the history of FIFA, European delegates spoke for a 'group of European associations' (FIFA, FIFA Congress, November 14–15, 1953). During the meeting other discussions were held, and for the first time with associations coming from across the Iron Curtain. The proactive South American associations engineered a compromise with European associations in the evening of the second day of the Congress. On the final day, Thommen passed the resolution to earmark two vice-presidencies and four member seats for Europeans (FIFA, FIFA Congress, November 14–15, 1953). Thus, European football administrators had finally accepted South American recommendations.

A majority of the Congress participants accepted the new ideas. In fact, only the Soviet Bloc associations were opposed to the proposed reorganization. Their expectation of more equality inside FIFA – the same wish to have underwrote their dealings with the International Olympic Committee (Parks 2014) – and empowerment of the emergent Asian and African countries were not fulfilled. This situation is interesting and shows that the Soviet Bloc was in fact isolated within FIFA because the other associations, particularly those from South America, did not concur with how the Soviet football leaders acted. For example, some month later, discussions between Argentina and Soviet Union about playing friendly games fell apart due to the way their respective national teams were composed. Soviet Union had no national team and it was still a club that represented the country (for instance Dynamo Moscow) on the international scene, which the Argentine football administrators refused to recognize as a 'national' team (*France Football*, June 8, 1955).

The creation of a European group: following the South American model?

The new article 17 of the FIFA statutes entailed the creation of a European group. Its fifth subparagraph stipulated that 'the members of the executive committee (vice-president and members) [would be] appointed by the national associations groups' (FIFA, FIFA Statutes, 1953 edition), which would be implemented during the first part of 1954. Considering the context in which the decision was taken, gathering all the European football associations was not easy. Moreover, if the European associations finally found an arrangement to create an organization, should they realize a group dedicated only to elect European members at the FIFA's Executive Committee or something more ambitious that could develop synergies among European federations?

After the first discussion among members of the Permanent Commission (Barassi, Crahay and Delaunay) (FFF, Executive Committee meeting, January 11, 1954), a meeting was held in Paris in April 1954. Twenty-two Associations were present, including Czechoslovakia and Hungary from Eastern Europe. The delegates failed to come to an agreement (FIFA, Letter from E. Thommen to Jules Rimet, April 25, 1954) and fixed another meeting, to be held before the next FIFA Congress in June. Days later, Henri Delaunay, secretary of the Permanent Commission, wrote in a letter to the secretary of the GDR football association about the discussions and the possibility of a regroup. He proposed forming a confederation duplicating the South American model (GDR, Letter from H. Delaunay to the secretary of the GDR football association, April 20, 1954). He was confident of success as 22 associations had responded to his proposal (GDR, 'Answer of the National association to the questionnaire to create a European organisation', no data)

Finally, members of the Permanent Commission drew the first draft of the statutes proposing change and in a new meeting held in Basel on 15 June 1954, 25 (in fact 27, two officials were represented by others) European associations agreed to creation of a new group. The activities of the Soviet Bloc's members were not documented separately but they probably understood joining the new European group was necessary for them, a small group of ten associations, to be taken seriously. Moreover, the political transition in the Soviet Union following Stalin's death increased possibilities of sporting exchange between the East and the West. Following the end of the Korean War (1953), the Berlin conference (1954) in which the foreign ministers of the United States, Great Britain, France and the Soviet Union came together for the first time since 1948 evinced the wish to initiate new dialogues. Since football had already taken strides towards this direction, notably by the resumption of the International Cup, creation of a European group could be a timely intervention to connect countries culturally. Even though no western European organization had yet managed to cross the Iron Curtain, the 'two blocs' were linked in more ways than was acknowledged at that time (Hochscherf, Laucht, and Plowman 2010; Major and Mitter 2003).

During its first month, the organization, renamed UEFA in October 1954, was hardly an authoritative voice of football administration. For example, the idea of a European Championship it mooted in 1955 was rejected by the majority of the associations (Mittag and Legrand 2010). However, some members, notably the president Ebbe Schwartz wanted to consolidate the organization quickly. A first step was starting the European Champion Clubs' Cup, an idea first proposed by Gabriel Hanot, editor of the Parisian newspaper *L'Equipe* (Vonnard 2014), modelled after the South American Championship of Champions held in Chile in 1948. This gave more legitimacy and new stakes to the organization (Vonnard 2016). Secondly, UEFA needed to consolidate its financial resources. A possibility was to ask FIFA to remit half of the percentage (2%), equivalent to what the South American confederation earned, that it received from games played among European countries. UEFA–FIFA correspondences show that this was discussed for one year and caused tensions between the two organizations. Finally, Ernst Thommen, now vice-president of FIFA and president of its Financial Committee, brokered a deal for FIFA to give UEFA (and other confederations, such as the Asian confederation created in 1956) the same right as the South American confederation.

Creation of a championship of European nations was a strong motivation for people ranging from Gustav Sebes (Hungary), one of the new generation of open-minded football administrators from eastern Europe, to the son of Henri Delaunay, Pierre, the new secretary of UEFA, succeeding his father in 1955. They considered it important to develop the structure of UEFA and also to create football tournaments and stronger connection between European associations. After numerous discussions in the 1957 and 1958 UEFA Congress (UEFA, General Assemblies, 1957 and 1958), a majority, influenced by Copa America, decided to create a European tournament that begun in 1959 (final round took place in 1960) (UEFA, UEFA General Assembly, June 4, 1958). Hence, from 1954 to 1958, the South American confederation directly influenced the decisions taken by European football administrators, leading to the creation of UEFA and the European Nations Cup. At the end of the decade, UEFA started to become an important actor in FIFA as the representative of European football and a powerful counterpart to the South American confederation. These new actors in global football augured a new age in the history of FIFA.

Conclusion: understanding transnational influence in the organization of football

The creation of UEFA was important for European football and could be seen as a step forward to football's globalization in the post-war period, compared to the inter-war years when regional loyalties outweighed transnational and transcontinental connections (Dietschy 2015). In fact, by organizing competitions (European Cups for clubs, European championship of nations, tournaments for youth), passing regulations (for example about broadcasting) and preparing even courses for referees and trainers, UEFA became the legitimate organization for control of European football in the 1960–70s. By helping to develop better network among associations, it played an important part in the 'Europeanisation of football' (Vonnard, Quin, and Bancel 2016) during the cold war and beyond. Its popularity and effective management of sporting exchange through continental competitions have made some authors ponder about its role in the establishment of a European identity (Sonntag 2008). More recently, others have touched upon its role in the creation of 'European sites of memory' (Groll 2014).

This article has explored from a global perspective the influence of the South American model of football organization on European football administration. The ascension of the South American confederation within FIFA undoubtedly inspired the new generation of European administrators in the beginning of the 1950s. Thereafter, the confederation was seen as a model, firstly to integrate European football associations, and secondly for a reorganization of FIFA. It is also important to notice what historians specialized in global history have called the 'back effect' (Douki and Minard 2007). UEFA's undertakings in football governance from the mid-1950s began to be perceived as a model for administrators from Asia, Africa and even South America. At the end of 1950s, South America followed the European example when they put in place a club football competition, the *Copa Libertadores*. Hence, as Eisenberg (2011) has already indicated, knowledge of transcontinental connections could be really helpful to understand the development of football structures all over the world.

References

Alabarces, Pablo. 2002. *Soccer and Nations. The Image of the Nations through Soccer in the Argentina's newspapers*. Buenas Aires: Prometeo Libros.

Diaz Alejandro, Carlos F. 1984. "The 1940s in Latin America." In *Economic Structure and Performance*, edited by Moshe Syrquin, Lance Taylor, and Larry E. Westphal, 341–362. New York, NY: Harcourt.

Archambault, Fabien. 2012. "The difficult development of the Europeanization of Football during the 1950's". In *Making Europe. Cultural Aspects of European integration (1957–2007)*, edited by Pamela Anastasio and Charles Bossu, 85–96, Rome: Unione Internazionale degli Istituti di Archeologia.

Archambault, Fabien. 2014. "The continent of football." *Cahiers des Amériques latines* 74: 15–35.

Armus, Diego, and Stefan Rinke. 2014. *The History of Argentina, Brasillian and Uruguyan football*. Frankfurt am Main: Vervuert.

Barcelo, Laurent. 2004. "Europe of 52.... The Union of European Football Associations (UEFA)." *Gueres mondiales et conflits contemporains* 228 (4): 119–133.

Beck, Peter J. 2000. "Going to War, Peaceful Co-existence or Virtual Membership? British Football and FIFA, 1928–46." *The International Journal of the History of Sport* 17 (1): 113–134.

Berthoud, Jérôme, Grégory Quin, and Philippe Vonnard. 2016. *The Swiss Football. From the Pioneers to Professionnals*. Lausanne: PPUR.

Breuil, Xavier, and Constantin Pompiliu-Nicolae. 2015. "The Balkan Cup as a Vector of European Integration, 1929–1994." *Sport in History* 35 (4): 591–603.

Cavallaro, Maria Elena. 2009. "The Spanish European Integration: The First Steps of a Long Journey." In *The Two Europes*, edited by Michele Affinito, Guia Migani, and Christian Wenkel, 149–163. Brussels: Peter Lang.

Charitas, Pascal. 2015. "Imperialisms in the Olympics of the Colonization in the Postcolonization: Africa into the International Olympic Committee, 1910–1965." *The International Journal of the History of Sport* 32 (7): 909–922.

Collins, Tony. 2015. *The Oval World. A Global History of Rugby*. London: Bloomsbury.

Compagnon, Olivier. 2013. *Goodbye Europe. The Latin America and the First World War*. Paris: Fayard.

Compagnon, Olivier. 2015. "Beyond the War? The Latin Americas." In, *The Global-War. First Volume*, edited by Alya Aglan and Robert Frank, 565–598, Paris: Gallimard.

Davies, Darién J. 2000. "British Football with a Brazilian Beat: The Early History of a National Pastime (1894–1933)." In *English-speaking Communities in Latin America*, edited by Oliver Marshall, 261–284. London: Institute of Latin American Studies.

Dichter, Heather. 2013. "Kicking Around International Sport: West Germany's Return to the International Community through Football." *The International Journal of the History of Sport* 30 (17): 2031–2051.

Dichter, Heather, and Andrew Johns, eds. 2014. *Diplomatic Games: Sport, Statecraft, and International Relations since 1945*. Lexington, KY: University Press of Kentucky.

Dietschy, Paul. 2006. "Football and Total War: The Case of the Second World War." In *The Football in our Societies*, edited by Yvan Gastaut and Stéphane Mourlane, 159–173. Paris: Autrement.

Dietschy, Paul. 2010. *History of Football*. Paris: Perrin.

Dietschy, Paul. 2013. "Making Football Global? FIFA, Europe, and the Non-European Football World, 1912–74." *Journal of Global History* 8: 279–298.

Dietschy, Paul. 2015. "Did a "Europe of football" Exist in the 1930's?" *Sport in History* 35 (4): 515–530.

Dietschy, Paul, Yvan Gastaud, and Stéphane Mourlane. 2006. *A Political History of the football's Worlds Cups*. Paris: Perrin.

Douki, Caroline, and Philippe Minard. 2007. "Global History, Connected History: A Change of Scales in Historiography?" *Revue d'histoire moderne et contemporaine* 54 (5): 7–21.

Dumont, Juliette. 2009. *The Brazil and the International Institut of Intellectual Cooperation. 1924-1946. A Tool of Cultural Diplomacy*. Paris: Éditions de l'IHEAL.

Dumont, Juliette. 2012. "From Intellectual Cooperation to Cultural Diplomacy: The Brazil During the Interwar period." *Caravelle. Cahiers du monde hispanique et luso-brésilien* 99: 217–238.

Eisenberg, Christiane. 2011. "Towards a New History of European Sport?" *European Review* 19 (4): 617–622.

Eisenberg, Christiane, Pierre Lanfranchi, Tony Mason, and Alfred Wahl. 2004. *100 Years of Football: The FIFA Centennial Book*. London: Weidenfeld and Nicolson.

Fontes, Paulo, and Bernardo Buarque de Hollandia. 2014. *The Country of Football: Politics, Popular Culture and the Beautiful Game in Brazil*. London: C. Hurst & Co.

Giulianotti, Richard, and Roland Robertson. 2009. *Globalization and Football*. London: Sage.

Gleaves, John, and Thomas M. Hunt. 2015. *A Global History of Doping in Sport*. London: Routledge.

Goldblatt, David. 2006. *The Ball Is Round: A Global History of Soccer*. London: Viking.

Grainey, Timothy. 2012. *Beyond Bend It Like Beckham. The Global Phenomenon of Women's Soccer*. Lincoln, NE: University of Nebraska Press.

Groll, Michael. 2014. "UEFA Football Competition as European Site of Memory – Cups of Identity." In *European Football and Collective Memory*, edited by Wolfram Pyta and Nils Havemann, 63–84, Basingstoke: Palgrave Macmillan.

Gygax, Jérôme. 2012. *Olympism and Cold War. The Prize of the US Victory*. Paris: L'Harmattan.

Helleiner, Eric. 2014. *The Forgotten Foundations of Bretton Woods: International Development and the Making of the Postwar Order*. New York, NY: Cornell University Press.

Hémeury, Lucie. 2014. "Between Stands and Pitch. The Sportives Cultures of the Argentinians Political Leaders 1880–1990." *Histoire@Politique* 23 (2): 97–122.

Hochscherf, Tobias, Christoph Laucht, and Andrew Plowman. 2010. *Divided, but Not Disconnected: German Experiences of the Cold War*. New York, NY: Berghahn Books.

Homburg, Heidrun. 2008. "Financing World Football: A Business History of the Fédération Internationale de Football Association (FIFA)." *Zeitschrift für Unternehmensgeschichte* 53 (1): 33–69.

Klein, Alan. 2007. "Towards a Transnational Sports Studies." *Sport in Society* 10 (6): 885–889.

Kowalski, Ronald, and Dilwyn Porter. 2003. "England's World Turned Upside Down? Magical Magyars and British Football." *Sport in History* 23 (2): 27–46.

L'Hoeste, Fernández Hector, McKee Irwin, Robert, and Juan Poblete. 2015. *Sports and Nationalism in Latin/O America*. Basingstoke: Palgrave MacMillan.

Laborie, Léonard. 2010. *Networking Europe. The France and the International Cooperation in Postal and Telecommunications (1850–1950)*. Brussels: Peter Lang.

Loth, Wilfried. 2004. *Europe, the Cold War and Coexistence, 1953–1965*. London: Routledge.

Major, Patrick, and Rana Mitter. 2003. "East is East and West is West? Towards a Comparative Sociocultural History of the Cold War." *Cold War History* 4 (1): 1–22.

Malz, Arié, Rohdewald, Stefan, and Stefan Wiederkehr. 2007. *Sport Between East and West. For an History of Sport in Eastern Europe. 19 and 20 Century*. Osnabrück: Fibre Verlag.

Marston, Kevin. 2015. "A Lost Legacy of Fraternity? The Case of European Youth Football." In *Routledge Handbook of Sport and Legacy: Meeting the Challenge of Major Sporting Events*, edited by Richard Holt and Dino Ruta, 176–188. London: Routledge.

Mason, Tony. 1995. *Passion of the People? Football in South America*. London: Verso.

Mittag, Jürgen. 2015. "Negociating the Cold War? Perspectives in Memory Research on UEFA, the Early European Football Competitions and the European Nations Cups." In *European Football and Collective Memory*, edited by Wolfram Pyta and Nils Havemann, 40–63. Basingstoke: Palgrave Macmillan.

Mittag, Jürgen, and Benjamin Legrand. 2010. "Towards a Europeanization of Football? Historical Phases in the Evolution of the UEFA Football Championship." *Soccer & Society* 11 (6): 709–722.

Mittag, Jürgen, and Jörg-Uwe Nieland. 2013. "Searching Europe: UEFA and EBU as Vector of Europeanization of sport." In *Friend or Foe? Sport Between East and West During the Cold Wars*, edited by Christoph Bertling and Evelyn Mertin, 208–229. Gütersloh: Medienfabrik Gütersloh.

Parks, Jenifer. 2007. "Verbal Gymnastics: Sports, Bureaucracy, and the Soviet Union's Entrance into the Olympic Games, 1946–1952." In *East Plays West: Sport and the Cold War*, edited by Steven Wagg and David Andrews, 27–44. London: Routledge.

Parks, Jenifer. 2014. "Welcoming the 'Third World'. Soviet Sport Diplomacy, Developing Nations and the Olympic Games". In *Diplomatic Games: Sport, Statecraft, and International Relations since 1945*, edited by Heather Dichter and John Andrew, 85–114, Lexington, KY: University Press of Kentucky.

Péchoux, Pierre-Yves. 2004. "Which Frontiers for Europe?" In *Thinking on the Frontiers of Europe. From 19 to 20 Century. Historical Approaches*, edited by Gilles Pécout, 119–136. Paris: PUF.

Quin, Grégory. 2013. "The International Cup. 1927-1938. A Forgotten International Competition" *Stadion. Revue Internationale d'Histoire du Sport* 37 (2): 285–304.

Racine, Nicole. 2008. "The International Associations of Writers During the Cold War: The Exemple of French PEN club." In *Despite Europe, 1945–1990*, edited by Antoine Fleury and Lubor Jilek, 139–152. Brussels: Peter Lang.

Rider, Toby. 2011. "The Olympic Games and the Secret Cold War: The U.S. Government and the Propaganda Campaign against Communist Sport, 1950–1960." Thesis, Western Ontario University.

Rothenbühler, Rudolph. 1979. *UEFA. 25 Years*. Berne: UEFA.

Sbetti, Nicola. 2016. "Quest for Legitimacy: the Road to Redemption of Italian Football in Europe after the Second World War (1943–1949)." In *Building Europe with the Ball: Turning Points in the Europeanization of Football. 1905–1995*, edited by Philippe Vonnard, Grégory Quin and Nicolas Bancel. 101–119. Oxford: Peter Lang.

Senyuva, Özgehan, and Sevecen Tunç. 2015. "Turkey and the Europe of Football." *Sport in History* 35 (4): 567–579.

Singaravélou, Pierre, and Julien Sorez. 2010. *The Sport's Empire. An History of the Cultural Globalization (19 and 20 Centuries)*. Paris: Belin.

Sonntag, Albrecht. 2008. "Shared Passion, Ambiguous Identities. European Stakes of Contemporary Football." *Politique européenne* 26 (3): 191–209.

Sudgen, John, and Alan Tomlinson. 1997. "Global Power Struggles in World Football: FIFA and UEFA, 1954–74, and Their Legacy." *The International Journal of the History of Sport* 14 (2): 1–25.

Svetozar, Rajak. 2011. *Yugoslavia and the Soviet Union in the Early Cold War: Reconciliation, Comradeship, Confrontation, 1953–1957*. Londres: Routledge.

Taylor, Matthew. 2006. "Global players? Football, Migration and Globalization, c. 1930–2000." *Historical Social Research* 31 (1): 7–30.

Taylor, Matthew. 2013. "Editorial – Sport, Transnationalism, and Global History." *Journal of Global History* 8 (2): 199–208.

Taylor, Matthew. 2016. "English Football and 'the Continent' Reconsidered, 1919–1960." In *Building Europe with the Ball: Turning Points in the Europeanization of Football. 1905–1995*, edited by Philippe Vonnard, Grégory Quin, and Nicolas Bancel. 75–97. Oxford: Peter Lang.

Thorp, Rosemary. 1994. "The Latin American Economies in the 1940s." In *Latin America in the 1940s. War and Postwar Transition*, edited by David Rock, 41–58. Berkeley: University of California Press.

Tiesler, Nina Clara, and Joao Nuno Coelho. 2008. *Globalized Football: Nations and Migration, the City and the Dream*. London: Routledge.

Vonnard, Philippe. 2014. "A Competition That Shook European Football: The Origins of the European Champion Clubs' Cup, 1954–1955." *Sport in History* 34 (4): 595–619.

Vonnard, Philippe. 2016. "How did UEFA Govern the European Turning Point in Football? UEFA, the European Champion Clubs' Cup and the Inter-Cities Fair's Cup Projects (1954–1959)." In *Building Europe with the Ball: Turning Points in the Europeanization of Football. 1905–1995*, edited by Philippe Vonnard, Grégory Quin and Nicolas Bancel, 165–186. Oxford: Peter Lang.

Vonnard, Philippe, Quin, Grégory, and Nicolas Bancel. 2016. *Building Europe with the Ball: Turning Points in the Europeanization of football. 1905–1995*. Oxford: Peter Lang.

Wahlig, Henry. 2010. *A Goal for the World. The German Football and the FIFA. 1945-1950*. Göttingen: Verlag die Werksatt.

'Yes to Football, No to Torture!' The politics of the 1978 Football World Cup in West Germany

Felix A. Jiménez Botta

ABSTRACT

In the run-up to the 1978 World Cup, the West German section of Amnesty International launched a campaign called 'Yes to Football, No to Torture!' which sought to raise awareness of human rights violations in Argentina by taking advantage of the popularity of the XI World Cup. This article demonstrates that the Football Federation (*Deutsches Fussball Bund*) and its president Hermann Neuberger, in connivance with the West German Government, actively opposed one of the first large-scale human rights campaigns in 1970s West Germany, but were unable to prevent its success. 'Yes to Football, No to Torture!' sparked a significant discussion on the relationship of sports and politics, and rallied tens of thousands of people for the cause of human rights violations in Argentina.

Introduction

The XI FIFA World Cup, held in Argentina in June 1978, has gone down in history as one of the most controversial sports events to have ever taken place. The World Cup was organized by a military junta that ruled the country with an iron fist from 1976 until 1983, and that was subject to intense international criticism for its violations of human rights. The junta believed that Argentina was the victim of an 'international campaign of slander',[1] and envisioned the World Cup as part of a counteroffensive against foreign and domestic critics. Gorini (2015) has argued that 'the popular attachment to sports [in Argentina], and the international character of the event offered the [World Cup] ideal attributes to be utilized as a colossal propaganda operation'. The Argentinean junta hoped that a successful World Cup would promote the image of a welcoming, effective, orderly, and peaceful country abroad, and rally the passions of the football-crazed Argentine people for the benefit of the government (Smith 2002). As Grix (2012a, 2012b) has amply showed, many governments since have sought the manufacturing of social consensus by staging mega sports events such as the Olympics and the FIFA World Cup.

West German human rights activists hoped that the World Cup would have a very different effect than the one the Argentinean generals anticipated. A movement of solidarity with the Argentine public, similar to the one mobilized against human rights violations in Chile after the military coup of 11 September 1973, had failed to materialize in West Germany. Activists knew that the World Cup would generate larger-than-average interest in Argentina, since West Germany was the defending champion and many hoped for a new title. Activists hoped to channel this interest towards the human rights violations occurring there. This article analyses the campaign 'Yes to Football, No to Torture!' that the West German section of Amnesty International and smaller activists groups organized on the eve of the XI World Cup. The campaign was successful in that it mobilized tens of thousands to protest human rights violations in Argentina, but it encountered resistance from the West German Government and the national Football Federation, the *Deutsches Fussball Bund* (DFB). West German diplomats and sports officials alike believed that human rights activists were troublemakers who were politicizing sports. Nevertheless, 'Yes to Football, No to Torture!' achieved its aims, and marked a watershed in the history of human rights activism in the Federal Republic of Germany and in public debate about sports, politics and human rights.

The sports tournament fulfilled the junta's aspirations in part. The Argentinean national team defeated the strong Dutch squad in the final. Argentines filled the streets waving the national flag and chanting 'Argentina, Argentina' (Archetti 2004; Bayer 1996; Gilbert and Vitagliano 1998). The World Cup propelled the junta to the peak of its popularity and power. It earned enough public support to rule another four years, until economic crisis forced the military to manufacture popular consent once again. The failed 1982 invasion of the British-held Malvinas/Falkland Islands brought the people to the streets once more but this time to protest against the military, forcing it to give up power the following year (Ciria 1984).

At the same time, the World Cup was a setback for the ambitious counteroffensive against an alleged 'Anti-Argentine campaign' that the junta had envisioned. As Rein (2014) has showed, activists in France, the Netherlands, Israel, Spain, West Germany and Sweden were 'successful in promoting a public debate … on ties with the Argentinean dictatorship, on issues of human rights and international relations, as well as on the use and abuse of sports for political purposes'. The West German campaign 'Yes to Football, No to Torture!' was a local expression of an international movement for human rights that rocked the global political landscape of the 1970s. The World Cup put human rights activists at odds with DFB president Hermann Neuberger and with government officials. Historian Nils Havemann interprets the campaign from the lens of domestic West German politics. He avers that critics of the DFB and president Neuberger were actually 'left-wing propagandists' who mounted an 'excessive' campaign against the DFB president that morphed into a 'propagandistic myth'. Havemann argues that Neuberger supported Amnesty's cause, but that he was compelled by the West German Government to refrain from public pronouncements on behalf of human rights (Havemann 2013, ch. 4, loc. 7242).

After analysing the arguments of human rights activists, West German sports officials, government representatives and the press in the run-up to the 1978 World Cup, I arrive at a different conclusion. Interpreting West German human rights activism as a mere expression of domestic politics, as Havemann does, elides the fact that 1970s human rights activism was an international phenomenon. Unbound by the constraints of the nation state, transnational activists carried the discourse of human rights across national and continental borders (Cmiel 1999; Keck and Sikkink 1998). Scholars such as Moyn (2010) and Eckel (2012, 2014) have made convincing arguments that there was a global turn to human rights from the late 1960s to the 1980s. The reasons were manifold: a desire to overcome stale Cold

War discourses and the failure of previous political projects led to novel iterations of earlier discourses of human rights. Regimes such as Argentina's, that trampled on the most basic rights, were anathema to human rights activists (Eckel and Moyn 2014).

As I will show also, the DFB and its president, similarly to West German government officials and the conservative press, opposed the 'Yes to Football, No to Torture!' campaign, and trivialized the repression carried out by the Argentinean military junta. I argue that they did so in order to counteract a human rights movement that threatened to turn public opinion against the lucrative sports event by highlighting the connection between sports and politics, and criticizing organized football's willingness to work with dictators that were misusing sports to hide their systematic violations of human rights. This article proposes further that the 'Yes to Fooball, No to Torture!' campaign was a decisive turning point in the effort of raising public awareness in West Germany about human rights violations in Argentina.

West Germany and the Argentinean 'Dirty War', 1976–1983

Terrorism from the left and the right shook Argentina in the 1970s, a consequence of decades of military rule and popular resistance that had transformed Latin America's most stable democracy into a nest of political violence. The military government or junta, that took power on 24 March 1976, claimed that it would save Argentina from terrorism. Their 'Process of National Reorganization', most commonly known as the 'Dirty War', was born of a toxic mixture of fascism, anti-populism, religious extremism and anti-Semitism that pervaded the Argentinean right. Once in power the military engaged in a campaign of state terrorism that surpassed the terrorist threat that they had allegedly set out to destroy by far (Novaro and Palermo 2003; Wright 2007). The Doctrine of National Security permeated the Argentine armed forces that believed themselves to be at war with a host of foreign and domestic enemies. The 'Dirty War' targeted not only guerrilla members from the ERP and Montoneros but also trade unionists, left-wing students, academics, left-wing lawyers and jurists, human rights activists, Jews, liberal politicians and the relatives of real and imagined subversives (Finchelstein 2014). The governor of the Province of Buenos Aires, General Ibérico Saint Jean, infamously proclaimed in 1976: 'First we will kill all the subversives, then we will kill their collaborators, then … their sympathizers, then … those who remain indifferent; and, finally, we will kill the timid' (emphasis in original) (quoted in Feitlowitz 2011, 36). The 'Dirty War' lasted from 1976 to 1983, with an estimated 30,000 deaths and tens of thousands victims of torture, rape and lengthy imprisonment.

West German diplomats perceived the latest coup as a symptom of Argentina's pervasive political instability and violence since 1930. The Argentinean coup was the sixth in only 46 years and by 1976, all but two South American nations were ruled by jackbooted officials. Jörg Kastl, then West German ambassador in Buenos Aires, believed that military rule was 'the only viable way' and encouraged his superiors to show goodwill towards the new regime. If West Germany wanted to prevent Argentina from falling 'into leftist authoritarian adventures', the ambassador emphasized, 'we will have to work with the new regime'.[2] Even as the crimes of the military regime became well known by 1977, Kastl maintained that either 'Videla's experiment of national reorganization' was successful or 'the country will succumb to a leftist dictatorship'.[3] Karl Alexander Hampe, head of the Foreign Ministry's Referat 330, responsible for relations with Latin America's Southern Cone, argued that the generals were 'helpers in an emergency situation marked by impending economic breakdown and political chaos'.[4] Targeted by the left-wing terrorists of the Red Army Faction, the Social Democratic–Liberal (SPD/FDP) administration showed understanding towards the junta's self-proclaimed war on subversion. West Germany opted for a 'silent diplomacy' that would enable Bonn to intervene on behalf of West German citizens to have fallen victim to the repression, while maintaining friendly relations, which secured profitable economic deals and weapon sales. Bonn approved nearly 4.5 billion Deutschmarks in armament sales to the junta from 1976 to 1983.[5] Grassroots campaigns exposing the junta's human rights violations were incompatible with the 'silent diplomacy' approach towards Buenos Aires and thus undesirable from a government standpoint.

The West German Government's reaction to Argentina was different from its earlier response to the 1973 coup in Chile, which became a *cause célèbre* of the West German left, including parts of the ruling Social Democratic Party and the politically important federation of trade unions Deutscher Gewerkschaftsbund (DGB) (Dufner 2014). The Willy Brandt administration had set up an asylum programme for Chileans that continued under his successor Helmut Schmidt. While 2500 refugees from Chile had arrived in West Germany by 1980, Argentineans were denied asylum. Moreover, civil society as a whole evinced little interest in Argentinean political violence. West German citizens had not mobilized in large numbers on behalf of Argentina, as they had for Vietnam and Chile in the 1960s, and after 1973, respectively. An Argentinean activist examining the possibilities for mobilizing West German citizens faced a desolate situation: 'Solidarity with Argentina is very weak and hardly developed, a comparison with Chile or Vietnam is absurd … there is not a single committee of solidarity with Argentina'. The activist further bemoaned that the few who were engaging in solidarity with Argentina were Argentinean exiles, of whom there were very few because of the strict asylum restrictions against them.[6]

This caused significant frustration amongst human rights activists, primarily members of Amnesty International, who were painfully aware of the human rights violations in Argentina. As early as December 1975, Amnesty International had informed Interior Minister Werner Maihofer about violence in Argentina and that Chilean refugees, who had arrived after September 1973, were being harassed by a right-wing death squad that styled itself the Argentine Anti-Communist Alliance or AAA. Amnesty requested that West Germany cease to sell weapons to Argentina and that it admit at least some of these refugees.[7] The United Nations High Commissioner for refugees, Sadruddin Aga Khan, also lodged a similar request to Chancellor Schmidt.[8] Maihofer disputed that Chilean refugees were being harassed and, arguing that Argentina was a safe country, rejected Amnesty's request.[9] The upcoming World Cup was therefore a one-of-a-kind opportunity for human rights activists. They hoped that it would encourage mass activism on behalf of Argentinean refugees, and against human rights violations occurring in Argentina, which would, in turn, translate into state policy.

Debating human rights and sports on the eve of the World Cup

Activists reasoned that football might be the key to get the average West German interested in the conditions in Argentina, if they could transform football excitement into moral outrage somehow. Amnesty had already gained international attention for its signature drives, 'urgent actions' and human rights events that resembled secular church services since the creation of the organization by British lawyer Peter Benenson in 1961. Since the late 1960s, when the Nigerian Civil War rallied the passions of many 'western' humanitarians, the discourse of 'human rights' had risen in prominence. Some historians speak of a veritable 'revolution' as regular citizens and even governments, under Joop den Uyl in the Netherlands and under Jimmy Carter in the United States, embraced the cause of political prisoners and victims of state persecution, a movement that Samuel Moyn has termed 'the last utopia' (Eckel 2014; Eckel and Moyn 2014; Hoffmann 2011; Iriye, Goedde, and Hitchcock 2012).

The West German section, with 6000 members organized in 520 local groups across the country, was a civil society force to be reckoned with. But Amnesty's concerns, and particularly its methods, had its fair share of detractors. The West German Government, which was engaged in a process of detente with Eastern Bloc countries, and pursued a similar approach towards human rights violators in the 'Third World' was dismissive of the organization (Rock 2010). The Foreign Ministry believed that Amnesty International's purpose was to 'damage our relations with the military government in Argentina' rather than 'humanitarianism'.[10]

Moreover, ever since Amnesty signalled its intention to take advantage of the World Cup for their Argentina campaign, the German Football Federation and its president, Neuberger, resolutely opposed it. The DFB's stance became evident on the occasion of a friendly between the West German and Argentinean national selections on 3 June 1977. After the match, that the West German team won with three goals to one, theologian Helmut Franz proposed in the popular radio show, *Wort zum Sonntag* (Word on Sunday), that the fact that the national team had gone to Argentina should have been a chance to criticize the human rights violations in that country. After all, 'it was a friendly! Friendship! Who are our "friends" over there? The oppressors or the oppressed?' The theologian wondered why 'our sports functionaries' did not go into the presidential palace, 'confronted the military dictators with the human rights violations in their country and demanded the freedom of political prisoners?' The commentary irked Neuberger who saw the integrity of sports threatened. He 'protested with all resoluteness' against the 'political phrasing of this *Wort zum Sonntag*', a programme that he believed should stick to religious questions. Human rights violations occurred all over the world and focusing 'disproportionately' on Argentina smacked of left-wing political bias. Humanitarianism had seemingly no place in a religious commentary. Worse, 'misusing' football for human rights advocacy threatened the future of international sports because there would soon be no teams against whom to play. The Director of Saarland Radio, at whom the protest was lodged, responded amiably to Neuberger's diatribe, calling the commentary 'ideological' and 'pseudo-Christian', and promised Neuberger that had he been informed about the content previously, the theologian's message would not have been aired (Pramann et al. 1978).

This episode foreshadowed what was to come from sports officials in the spring and summer of 1978. Human rights activists were undeterred however. Konstantin 'Tino' Thun, a leading member of Amnesty International, contended,

> We must not be silent, when in a country, to which we are all going to be looking at in a few weeks, 15,000 people have been kidnapped and since disappeared … in Argentina are 8,000 to 10,000 political prisoners in jail without having ever been accused, not to speak of having been charged.

The activist argued further,

> it must not be that [the image] of this military junta is being glossed over only so that a World Cup may take place. For me, who receives daily information about the horrible persecution

in Argentina … statements [such as Neuberger's] are really impossible to accept. (Pramann et al. 1978, 67)

For activists, Neuberger's arguments rung hollow. After all, it was the junta which was using the World Cup for its propaganda campaign in the first place. Moreover, Neuberger's charge that activists criticizing human rights violations in Argentina were politicizing sports, or engaging in political propaganda, was contrary to human rights activists' own conceptions of their work. Amnesty International criticized the treatment of dissidents and of Jews in the Soviet Union, South African Apartheid and South American military juntas alike (Eckel 2012). Activists' image of Neuberger did not improve in the least after he told the sports magazine *Sports Illustrierte,* when asked if Argentina was being ruled by a dictatorship, 'I am very careful with the term dictatorship', and argued that the Argentinean Junta was merely in the process of shaking people up for 'healthy democracy' (Pramann et al. 1978, 34–35).

Amnesty was careful to declare that its campaign was not aiming for a boycott. The very name of the campaign 'Yes to Football, No to Torture!' denoted a positive attitude to the game. General Secretary Helmut Frenz declared early on,

Amnesty International is not against the World Cup. We are opposed that the roar of football fans be used to drown out the screams of those being tortured in Argentina … we are not making propaganda for or against the World Cup … [Amnesty will] utilize this sports event to inform world opinion about the true conditions in Argentina. (*Berliner Stimme*, April 15, 1978)

Frenz made clear that activists were all for sports as long as tournaments were not utilized to cover up crimes, but this positive attitude towards the sport itself did not change the DFB's hostile attitude. Amnesty decided therefore to bypass the football hierarchy, and engaged the players themselves in the discussion. Each football player slated to play at the World Cup received a letter saying that Amnesty International was not calling for boycott, but that its aims were that the 'strong media interest in Argentina is to be used to propagate information about these repressed people'. Players were informed that 'with an enormous effort, [and] with the help of the World Cup, the junta is attempting to present the world with a peaceful image of Argentina'. The letter informed them about the staggering numbers of political prisoners, of the kidnapped and disappeared, and that over one hundred Europeans, including seventeen Germans were either known to have been killed, or were disappeared or incarcerated. Also shocking was the existence of torture facilities but a few hundred metres away from the one of the main venues of the World Cup, CA River Plate's *Estadio Monumental.* The players were reminded that the Nazis had set out with a similar mission in the 1936 Olympics, and that they, as sportsmen, had a chance in preventing the junta to get away with it. Amnesty asked the players to sign a petition demanding the end of human rights violations in Argentina and requesting the West German Government to accept five hundred Argentinean refugees. The letter ended with the Amnesty mantra: 'We know that publicity is the worst enemy of torture' (Pramann et al. 1978, 21–22).

Even though most players were indifferent to the petition, Amnesty had chosen the right tactic by engaging them directly. Player's responses, aired on the prime-time TV programme 'Monitor', and printed on the biweekly magazine *Stern*, became an immediate media sensation. Klaus Fischer, a striker for Schalke 04, refused to sign the petition, saying, 'political conditions in Argentina do not interest me in the very least' (Breitner, *Stern*, April 6–12, 1978). Defender Berti Vogts, World Champion in 1974 and team captain, replied to a journalist's entreaty about whether he intended to sign Amnesty's petition with a question of his own 'if the World Cup was being held in the Soviet Union, would you make the same interview?' (Breitner, *Stern*, April 6–12, 1978). Vogts' response reflected the standard West German conservative reaction towards human rights activists who focused their energies against right-wing dictatorships, rather than 'Real Existing Socialism' in Eastern Europe. Conservatives made human rights activism into a Cold War issue, which was precisely what Amnesty sought to avoid by maintaining a critical stance towards human rights violations regardless of their source of origin. Vogts' comment provoked derision by critics who saw in his 'mean aggressiveness … a justification of the conditions in Argentina' (*Frankfurter Allgemeine Zeitung*, March 30, 1978). Others defended Vogts' rejection of 'cheap one-sided … left-wing[ers]' who were allegedly blind to human rights violations in Socialist countries (*Die Welt*, March 31, 1978). But it was Midfielder Paul Breitner, Vogt's teammate in the winning team of 1974, who stole the show by energetically supporting Amnesty's petition. His broadside against the DFB, Neuberger and coach Helmut Schön, whom he qualified as 'political ignorants', because they ignored conditions in Argentina, had all the ingredients that fed the tabloid press. The sensationalist *Bild* intimated that Breitner was just trying to profile his 'bad boy' image and stand in the centre of attention (*Bild am Sonntag*, May 14, 1978; *Frankfurter Rundschau*, April 6, 1978). In an op-ed in *Stern*, however, Breitner revealed a sophisticated awareness of the political role of sports. He opposed a boycott, but demanded that all players should refuse the customary handshake with the head of the state, in this case Junta-chef Jorge Rafael Videla. He said, 'Our team will go to Argentina to play football, not make politics. But it can prevent being used as a marionette for the political games of Argentinean generals'. Goalkeepers Seep Meier, Rudi Kargus and Berndt Franke, midfielder Rudi Seliger, and striker Manfred Burgsmüller, also showed solidarity towards Amnesty's campaign (Breitner, *Stern*, April 6–12, 1978; 'Folter-Bedrückt sie das?', *Stern*, April 6–12, 1978).

DFB officials made their opposition to Amnesty's petition clear. Even though Amnesty repeated on multiple instances that they were not pursuing a boycott, sports officials continued to argue against the straw man of the boycott. The General Secretary of the DFB, Karlheinz Gieseler, argued that sports had no ability to bring about political change. Anyone who doubted this had a 'false idealization of sports' and harmed its ability to establish links between peoples, nations and political systems. The 'freedom of action [of sports] is just as limited as other powers that be'. The West German football team was not going to play for 'General Videla, Leonid Breschnev, Erich Honecker, or [Ugandan] dictator Idi Amin', but to demonstrate their abilities in the hope that a better world may be created (Pramann et al. 1978, 42, 44). Wilfried Gerhart, public relations officers of the DFB, argued, 'We know that there is much wrong in South America and in other parts of the earth. We resist the belief, however, that sports … can be turned into a tool for applying pressure'. This would have dire consequences, less interaction, less tournaments and a 'world more grey and gloomy as it already is' (Pramann et al. 1978, 54). Neuberger endorsed his colleagues' views in an interview with *Spiegel*. Even as he assured the interviewer that West German players had the freedom to support Amnesty International, perhaps even intercede on behalf of political prisoners, and that he personally intended to bring up the issue himself in Buenos Aires, Neuberger maintained that 'politics cannot unduly encroach upon the freedom of sports … what politics cannot solve, cannot be pushed onto us sportsmen' (*Der Spiegel*, April 24, 1978).

These views echoed amongst politicians. The CDU/CSU Bundestag delegate, Willi Weisskirch, hyperbolically argued that

> if one really believes that there should not be any international sports events, no World Cups, and not Olympic Games held in dictatorships or in countries with obscure political conditions, then one would need to stop all international sports events. (Weisskirch 1978)

Hildegard Hamm-Brücher, FDP State Minister in the Foreign Ministry, argued in Parliament that the government would not be 'supporting' the campaign because it would represent an intromission in the internal affairs of Argentina, and therefore, the government was not encouraging players or fans to do the same. Historian Nils Havemann has posed that Hamm-Brücher's statement reflected the government's opposition to Neuberger's statements seemingly supporting Amnesty's campaign to the *Spiegel* and that it forced Neuberger to change his stance (Havemann 2014). This is a problematic interpretation, considering Hamm-Brücher did not criticize Neuberger or his comments to the *Spiegel* explicitly, and there is no evidence that the DFB received a private reprimand from the government. Rather, Hamm-Brücher acknowledged that each player had the right to speak his mind. Her statements reflected the government's attitude; it would not encourage engagement for human rights, but knew that it could not prohibit it.[11]

The DFB and the government were on the same page. Both believed that the World Cup should remain a strict sports affair, and that any efforts on behalf of political prisoners were to occur as private initiatives. Their attitude fit perfectly in the plans of the Argentinean junta, which suppressed any critical voices that would damage their carefully choreographed sports event. They hoped that the World Cup would blind the world to the human rights abuses going on, not shed more light on them. The mothers of the 'disappeared', who had begun to walk in circles around the obelisk in the Plaza de Mayo in protest since the previous year, were subjected to especial harassment in the weeks prior to the World Cup, and slandered as unpatriotic and 'anti-argentine' (Gorini 2015).

The 'Yes to Football, No to Torture!' campaign and its repercussions

A campaign such as 'Yes to Football, No to Torture!' had no precedent in West Germany, therefore, West German Amnesty activists received help from their British peers who taught them how to seize public attention and direct it towards human rights violations in faraway countries.[12] At the heart of the campaign was a travelling exhibition about conditions in Argentina with images and statistics of the repression that aimed at changing the 'image of Argentina [as a country of] Tango, Steaks and temperament' and investigate the 'connection between sports and politics, between "Football and torture" (without opposing football)'.[13] Amnesty spearheaded the campaign, but numerous activist groups, which had previously spoken out for Chile, collaborated in financing the travelling exhibition and developing ways of reaching a wider audience. Bonn campaigners, for example, designed a write-in quiz where football fans that mailed in the right keyword could win a basket filled with Argentinean souvenirs, Tango records, a Gaucho's lazo, and a poncho. The questions in the quiz-brochure ranged from 'What is the name of the most popular football team in Argentina?' to 'how many people ... are incarcerated out of political reasons?' To win, one needed to accurately answer all questions and then fill-in the letters in the keyword box provided in the brochure, which was nothing other than the campaign's motto: 'FUSSBALL JA FOLTER NEIN'.[14] Activists then attempted to bring these quizzes and anti-Argentinean junta posters to West Germany's professional league (Bundesliga) games. Here they encountered open hostility by sports officials and stadium staff. Campaigners suffered expulsion, violence, and in at least one occasion, the Bundesliga team Borussia Mönchengladbach sued them on charges of undisciplined behaviour during a sports event.[15] Similarly, demonstrators who entered the Argentinean consulate in Düsseldorf bearing 'Yes to Football, No to Torture!' banners were evicted by the police and threatened with a civil suit for trespass (*Die Welt*, June 22, 1978).

Others engaged themselves in less spectacular, but still effective ways. On 1 June 1978, the first day of the World Cup, the West Berlin-based Chile–Latin America Documentation Centre published a two-page appeal in the *Franfurter Rundschau* calling the situation in Argentina 'worse as in Chile!' and supporting Amnesty International's campaign. The appeal was signed by numerous personalities from West German civil society including writer Ingeborg Drewitz, theologians Helmut Gollwitzer and Norbert Greinacher, movie directors Volker Schlöndorff and Margarete von Trotta, graphic designer Klaus Staeck and the CDU politician Norbert Blüm (*Frankfurter Rundschau*, June 1, 1978). The Bonn-based working group 'Journalists Help Journalists' kept its members informed regularly about conditions in Argentina. On 16 May, the working group's members were informed that there were '29 murdered, 40 disappeared, 70 imprisoned and 400 exiled argentine journalists'. Solidarity between Journalists was certainly an important reason for why so many newspapers reported on the campaign, and why many were overwhelmingly critical of the DFB and Neuberger.[16]

Numerous publications wholeheartedly supported the 'Yes to Football, No to Torture!' campaign and criticized the DFB. The trade unionist magazine *Solidarität* editorialized that 'sport and politics are old bedfellows' and criticized sports functionaries that act as 'if sports and politics are two completely different things' (*Solidarität*, May 1978). The magazine *Blickpunkt* contended that 'the DFB, as a powerful Football Federation, has [the] ability ... to do something about human rights' but since it failed to distance itself from the conditions in Argentina, the DFB 'is complicit with what is going on' (*Blickpunkt*, May 3, 1978). The *Anti-Imperialist Information Bulletin* contrasted Neuberger's statements about the neutrality of sports, with the fact that Argentinean generals themselves had openly proclaimed the political nature of the world Cup, quoting General Antonio Merlo's famous remark that 'hosting the world cup is a political decision which has the goal of improving the image of Argentina in the world' (*Antiimperialistisches Informationsbullettin*, June 6, 1978). The editors of the *Informationsbulletin* argued that as the defending champion, the German Football Team had the moral duty of standing up for human rights. The *Frankfurter Rundschau* compared watching the World Cup to the profoundly uncomfortable act of having to swallow a toad. The sports event deserved the criticism of upstanding citizens worldwide, but in the end it was up to politicians to bring about a meaningful change in Argentina, the viewers were powerless (*Frankfurter Rundschau*, March 31, 1978).

The TV Channel *Westdeutscher Rundfunk* informed its viewers in a televised reportage on 21 February 1978 that 'a military regime is attempting to make itself socially acceptable through football', adding that

> football is no longer simply an occasion for ordinary people to wave flags, but thanks to mass media, it is an [important] vehicle for propaganda. [Dictators] want to attract world opinion with spectacular events and suppress human rights violations, torture, concentration camps and political prisoners.[17]

Konkret's criticism was more incisive. Looking at the history of the DFB under the Third Reich – the football association had undergone swift *Gleichschaltung* under the Nazis – the magazine found that DFB officials had always catered to dictators. It criticized Neuberger's stance towards the Argentinean junta, but reserved special reproach towards coach Helmut Schön, who had told the press that he had not seen anything that 'identified [Argentina] as a dictatorship in the full meaning of the term'. The magazine featured a picture of the German football team, which had included Schön, saluting Hitler with the 'German greeting', the raised right arm, after winning the gold medal the Olympic games of 1936 (*Konkret*, May 1978).

The reference to the 1936 Olympic Games, which the Nazis used with similar purposes as the Argentinean junta, was a staple of the global solidarity campaign countries and in West Germany as well (Franco 2005). A pamphlet by the 'Pforzheim Chile Working Group', for example, analysed the similarities between the Nazi Olympics and the 'Torture-Generals in Argentina' showing how the Nazis had polished their international image by removing anti-Semitic signs from stores and establishments, and juxtaposed these efforts with the junta's similar attempt to sell the world a clean image of Argentina. It highlighted the similarities between Nazi efforts to boost nationalism and the 'People's Community' in 1936, with the junta's concept of a 'patriotic union', where fandom of the national football team was supposed to erase all political cleavages. For activists there was no distinction between the Nazis and the Argentine generals: 'People's Community or "Patriotic Union": the difference lays almost only in the word choice!'[18]

Conservative newspapers criticized Amnesty International for its alleged bias against right-wing authoritarians while supposedly failing to criticize left-wing totalitarians. Conservatives agreed that the junta intended the World Cup to have a positive effect for its image, but argued, paradoxically, that it was primarily left-wing critics and human rights activists who were politically misusing sports with their 'Yes to Football, No to Torture!' campaign. *Die Welt* stated that it was a laudable effort by the Argentinean generals to improve their image because the military had 'prevented chaos, restored order in the country, [and] ensured the security of the average citizen'. Using sports for political purposes was a time-honoured practice, from the Nazis to the Soviet Union, a feature common to totalitarian and authoritarian states. Amnesty International's campaign was being 'selective' in its treatment of Argentina (*Die Welt*, March 28, 1978; *Welt am Sonntag*, April 9, 1978).

The *Frankfurter Allgemeine Zeitung* argued that even though 'there is no denying that sports plays a political role', it did not mean that 'sports should be misused politically'. The *FAZ* argued that 'Yes to Football, No to Torture!' was misusing sports, and averred that 'our players should go play sports in Argentina, not politics'. The newspaper wondered if the same activists who were criticizing the world cup with shouts of 'Yes to football, no to torture!' would respond to the 1980 Olympic Games to be held in Moscow with cries of 'Yes to medals, No to barbed wire!' (*Frankfurter Allgemeine Zeitung*, April 8, 1978).

The tabloid *Bild* was even more overt in its support for the junta. Ten days before the start of the tournament, the newspaper published an interview with Videla who argued that there were no political prisoners in Argentina but '3500 subversive terrorists, helpers, and sympathizers'. This was the same discourse employed in West Germany to refer to domestic left-wing terrorists of the Red Army Faction and its network of accomplices. Videla argued that human rights activists were part of an international campaign of calumny bankrolled by 'international terrorism! The same people that killed [former Italian Prime Minister Aldo] Moro, who executed [West German industrialist Hanns Martin] Schleyer' (*Bild am Sonntag*, May 21, 1978).

The campaign also provoked substantial reactions in the population. Football and torture became a regular topic of conversation in middle and high schools, church youth groups and amongst concerned citizens. The schoolboys and girls from a Cologne secondary school bluntly asked the Foreign Ministry in a letter: 'what are you going to do against' the fact that the Argentinean junta had incarcerated thousands and controlled 'every facet of public life?'[19] Frieder S., a Coast Guard sailor, wrote to Chancellor Schmidt about his frustration with West Germany's overly friendly policy towards the Argentinean junta: 'As a nation, that advocates for freedom and equality in the world, we have to engage critically with the conditions in Argentina'. The sailor added that the Federal Republic should own up to its role 'as a state that stands for freedom and human rights', openly criticize the torture, and accept refugees.[20] Others focused on the responsibilities that, according to them, Germany's past of war of genocide delegated onto future generations. The Evangelic youth group of Kirch-Brombach in Hesse, for example, argued that Argentina's junta was similar to the Third Reich. The efforts to politicize the World Cup were tantamount to the 'dishonest propaganda' show that the 1936 Olympic Games had been. Consequently, the group demanded that Bonn engage itself for human rights and free elections in Argentina.[21] The government had to put up with the reproach of a seventh grade class from Bielefeld that 'not enough is being done' for tortured people in Argentina.[22] A petition bearing 52,899 signatures in support of the campaign reached the Foreign Ministry in June.[23] By then, Bonn had reversed its earlier opposition to accepting political refugees from Argentina, announcing in April that it would accept Amnesty's plea for the admission of five hundred political refugees from Argentina (*Deutsche Presse Agentur,* April 21, 1978).

The campaign also grabbed the attention of parliamentarians such as Horst Seefeld, a Social Democratic member of the European Parliament, who criticized the skewed image of 'Pampas, Gauchos, Señoritas, – the wonderful and idyllic world' that the junta was selling to the world, and contended that the Argentinean propaganda campaign 'must be confronted' (Seefeld 1978). Seefeld co-sponsored a hearing on human rights violations in Argentina, held at the European Parliament in Strasbourg on 25–26 May, where witnesses gave their reports on human rights violations in Argentina, on the fate of the disappeared, and on the condition of Argentinean refugees. Ernst Käsemann, theologian at Tübingen University, whose daughter Elisabeth had died the previous year under mysterious circumstances at the hands of the Argentinean military in Buenos Aires, was one of these witnesses (*Deutsche Welle,* May 21, 1978; Weitbrecht 2013).[24]

Even the DFB found itself compelled to relent somewhat. DFB officials met with Amnesty's representatives Frenz and with 'Tino' Thun in May. At the meeting, the DFB president agreed to intervene for approximately 13 German citizens who were either sitting in Argentine prisons or had 'disappeared'. Neuberger clarified his earlier statement to *Der Spiegel.* He would carry out these efforts as a private citizen and not in his capacity as DFB president. Just how thin Neuberger's interest was became obvious in his refusal to accept a list of eight imprisoned Argentinean sportspersons. He also snubbed signing a petition to the West German Government to earnestly pursue the acceptance of the five hundred refugees, and further declined to make a joint statement on human rights violations in Argentina, or to consider Amnesty's proposal to host a solidarity match between West German players and Argentinean refugees (Kuhlwein 1978).

By now Neuberger and the DFB had alienated Amnesty International and solidarity activists. His promise to undertake efforts as a private citizen on behalf of a few selected political prisoners resembled the Foreign Ministry's silent diplomacy. It was insufficient for 'Yes to Football, No to Torture!' campaigners, who aimed, however quixotically, at ending human rights violations in Argentina by means of international pressure. The appearance of Hans Ulrich Rudel – dive bomber in the Second World War and known for his unapologetic Nazi views and his friendly disposition towards the military junta – at the West German team's headquarters in Ascochinga, confirmed the worst fears of those concerned about human rights violations in Argentina, and the role that the West German Government and the DFB were playing in disregarding them. It seemed as if the DFB, which had opposed Amnesty's campaign, was now demonstrating blatant support for the junta by inviting one of its most (in)famous admirers. After visiting the training camp, Rudel threw fuel into the fire by giving an interview to the public channel ZDF, where he claimed that the Argentinean military was doing its duty, just 'as we did ours' (Havemann 2014).[25] The former coronel of Hitler's Air Force had equated the 'Dirty War' to the Wehrmacht's brutal war of extermination in the Soviet Union, and his comment was ambiguous enough that it could be interpreted as a defence of the Holocaust as well.

Rudel's visit outraged the Left and the Jewish community in West Germany. The future Chancellor, Gerhard Schröder, then head of the Social Democratic Jusos, criticized the visit as a 'provocation of all democrats'. Heinz Galinski, head of the Jewish Community in Berlin, called it a scandal. Neuberger certainly did not help his cause by stating that 'Mr. Rudel is a German citizen with as many rights as protesters and as myself. I do hope that he is not being reproached for his actions as a combat pilot in the Second World War' (*Frankfurter Rundschau*, June 12, 1978). Hans Lamm, speaking for the Munich Israeli Cultural Community, lambasted Neuberger's defence of Rudel's appearance in Ascochinga, which had already earned the dubious distinction of being praised by the far-right newspaper *National Zeitung*. Lamm argued that 'Mr. Rudel is not just an apolitical hero of the Second World War. He is the idol of old and new Nazis', adding that Rudel had engaged in a 'brazen defence of a military regime that has violated human rights, [engaged] in kidnapping and terror, as Amnesty International has proven' (*Süddeutsche Zeitung*, June 24, 1978). A letter-writer to *Süddeutsche Zeitung*, one Jochen Ebner, stated what many were now thinking:

> It is obvious that the meeting that the DFB held with representatives from Amnesty International was a farce ... the DFB naturally recognized that terror and torture occur daily [in Argentina]. But that was only lip service by some [DFB] functionaries [due to] public pressure. (*Süddeutsche Zeitung*, June 24, 1978)

In a book and a subsequent article, Havemann argues that critics of Neuberger and the DFB were left-wing propagandists who had been waiting for the perfect opportunity to 'tackle the DFB president in the legs with full power from behind' (Havemann 2013, ch. 4, loc. 6491). Havemann claims that the DFB president cared for the human conditions in Argentina and that his views were misconstrued because of Neuberger's authoritarian and rude personality that tended to attract enemies. The fact that journalists focused their anger on Neuberger, even to the point of ad hominem attacks, rather than the 'working-class' Schön or his predecessor Sepp Herberger, both of whom had entertained friendly relations with Rudel, is supposed to be evidence of their malicious intention (*Der Spiegel*, July 3, 1978; Havemann 2014; *Stern*, June 22, 1978). In fact, at a post-World Cup parliamentary hearing, it became clear that the DFB had not invited Rudel, that Neuberger had not welcomed the known Nazi as some papers had reported, and that there were no secret ties between the DFB and the junta.[26]

To speak of a 'propagandistic campaign', however, as Havemann does, is grossly exaggerated and unscholarly. Neuberger had after all maintained that the junta was not a dictatorship, and had unapologetically opposed Amnesty International and the 'Yes to Football, and No to Torture!' campaign. His attempt to defend the war record of a known unrepentant Nazi, finally, made it seem as if West German sports officials were in league with Rudel and the Argentine junta.

Conclusion

The 'Yes to Football, No to Torture!' campaign was not an isolated event. It was part of an international trend that had begun with the Biafra campaign in the late sixties, continuing with the campaigns against torture in Greece, South African Apartheid and the military coup in Chile (Eckel 2011; Heerten 2015; Hoffmann 2011; Simpson 2012). As in these previous campaigns, West Germans activists, by means of the 'Yes to Football, No to Torture!' campaign, were able to make atrocities in Argentina, even if for a fleeting moment, a matter of national debate and criticize the stance of their government and of the DFB. The uniqueness of the campaign lays in the novel use of culture, in this case sports, for attracting the attention of the average West German for atrocities in a far-off country. The discussion about human rights and sports reached a level and diffusion hereto unseen. Joachim Jaenicke, Bonn's ambassador in Buenos Aires since 1977, noted that 'the problem of the relationship between sports and politics in an in international sports competition has never been posed as sharply as by the World Cup 1978'.[27]

Activists encountered substantial resistance from government representatives, the conservative press, but especially from the DFB and president Neuberger. The sports hierarchy maintained that activists were politicizing sports, ignoring the fact that the junta had politicized the World Cup already, as they aimed to broadcast a peaceful and welcoming image of Argentina. Ultimately, the visit of the retired combat pilot, supporter of the junta and unapologetic Nazi, Hans-Ulrich Rudel, to the West German National Football Team headquarters became a scandal because it dovetailed with the attitude the DFB and chairman Neuberger had taken towards the human rights campaign. While there was misreporting and exaggeration involved in the reporting of some journalists, it occurred less out of a malicious desire to calumniate the DFB but rather because sports officials had spoken out regularly against human rights activists and had expressed sympathy towards the Argentinean Junta.

The campaign 'Yes to Football, No to Torture!' must be seen as a watershed in West German human rights activism. Post-1945 West German society was no stranger to mass demonstrations and political campaigns and the language of human rights had been used previously, but never with the intensity of the spring and summer of 1978 (Wildenthal 2013).

Notes

1. Ministerio de Relaciones Exteriores y Culto to Argentine Ambassador in Bonn, Enrique J.L. Ruiz Guiñazú, Archivo Histórico de Cancillería, Buenos Aires. Online Declassified documents. http://desclasificacion.cancilleria.gov.ar.
2. Jörg Kastl, Embassy Buenos Aires, to Foreign Ministry, 'Betr.: Argentinischer Staatsreich vom 24.3.76; hier: Möglichkeiten und Gefahren', 2 April 1976, in *1. Juli Bis 31. Dezember*

GLOBAL AND TRANSNATIONAL SPORT

1976. Akten Zur Auswärtigen Politik der Bundesrepublik Deutschland, hrsg. im Auftr. des Auswärtigen Amts vom Institut für Zeitgeschichte; 1976/I (München: Oldenbourg, 2007), 449.

3. Jörg Kastl, 'Zwei Jahre in Argentinien: Ein Erfahrungsbericht', undated report [1977], Politisches Archiv Auswärtiges Amt, Berlin (henceforth PA-AA, ZA), B 33, 107921.

4. Karl Alexander Hampe, 'Gewalttätigkeit in Argentinien und ihre Auswirkungen auf das deutsch-argentinische Verhältnis', 1 August 1977, PA-AA, ZA, B33, 107921.

5. Hans Jürgen Wischnewski to Ottfried Hennig (CDU/CSU), 10 Juni 1982, Friedrich Ebert Stiftung (henc. FES), Archiv der Deutschen Sozialdemokratie (henceforth AdsD), Bonn-Bad Godesberg, Bestand Helmut Schmidt, 1/HSAA006834.

6. Mario Weitmann, 'Los fundamentos o el Marco de solidaridad con el pueblo argentino', 1978, Ordner 'Argentinien Solidarität 1976–1977', Forschungs und Dokumentationszentrum Chile Lateinamerika, (henceforth FDCL), Berlin.

7. Herbert Ladwig (ai) to Werner Maihofer, 'Betr.: Aufnahme Lateinamerikanischer Fluechtlinge aus Argentinien', 10 December 1975, PA-AA, ZA, B33, 103590.

8. Oldenkott, 'Vermerk über das Gespräch des Bundeskanzlers mit dem Hohen Flüchtlingskomissar der Vereinten Nationen, Prinz Sadruddin Aga Khan, am 30. Januar von 9.05 bis 10.00 Uhr im Palais Schaumburg', 30 Januar 1976, FES, AdsD, Bestand Helmut Schmidt, 1/HSAA007156.

9. Werner Maihofer to Herbert Ladwig, 'Betr.: Aufnahme Lateinamerikanischer Fluechtlinge aus Argentinien', 15 January 1976, PA-AA, ZA, B33, 103590.

10. On West German foreign policy and human rights see Rock (2010). [Karl Alexander] Hampe, 'Betr.: Zieschank', 20 August 1976, PA-AA, B33, ZA, 103591.

11. Deutscher Bundestag, 8 WP, April 27, 1978, *Sten.Ber.,* 7009.

12. 'Rückschau: Die Argentinien Kampagne!' *Argentinien-Info 15/16*, 12 May 1978, Box 'ai-Info Argentinien, 1977–1982,' FDCL.

13. See letter to 'Gerald', 12 February 1978, and Leaflet 'Was hat Fußball mit Folter zu tun? Argentinien-Woche in Konstanz vom 8. bis 13.4. anlässlich der Fußball Weltmeisterschaft 1978', Folder 'Argentinien Solidarität 1976–1977', FDCL.

14. Informationsstelle Lateinamerika, I.L.A, Bonn, 'ein Fußballquiz für Kenner!', Quiz brochure in Folder 'Argentinien Solidarität 1976–1977', FDCL.

15. See Argentinien–Solidaritätsgruppe Münster, 'Menschenrechte sind unteilbar', Leaflet, Folder 'Argentinien Solidarität 1976–1977', and Rainer Kursch, 'WM Nachspiel: Protest gegen Folter: Borussia Mönchengladbach fordert Geldstrafe', Leaflets in Folder 'Argentinien Solidarität 1976–1977', FDCL.

16. Arbeitskreis Bonn, Journalisten Helfen Journalisten, 16 May 1978, Presse Archiv Argentinien 0/073, Argentinien, Konrad Adenauer Stiftung (KAS).

17. 'Argentinien vor der Fußballweltmeisterschaft', III. Fernseheprogramm des Westdeutschen Rundfunks, 21 February 1978, Caja AH/0021, Archivo de Cancillería, Buenos Aires.

18. Chile-Arbeitsgruppe Pforzheim, 'Von der Olympiade '36 zur Fussball-WM Argentinien '78', undated pamphlet, 2–6, S BRD und Ausland. Lateinamerika Süd, 1966–1990, Signatur 808, Archiv der Ausserparlamentarische Opposition und Neue Soziale Bewegungen (APO-Archiv), Freie Universität Berlin.

19. Schüler der Hauptschule Buschfeldstrasse 46 (Köln) to AA, 21 April 1978, PA-AA, ZA, B33, 111.038.

20. Frieder S. to Chancellor Schmidt, 29 May 1978, PA-AA, ZA, B33, Bd. 111.057.

21. Evangelische Jugendgruppe Kirch-Brombach to Genscher, 22 July 1978, PA-AA, ZA, B33, 111.057.

22. Klasse 7c (Oerlingshausen bei Bielefeld) to President Scheel, 7 July 1978, PA-AA, ZA, B33, 111.057.

23. Michael Klein (AI) to Chancellor Schmidt, 26 June 1978, PA-AA, ZA, B33, 111.056.

24. Deutsche Welle, ZD Politik/Wirtschaft, Features/Dokumentation, 'Argentinien– WM und Menschenrechte', 31 May 1978, FES, ADSD, Bestand Horst Seefeld.

25. 'Hans-Ulrich Rudel, Oberst a.D., z.Zt. Argentinien, zu seinem Besuch im Trainingslager der deutschen Fussballnationalmannschaft in Argentinien,' 15 June 1978, PA-AA, ZA, B33, 107941.
26. Deutscher Bundestag, Sportausschuß, 'Kurzprotokoll 19 Sitzung am Mittwoch, dem 8. November 1978, 15.15 Uhr Bonn-Bundeshaus,' 106/86882, Akte 8, Bundesarchiv Koblenz.
27. Jaenicke, 'Vorschau auf die Fußball-WM 1978 in Argentinien,' 11 May 1978, PA-AA, ZA, B33, 107941.

Funding

This work was supported by Boston College.

References

"AIB-Aktuell: Buenos Dias Argentina?" 1978. *Antiimperialistisches Informationsbulletin*, 9 Jahrgang, Nr. 6, Juni.
Archetti, Eduardo P. 2004. "El Mundial de Futbol de 1978 En Argentina: Victoria Deportiva y Derrota Moral" [The World Cup 1978 in Argentina: A sports victory and a moral defeat.] *Memoria y Civilización* (7): 176–194.
"Argentinien 78: Fußball 'total'itär?" [Argentina 78: Football Total'itarian?] 1978. *Solidarität, Nr.5, Monatszeitschrift für Gewerkschaftliche Jugendarbeit*, 29 Jahrgang, May.
"Argentinien: Die Wahrheit über das Land, in dem wir siegen wollen" [Argentina: The truth about the country where we want to win.] 1978. *Bild am Sonntag*, May 14.
Bayer, Osvaldo. 1996. *Futbol Argentino*. Buenos Aires: Editorial Sudamericana.
"Berti Vogts in Zwielicht" [Berti Vogts in twighlight.] 1978. *Frankfurter Allgemeine Zeitung*, March 30.
Breitner, Paul. 1978. "Kein Handschlag: Die deutsche Fußballnationalmannschaft soll sich bei der Weltmeisterschaft in Argentinien nicht für das politische Schauspiel der Generäle mißbrauchen lassen" [No handshake: The German Football National Team should not allow itself to be missapropiated for the Generals' political spectable.] *Stern* Nr.15, April 6–12.
"Breitner Attacke: DFB ist politisch Ahnungslos" [Attack from Breitner: The DFB is politically naïve.] 1978. *Frankfurter Rundschau*, April 6.
Ciria, Alberto. 1984. "From Soccer to War in Argentina: Preliminary Notes on Sports as Politics under a Military Regime, 1976–1982." In *Latin America and the Caribbean: Geopolitics, Development, and Culture*, 80–95. Ottawa.
Cmiel, Kenneth. 1999. "The Emergence of Human Rights Politics in the United States." *The Journal of American History* 86 (3): 1231–50.
"Das Exklusiv-Interview: Argentiniens Staatspräsident Videla 10 Tage vor der Fussball-Weltmeisterschaft. Niemand braucht Angst zu haben" [The Exclusive Interview: Argentina's state president Videla 10 days before the World Cup. No one needs to be afraid.] 1978. *Bild am Sonntag*, May 21.
"Demonstranten besetzen argentinisches Konsulat" [Protesters occupy the argentinean consulate.] 1978. *Die Welt*, June 22.
Deutsche Presse Agentur. 1978. "Bonn zur Aufnahme politischer Gefangener aus Argentinien bereit" [Bonn ready to admit political refugees from Argentina.] April 21.
Dozert, Ludwig. 1978. "Die WM-Kröte" [The World Cup toad.] *Frankfurter Rundschau*, March 31.
Dufner, Georg. 2014. *Partner im Kalten Krieg: Die Politischen Beziehungen zwischen der Bundesrepublik Deutschland und Chile* [Partners during the Cold War: The political relations between the Federal Republic of Germany and Chile, 1945–1980.] Frankfurt: Campus Verlag.
Eckel, Jan. 2011. "'Under a Magnifying Glass' The International Human Rights Campaign against Chile in the Seventies." In *Human Rights in the Twentieth Century*, edited by Stefan-Ludwig Hoffmann, 321–341. Cambridge: Cambridge University Press.
Eckel, Jan. 2012. "Humanitarisierung der internationalen Beziehungen?" [Humanitarization of Foreign Relations?] *Geschichte und Gesellschaft* 38 (4): 603–635.

GLOBAL AND TRANSNATIONAL SPORT

Eckel, Jan. 2014. *Die Ambivalenz des Guten: Menschenrechte in der internationalen politik seit den 1940ern* [The ambivalence of good: Human Rights in international politics since the 1940s.] Göttingen: Vandenhoeck und Ruprecht.

Eckel, Jan, and Samuel Moyn, eds. 2014. *The Breakthrough: Human Rights in the 1970s*. Philadelphia: University of Pennsylvania Press.

"Elf deutsche Gewissen zwischen Tor und Terror" [Eleven German consciences between goal and terror.] 1978. *Welt am Sonntag*, April 9.

Feitlowitz, Marguerite. 2011. *A Lexicon of Terror*. Oxford: Oxford University Press.

Finchelstein, Federico. 2014. *The Ideological Origins of the Dirty War*. Oxford: Oxford University Press.

"Folter-Bedrückt sie das?" 1978. *Stern* Nr.15, April 6–12.

Franco, Marina. 2005. "Derechos Humanos, Politica y Futbol" [Human Rights, Politics and Football.] *Entrepasados* XIV (28): 27–46.

"Für die Verschwundenen gibt es keinen Anwalt: Ein Aufruf des Forschungs- und Dokumentationszentrum Chile–Lateinamerika zum Protest gegen Terror und Diktatur in Argentinien" [For the disappeared there is no attorney: A call by the Center for Research and Documentation Chile–Latin America to protest Terror and Dictatorship in Argentina.] 1978. *Frankfurter Rundschau*, June 1.

Gilbert, Abel, and Miguel Vitagliano. 1998. *El Terror y la Gloria: La Vida, El Fútbol y la Politica en la Argentina del Mundial '78* [The Terror and the Glory: Life, Football, and Politics in Argentina during the Wolrd Cup '78]. Buenos Aires: Norma.

Gorini, Ulises. 2015. *La Rebelión de Las Madres: Historia de Las Madres de Plaza de Mayo*. [The Mother's Rebellion: History of the Mothers of Plaza de Mayo.] Buenos Aires: Ediciones Biblioteca Nacional.

Grix, Jonathan. 2012a. "'Image' Leveraging and Sports Mega-events: Germany and the 2006 FIFA World Cup." *Journal of Sport & Tourism* 17 (4): 289–312.

Grix, Jonathan. 2012b. "The Politics of Sports Mega-events." *Political Insight* 3 (1): 4–7.

Havemann, Nils. 2013. *Samstags um Halb Vier: Die Geschichte der Fussball Bundesliga* [Saturdays at three thirty: The history of the German Bundesliga.] Munich: Siedler.

Havemann, Nils. 2014. "The Federal Republic of Germany and the 1978 Football World Cup in Argentina. Genesis and Deconstruction of a Propagandistic Myth." *The International Journal of the History of Sport* 31 (12): 1509–1518.

Heerten, Lasse. 2015. "A as in Auschwitz, B as in Biafra: The Nigerian Civil War, Visual Narratives of Genocide, and the Fragmented Universalization of the Holocaust." In *Humanitarian Photography*, edited by Heide Fehrenbach and Davide Rodogno, 249–274. New York: Cambridge University Press.

Heggen, Rolf. 1978. "Nach Argentinien zum Fußballspielen: Der Sport darf nicht überfordert werden" [To Argentina to play football: Sports should not be overburdened.] *Frankfurter Allgemeine Zeitung*, April 8.

Heizmann, Reinhard. 1978. "Fußball & Folter: Weltmeisterschaft in Argentinien, Menschenrechte in Abseits" [Football & Torture: World Cup in Argentina, human rights in offside.] *Blickpunkt, Das Jugend–Journal mit Durchblick*, Mai 3.

"Hinter der Fußball–Kulisse lauern die Folterknechte" [The torturers await behind the football show.] 1978. *Berliner Stimme*, April 15.

Hoffmann, Stefan-Ludwig, ed. 2011. *Human Rights in the Twentieth Century*. Cambridge: Cambridge University Press.

Iriye, Akira, Petra Goedde, and William I. Hitchcock, eds. 2012. *The Human Rights Revolution: An International History*. New York: Oxford University Press.

Keck, Margaret E., and Kathryn Sikkink. 1998. *Activists beyond Borders: Advocacy Networks in International Politics*. Ithaca, NY: Cornell University Press.

Kuhlwein, Eckart. 1978. "In Argentinien leider nur vornehme Zurückhaltung: Präsident Neuberger auf dem Rückzug" [In Argentina only respectful demureness: President Neuberger on the retreat.] *Sozialdemokratischer Pressedienst*, May 24.

Loewenstein, Enno. 1978. "Foulspiel an einen Verteidiger" [Foul against a defender.] *Die Welt*, March 31.

Moyn, Samuel. 2010. *The Last Utopia: Human Rights in History*. Cambridge, MA: Belknap Press of Harvard University Press.

Novaro, Marcos, and Vicente Palermo. 2003. *La Dictadura Militar (1976–1983): Del Golpe de Estado a La Restauración Democrática* [The Military Dictatorship (1976–1983): From the military coup to the Democratic Restoration.] Barcelona: Paidós.

"NS-Idol bei der Fußballmannschaft" [National Socialist Idol [visits] the National Football Team]. 1978. *Süddeutsche Zeitung*, June 24.

Pramann, Ulrich, Peter Fuchs, Hejo Heussen, and Monika López, eds. 1978. *Fußball und Folter: Argentinien '78* [Football and Torture...Argentina '78.] Rororo Aktuell. Reinbek bei Hamburg: Rowohlt.

Rein, Ranaan. 2014. "Football, Politics, and Protest: The International Campaign against the 1978 World Cup in Argentina." In *The Fifa World Cup, 1930–2010: Politics, Commerce, Spectacle and Identities*, edited by Kai Schiller and Stefan Rinke, 240–258. Göttingen: Wallstein.

Rock, Philipp. 2010. *Macht, Märkte und Moral. Zur Rolle der Menschenrechte in der Außenpolitik der Bundesrepublik Deutschland in den Sechziger und Siebziger Jahren* [Power, Markets, and Morality. The Role of Human Rights in the Foreign Policy of the Federal Republic of Germany in the Sixties and Seventies.] Frankfurt: Peter Lang.

"Rudels Besuch im deutschen WM-Quartier 'Provokation aller Demokraten': Jüdische Gemeinde spricht von Skandal/Jünge Europäische Föderalisten fordern Rücktritt des DFB-Vorstands/Fußball-Bund verteidigt seine Entscheidung" [Rudel's visit in German World Cup quarters 'Provocation of all democrats': Jewish community spekas about a scandal/ Young Europeans federalists demand resignation of the DFB executive board/ German Football federation defends its decision.] 1978. *Frankfurter Rundschau*, June 12.

Seefeld Horst. 1978. "Argentinischer Propagandarummel entgegentreten" [Argentinean propaganda campaign is to be confronted.] *Sozialdemokratischer Pressedienst*. March 28.

"Selektiv." 1978. *Die Welt*, March 28.

Simpson, Bradley R. 2012. "'The First Right': The Carter Administration, Indonesia and the Transnational Human Rights Politics of the 1970s." In *The Human Rights Revolution*, edited by Akira Iriye, Petra Goedde, and William I. Hitchcock, 179–200. Oxford: Oxford University Press.

Smith, Bill L. 2002. "The Argentinian Junta and the Press in the Run-up to the 1978 World Cup." *Soccer & Society* 3 (1): 69–78.

Unruh, Paul. 1978. "Fußball und Folter ... aber der Lederball rollte" [Football and torture...but the ball rolled.] *Konkret*, May.

Vetten, Horst. 1978. "Herr Schlauberger." *Stern* Nr. 26, June 22.

Weisskirch, Willi. 1978. "Fußballweltmeisterschaft in Argentinien– Deutsche nationalelf sieht sich politischen Attacken ausgesetzt" [Football World Cup in Argentina: the German National Team is being subjected to political attacks.] *Deutschland–Union–Dienst*, May 17.

Weitbrecht, Dorothee. 2013. "Profite versus Menschenleben: Argentinien und das Schwierige Erbe der Deutschen Diplomatie" [Profits versus human lives: Argentina and the difficult heritage of German diplomacy.] *Blätter für Deutsche und Internationale Politik* 58 (7): 93–104.

Wildenthal, Lora. 2013. *The Language of Human Rights in West Germany*. Philadelphia: University of Pennsylvania Press.

"'Wir vergattern keine Spieler' Fußballpräsident Hermann Neuberger über die Nationalmannschaft vor der WM in Argentinien" ['We do not censure any players' Football President Neuberger about the National Team before the World Cup in Argentina.] 1978. *Der Spiegel*, April 24.

Wright, Thomas C. 2007. *State Terrorism in Latin America: Chile, Argentina, and International Human Rights*. Lanham, MD: Rowman and Littlefield.

"Zunge zügeln." 1978. *Der Spiegel*, Nr. 27, July 3.

Learning in landscapes of professional sports: transnational perspectives on talent development and migration into Danish women's handball around the time of the financial crisis, 2004–2012

Sine Agergaard

ABSTRACT

This article contributes to breaking down the methodological nationalism in sport through which talent development is perceived and organized within a nation's borders. It develops an alternative transnational perspective on learning conditions in professional sport by using Etienne Wenger's concept landscape of practice. Wenger draws attention to the options for learning across communities and to the learning assets of boundary encounters. This approach will be deployed in a case study of the fluctuations in sport labour migration into Danish women's handball around the time of the financial crisis. Media reports and interviews with handball coaches suggest perceptions that changed from considering migrant athletes as barriers to domestic talent to migrant athletes becoming useful for enhancing local and national talent development. The article ends with a discussion about the options for and challenges in breaking down the methodological nationalism in sport governance.

Introduction

Immigration is at the centre of the political debate across Europe. Although the primary focus is on migration of Syrian civil war refugees into Europe, opinions about the problems of migration are also reflected in the debate on labour migration. It has often been argued in the Danish media that immigration of foreign labour has led to a crowding out effect on indigenous workers.[1] The public debate is particularly concerned with how migrant labourers challenge job opportunities of local young employees in the domestic labour market.[2] However, this debate hardly consider if labour migration could potentially enhance the openness of the host country, facilitate transnational exchange of goods and ideas, and promote new investments.

This article contends that sport labour migration offers interesting insights into various perceptions and realities of how migrant labourers influence the domestic population. Particularly, the fluctuating number of recruitment of highly skilled athletes from abroad offers an opportunity to study changing receptions of the latter's influence on domestic talent development. Moreover, sport labour migration, characterized by short-term careers and regular movement between the countries of the athlete's origin and destination,[3] may provide insight into the conditions of skills exchange between domestic and foreign labour.

Thus, the objective of this article is to contribute to develop a transnational perspective on the association between sport labour migration and talent development of domestic/ indigenous players. It intends to break down methodological nationalism through which talent development is perceived and organized within national borders. The research question is: how are migrant athletes perceived and related to domestic talent? The article will elaborate this through a case study that provides insight into changing perceptions of athlete immigration into Danish women's handball. Focus will be on the impact of immigrating athletes on domestic talent development as described by the media and coaches, who were interviewed about their first-hand experience of the environments inhabited by both domestic and foreign athletes.

This article focuses specifically on the changes occurring in Danish women's handball during 2004–2012, i.e. before and after the financial crisis. The immigrating athletes in this context came mainly from (neighbouring) European countries, hence not forming a racially and ethnically heterogeneous category of analysis, but eliciting invocations of the nation and nationalism in responses to their arrival and employment. This article does not discuss in detail the financial crisis, which was manifested not as a single pressure situation but with significant variations across nations and regions (Pratt and Hutton 2013). Economic slowdown and restructuring were evidenced as a common factor in the Nordic countries (Andersen, Bergman, and Jensen 2015), and such tendencies can also be found in the case of Danish women's handball. Under these conditions, aggressive hiring of top performers could be restricted and more creative responses to talent development introduced (Beechler and Woodward 2009), which this article ponders in connection with the perceptions of coaches about athletes.

State of the art

The literature on sport labour migration has developed much since the appearance of Bale and Maguire's (1994) pioneering edited volume on the global sports arena. The existing literature comprehensively presents a plethora of perspectives on the association between sport labour migration and talent development. The first wave of studies of sport labour migration was primarily concerned with emergent globalization theories and more particularly theories about world-systems and dependency (Cornelissen and Solberg 2007; Darby 2001, 2006; Darby, Akindes, and Kirwin 2007; Magee and Sugden 2002). These studies focused on talent drain from the Global South to the Global North, implicitly indicating the mechanisms of talent gain in the Global North. The seminal source here is Bale's (1991) book in which he uses the concept *brawn drain* to describe the migration of foreign student athletes into American universities.

A number of studies within the next wave of research have drawn attention to the intended and unintended consequences of migration for talent development in countries of destination (Maguire and Pearton 2000; Poli 2007). These studies are mainly informed by figurational sociology and network theory (Elliott and Maguire 2008; Falcous and Maguire 2005; Poli 2007; Poli, Ravenel, and Besson 2010). These perspectives have also helped to point out the interdependency among athletes, coaches and clubs at both ends of the migration spectrum.

Recent studies of sport labour migration, which may be identified as a third wave, have criticized macro-sociological perspectives on, for instance, talent drain from the Global South, and recast attention to spillover effects and skills exchange between domestic talent and immigrant athletes (Elliott and Weedon 2011). Thus, latest research on sport labour migration can be said to have shifted focus on the multidimensional life and work experiences of athletes, who migrate across national borders (Agergaard and Tiesler 2014; Carter 2011; Engh and Agergaard 2015; Klein 2009). It gives more attention to athletes' agency in producing mobility while they are embedded in specific spatial structures (Darby 2013; Engh 2014; Esson 2015). Still, further exploration into the complex ways in which power relations play out in transnational athletic migration is required. Studies have begun to scrutinize the ways in which immigrant athletes are both challenged and assisted by being perceived as foreigners, as ethnic and racial others, in the receiving contexts (Engh 2014; Ungruhe 2014).

In addition to studies of labour migration, this article is grounded in studies of labour economics that deal with the effect of sport labour migration on domestic workers in both the countries of origin and destination. It has not been possible to statistically document any negative effect of sport labour migration on the countries of origin. On the contrary, various studies have shown positive or no effect on the performance of national teams in countries of origin when players migrate abroad to foreign clubs (Baur and Lehmann 2007; Berlinschi, Schokkaert, and Swinnen 2013; Frick 2009; Gelade and Dobson 2007). Studies have also shown that the positive effect of player immigration increases with greater difference in the quality of training between foreign and domestic clubs, as players acquire more skill if they play for a good club (Berlinschi, Schokkaert, and Swinnen 2013). As immigrant players are shown to have returned regularly to play for their national teams in international tournaments, the muscle drain hypothesis does not seem to account for the complexity of the impact of transnational movement.

Studies of labour economics have also questioned whether sport labour migration has negative consequences for local co-workers or rather lead to positive spillover effects in the receiving countries (Alvarez et al. 2011). Some studies have documented the need for clubs to put a limit on the number of foreign players if the latter are to have a positive influence on indigenous players (Alvarez et al. 2011), else they run the risk of stalling development of local players. Much of the research on economics presumes the possibility of statistically isolating and measuring the effect on domestic workers. As a corrective, a qualitative perspective appears to be relevant to draw attention to the complex dynamics in which immigrating and domestic workers are entangled in particular cases.

Theory

This article uses Etienne Wenger's work to develop a theoretical framework that allows transnational contextualization when considering the options for talent development. Together with the anthropologist Jean Lave, Wenger has advanced a theory of situated learning in which the focus is on how learning develops in social relationships (Lave and Wenger 2001). Furthermore, Wenger (1998) has written about communities of practice that can be delimited to analyse groups for mutual engagement, joint activities and shared repertoire towards learning in schools, at work, etc. Sport teams have been described as communities of practice due to the members' mutual engagement in the collective enterprise of training and playing matches, development of a shared repertoire of sport-specific skills and terminology, understanding of tactics and participating in the shared history of the game and the club (Christensen, Laursen, and Sørensen 2011; Galipeau and Trudel 2006).

Recently, Wenger (2014, 13) has expanded his theory of communities of practice with the concept of *landscape of practice* – 'a complex system of communities of practice and the boundaries between them' – which he employs to arrive at a better understanding of 'the "body of knowledge" of a profession'. Thus, Wenger has developed a broader perspective which includes the complex constellation of various communities of practice and options of learning across the boundaries of specific communities. This article uses the concept of *landscape of practice* to examine how athletes often develop their professional knowledge not only in a local setting, but also through interactions across local and national communities. Rather than focusing on isolated communities of practice, the attempt is to interrogate local and methodological nationalism and consider professional athletes in transnational settings. This perspective helps to understand the narrative glossed over by the straightforward story of immigrant workers affecting domestic workers in one specific community. The options and barriers to the development of athletes are also linked to the possibility for them to operate and learn across communal boundaries. As observed before, even if their activities are not phrased as a landscape of learning, domestic athletes participate in several communities of sporting practices involving not only their club team, but also often regional and national training gatherings (Agergaard and Ronglan 2015). Moreover, domestic athletes may be able to travel to other clubs or to connect with players from abroad, thereby developing a broader understanding of their profession.

Wenger (2014, 13) explains the difference between the processes of learning in a specific community of practice and in the wider landscape of practice by making a distinction between competence and knowledgeability, saying 'Whereas we use competence to describe the dimension of knowing negotiated and defined within a single community of practice, knowledgeability manifests in a person's relations to a multiplicity of practices across the landscape'. While competence is developed in the local community, participation in various communities of practice appears to expand overall knowledge. Further, in specific communities of practice there are specific regimes of competence, since the latter is not merely an individual characteristic but depends on what is recognized as competence by members of a community of practice. Thus, there is a tendency that newcomers' experiences are transformed by the regime of competence, but their experience may also challenge and transform the idea of competence. This dynamic interplay can help to understand possible conflicts that may occur when immigrant athletes arrive in local clubs. From Wenger's perspective, newcomers are either transformed by the ways things are done in a specific community or contribute to transform local routines and social practices.

Another dimension in the recent theory development is the greater attention to the boundaries between communities of practice and options for boundary encounters and crossings. Thus, in a landscape consisting of several communities of practice the crossing of boundaries appears as 'learning assets' (Wenger 2014, 17). In other words, athletes may be able to access a wider body of knowledge by crossing specific communities of practice. Keeping this in mind, athletic immigration into a specific community of practice such as a handball team may be perceived as a boundary encounter that causes conflict among actors and also highlights previously undiscovered options of learning.

Method

This article is based on a case study of the development of migration into and away from Danish women's handball around the financial crisis, since it can provide insights into how sport migrants may be perceived to influence domestic talent development. In the 2000s, the immigration of foreign players into Danish women's handball league increased rapidly, followed by a remarkable decrease latter in the decade, particularly after the financial crisis. In the 1999/2000 season, 15% of the national league players were immigrants; the number rose to 40% in the 2007/2008 season; while in the 2010/2011 season, the number of foreign players decreased to below 25% (Agergaard and Ronglan 2015).

The international players came mainly from the neighbouring Nordic and/or European countries, while the numbers of Asian, African and South American players were very limited. Thus, ethnic and racial differences between the immigrating players and Danish players were not in focus in this study, unlike studies of, e.g. migration of female African soccer players into Nordic sports clubs (Engh, Settler, and Agergaard 2016). Previous studies have shown that several Danish women's handball clubs such as Aalborg DH have mainly recruited players from neighbouring countries to facilitate their easy assimilation into the Danish handball scene and wider society, while a few clubs such as Slagelse DH that was led by the former international player Anja Andersen, mainly recruited players from Eastern European countries (Agergaard 2008). This club also hired a former international player to manage the migrant players, contrary to the usual practice of employing Danish coaches and managers to deal with players on their arrival to Danish clubs.

Danish women's handball has experienced significant changes in professionalization and commercialization in the 2000s (Storm 2008; Storm and Agergaard 2014). Handball has been traditionally considered a Scandinavian game (Skjerk 2001; Von Der Lippe 1994). Moreover, Danish handball clubs are often based in provincial cities and are central to local identity. In the Nordic countries, talent identification and development is centred around these local sports clubs (Andersen and Ronglan 2012). Sport labour migration has immensely broadened the scope of talent identification. Following the argument of Beechler and Woodward (2009), sport managers in the Scandinavian countries have become part of a global war for talent. This meeting between local and global recruitment strategies may fuel conflicting perceptions of the significance of developing domestic talent compared to recruiting players from abroad.

This article will analyse media reports and interviews with sport managers and coaches concerning the impact of athletic immigration. Media reports have been accessed through the Infomedia database which covers all national, regional and local newspapers in Denmark as well as press releases from news agencies (eg Ritzau's Bureau), TV coverage and web-based sources. A database search with the keywords ('Danish women's handball') and ('international or foreign') and ('player') returned hundreds of articles, several of which apparently came from the same news agency releases. The search was limited to the coverage between 2004 and 2007, when the number of players from abroad increased rapidly, and the post-financial crisis years (2008–2012) which saw a downturn in the number.

Interviews were conducted with seven coaches after the financial crisis. The informants were selected in terms of maximum experience of coaching Danish national and/or regional women's handball teams and insight into conditions for domestic talent development in both the pre- and post-financial crisis periods. Interviews of both national- and club-level coaches were taken to diversify the context of the positioning of foreign athletes in relation to domestic talent development. The national team coaches were expected to be more critical of immigrant players due to their concern for domestic talent development. Club coaches, on the other hand, appeared keen to recruit players from abroad, and often found the latter's contribution essential for the club's good performance. Excerpts of their statements were categorized and analysed using the theoretical framework of Wenger, more particularly his new work on the positioning of newcomers and learning conditions in *landscapes of learning* as presented above. An inductive thematic analysis of the media reports covers the prevalent perceptions of athletic immigration as well as changes in the perceptions of 'foreigners' throughout the 2000s. Interviews with athletes about their experiences would have been interesting, but this article is concerned with the experience of people who recruited and trained them.

Analysis

In the middle of the 2000s, the media showed concern about the decline or at least unstable performance of the Danish national women's handball team in international tournaments. In a number of articles the increase in the number of immigrant players was held responsible for this. They presented an argument that foreign players constituted an obstacle to domestic talent development. The hostility was self-evident in headlines such as 'Danish women's handball suffers because of many foreigners' (*Fyns Stifttidende*, 1 September 2007) and 'Effervescent youth should be given the chance' (*Nordjyske Stifttidende*, 20 August 2007), the latter arguing against preferring the huge number of foreign players in the first elevens of teams playing in the Danish handball league.

Many of the articles mentioned the perceptions of national sport governing bodies towards athletic immigration. Among others the president of the Danish Handball Federation (DHF) and the director of the Danish elite sport institution Team Denmark were quoted to have blamed the clubs for recruiting too many foreign players. The representatives from the national sport governing bodies seemed to have overlooked the options for DHF and Team Denmark to structure better the national tournament and take initiatives for domestic talent development (Ritzau's Bureau, 14 December 2006). The only direct suggestion from the national sport governing bodies pertained to restricting athletic immigration, articulated not only in the context of handball but other sports too ('The president of the National Olympic Committee and Sports Confederation of Denmark wants a limit to the number of foreigners', Ritzau's Bureau, 1 November 2007), for schemes of domestic talent development to function properly. It came as a surprise that sport administrators as a whole failed to remember that restricting immigration of athletes from other European countries was not possible due to the Bosman law.

The decline in the performance of the Danish women's handball team was remarkably almost entirely linked to the immigration of players from abroad in media reports. Alternative explanations for the decline, such as (no) change of coach, advanced age of players and lack of attention to the talent development essential for international success, were only peripherally mentioned. The possibility for DHF to restructure the rules for national tournaments thus allowing domestic athletes more playing time was mentioned in the passing. Still, very few articles expressed alternative viewpoints on the current challenges in Danish women's handball. The coach of the rivalling Norwegian women's handball team, Marit Breivik, suggested that the national sport governing bodies should have tried to develop domestic talent simultaneously with hiring players from abroad ('It's the Danes' own fault', Ritzau's Bureau, 19 October 2007). The controversial former Danish women's handball player, Anja Andersen, who at that time coached a national league team comprising many international players that managed to win the Champions League three times, was quoted expressing similar views ('The Danish women's handball league needs foreigners', Ritzau's Bureau, 15 December 2006).

A remarkable discursive transformation in the perception of foreign athletes could be observed in the media reports following the financial crisis. Between 2009 and 2010, several articles commented that the Danish national team coach, Jan Pytlick, was pleased with the decrease in the number of foreign players. The article, 'The Danish league with more Danish players' (*Horsens Folkeblad*, 5 March 2009), quoted Pytlick as having said, 'While most Danes are worried about the financial crisis, the national team coach Jan Pytlick cheers the development'. Another article pointed out that the national team coach was pleased about the number of foreign players in the Danish handball league having reached its lowest level in several years ('More and more foreigners go home', *Politiken*, 7 September 2010). However, just one year later, Pytlick was quoted as having said that the local players might have received more opportunity at matches recently, but the standard of the Danish national handball league had declined considerably, displaying the disadvantages of not having quality foreign players ('Leaving star players set back European success', *Politiken*, 10 November 2011). He subsequently appeared to be concerned about many foreign players leaving Danish women's handball ('Pytlick worried about the future', *TV2/Finans Online*, 20 March 2012).

In the light of the financial crisis, the media reports seem to reflect the observation that reducing the number of immigrant players was not the only way to implement domestic talent development. On the contrary, even if domestic players seemingly received more match practice in the national league after the financial crisis, the sporting level appeared to have dropped. Reports of the fluctuating immigration around the time of financial crisis reflected a more nuanced picture of the role of 'foreigners' in the game. Still, the media continued to unevenly categorize immigrant athletes as barriers or contributors to domestic talent development.

The relationship between domestic and immigrant players

The interviews with coaches revealed a similar change of perception about the impact of immigration of foreign players on domestic talent development. When describing the conditions for the latter, the coaches mainly talked about how things were done in local clubs, within specific communities of practice, in ways that might be seen to reflect specific regimes of competence. However, the interviews also indicated their increasing awareness of the broader *landscape of practice* and the prospects (and challenges) of developing what appeared as broader knowledgeability. The description of the arrival of foreign players were sometimes quite similar to that of mobility of young domestic talents from junior teams, even if the latter seldom involved considerable geographical relocation. As newcomers, both domestic and immigrant athletes were required to adapt to specific social practices and regimes of competence, a passage in which past experience surely helped. Let us consider the social underpinnings of some of the statements made by coaches.

> No matter, if you're a league player or you're a U18 or U16 player here, then they are all told that our club means a lot. Here you welcome all, also the young people. It is not for the young players to come and say hello, but for you to welcome the young. (Club coach)

As indicated above, a specific community has established practices, in this case how to welcome players, which reflected a particular concern for the smooth transition for young players to their new community. The immigrant players (along with domestic players) with more experience and skills than young talents appeared to be positioned differently.

> There is a clear hierarchy where – of course – the experience and routine you have are very influential, as well as the game qualities you have – that is the level at which you perform. If you are a really skilled player, then you are placed high in the hierarchy. (Club coach)

Due to this hierarchy, national and club team coaches agreed about the likelihood for immigrant players to take on more central positions and be given more playing time in matches, which were seen as crucial for domestic talent development too.

While the club coaches hardly talked about alternative match playing options for domestic talents, the interviewed national team coaches suggested that DHF could change the structure of tournaments to give domestic talents better match practice. They pointed to the fact that domestic talents were not only present in one community of practice but could move across various communities, which appears as a landscape of handball practice. When considering talent development across local and national communities of practice, the athletes were found to have the option to move to other clubs that would provide them with more playing time, and to move to clubs abroad to receive training and develop as a professional handball player.

According to the coaches, the motivation for young domestic players to go abroad seemed to be somehow inhibited by financial incentives. Before the financial crisis, when the percentage of immigrant players in the Danish women's handball league was high, the clubs could afford to sign contracts with both immigrant and domestic talents. But the situation changed in the late 2000s as the clubs could not afford to do so anymore.

> If they (league clubs) had just had the money to buy the expensive foreigners, but not been able to afford to have young talents on contract, then domestic talents had been forced to go elsewhere. (National team coach)

Here, one of the national team coaches suggested that good salaries had kept young domestic players in the leading national league clubs along with players from abroad. Thus, finance appears to be the sole explanation, and talented domestic players appear to lack the agency to move to other clubs or to seek out options within their clubs or national team settings to develop skill and experience as handball players.

As the number of immigrant players decreased after the financial crisis, both club and national team coaches felt a greater need for young domestic talent in national league clubs: 'Nowadays, the clubs need the young players for training practices as well as matches' (National team coach). Nevertheless, several of the coaches observed that the declining sporting level in the national league was also problematic for domestic talent development. Some coaches further drew attention to the potential of players and coaches arriving from other communities of practice within the landscape of professional handball as an important source of inspiration to domestic talent.

> I hope that at some point we can again begin to pick up some, not only foreign players, but also a few foreign coaches. This would help to provide some inspiration for Danish handball and Danish talent. (National team coach)

Hence, in Wenger's framework, the chance for young domestic talents to develop knowledge-ability about international standard of handball appear to have reduced with the decrease in the number of skilled foreign players and the declining sporting level. The importance for local players to be competing against and sharing knowledge with the best international players to lift their own performance in international and domestic tournaments was now sensed profoundly. Several of the interviewed coaches pointed out that the presence of migrant players provided domestic talent with the option of apprenticeship in the craft of handball.

> We have some players who master the craft and we have some who would become able to do so on the long term. See, hear and learn. Try; develop your own experience using the experienced training partners. It is an apprenticeship like relationship. (Club coach)

This coach suggested possible 'learning assets' to elucidate the relation of apprenticeship between domestic talent and migrant athletes. To use Wenger's perspective, players who cross the boundaries between various communities of practice, in this case around junior and senior handball, and around domestic and international handball, respectively, are faced with both conflicts and considerably beneficial learning options.

It appears that in the light of the financial crisis the coaches were able to see the options for developing domestic talents as wider than what happened in specific local and national communities. Thus, a transnational perspective on professional handball as a *landscape of practice* and knowledge about the options for players to learn across communities may provide coaches, sport managers, etc. with better opportunities to organize and support talent development in 'the age of migration' (Castles & Miller 2009).

Discussion

Applying Wenger's concepts to a case of fluctuating sport labour migration has highlighted the relevance of understanding the association between sport labour migration and domestic talent development in a transnational perspective. Still, the theoretical perspective as well as the methodological approach is worth discussing. Firstly, Wenger's perspective on landscapes of practice has helped to explain the social learning processes that take place across specific communities, in this case sport teams, and the options to learn by movement across communities. However, the possible challenges of crossing communities and the options for young athletes to immigrate are not considered in detail. Also in some cases, acquisition of skill within a specific community, according to a well-developed regime of competence, may be the most relevant thing to do for young talents. Nevertheless, the concept of landscape of practice draws attention to the professional knowledge that an athlete may acquire throughout one's career. Crossing communities and/or meeting skilled players within one's community appear crucial for one's development as a professional athlete. However, the balance between developing wide knowledge as a professional player and reproducing established competence in a local club remains delicate.

Focusing on the context of fluctuating migration into Danish women's handball, the article has explored the changing perceptions and realities for domestic talent development. A similar insight was developed by comparable studies of similar cases such as Norwegian and Danish women's handball (Agergaard and Ronglan 2015). Still, this unique context offers the opportunity to see the transience of perspective on labour immigration. This article has demonstrated through analysis of media reports the role journalism plays in shaping public perception of sport labour migration. A discourse analysis that included not only media texts, but also statements and practices from people in political power and experts on current knowledge of talent development would be interesting. This could develop a wide-ranging model of the ways in which the association between sports labour migration and talent development is perceived and enacted. Interviews with immigrant and domestic players themselves, as well as participant observations about some of the teams that are populated by players of mixed origin would have thrown up interesting aspects of their experience at the ground level. Still, the descriptions presented by the coaches as experts in the field are based on long-standing experiences.

Concluding perspectives

In the middle of the 2000s, players from abroad, 'the foreigners', were perceived as a major obstacle to domestic talent development, somewhat masking the national sport administrators' lack of attention to development of national tournaments and domestic talent. The discursive transformation after the financial crisis – from satisfaction with fewer immigrant players to apprehension of the lowering sporting level, and finally acknowledgement of the importance of fielding immigrant players in the national handball league. This was elaborated by interviews with club and national team coaches that revealed the ways in which the development of domestic talent may be seen as a part of a wider *landscape of practice*. Even if the coaches referred to specific regimes of competence in specific handball communities, the interviews indicated the importance for players to develop a broader knowledgeability. The immigrant players provided the young domestic talents the chance to experience the approaches to professional handball that are prevalent in the wider landscape.

Even though a transformation was observed after the financial crisis, our case study suggests that athletes who are recruited from abroad are often perceived in the nationalist discourse as an intruder rather than transnationals connecting communities. Danish women's handball may not be a singular case, and the tendency to perceive immigration as a severe threat to domestic labour force may also be found in other contexts. This is linked to looking at domestic talent development through the lens of methodological nationalism. Talent development is perceived as something that takes place within national borders. The options for developing athletes in transnational settings are yet underexplored.

Even if sport policy is driven mainly by national administrative institutions, various alternatives exist for supporting the immigration of skilled athletes at various stages of their career, and for sharing acquired skills and technology across national borders (Berlinschi, Schokkaert, and Swinnen 2013). In the research on women's football migration, a range of perspectives is presented on how national sport governing bodies relate to domestic players' development (Agergaard and Tiesler 2014). The American Football Association has opted for the protectionist strategy, reserving a number of positions in the national league to North American football players. At the other end of the spectrum is the Japanese Football Federation which has supported their national team players for playing abroad. This kind of outsourcing of player and talent development happened just before the FIFA Women's World Cup in 2011 that Japan won.

Thus, our case studies suggest a range of possible approaches for national sport governing bodies towards players' development, taking into account the transnational reality of contemporary professional sport. Even at present moment when sport is ineluctably entangled in neoliberal capitalism, nationalist fervour drives much of the fan following and administrative decision-making. The circumstances of national protectionism or outsourcing of domestic players' development are contingent both upon European law, which inhibits setting up of borders to prevent migration of athletes from other European member states, and possibly also on limited transnational engagement among sport administrators. Intriguing studies on this development are awaited in the years to come.

Notes

1. http://www.dr.dk/nyheder/indland/flere-udenlandske-haender-tager-fat-paa-danske-arbejdspladser.
2. http://politiken.dk/debat/profiler/hummelgaard/ECE2431735/vi-skal-satse-mere-paa-vores-laerlinge-end-udenlandsk-arbejdskraft/.
3. Movements, which involve the country of origin as well as country of destination, are particularly apparent among national team players, who regularly travel back and forth to participate in national team camps and tournaments.

Disclosure statement

No potential conflict of interest was reported by the author.

References

Agergaard, Sine. 2008. "Elite Athletes as Migrants in Danish Women's Handball." *International Review for the Sociology of Sport* 43 (1): 5–19. doi:10.1177/1012690208093471.

Agergaard, Sine, and L. T. Ronglan. 2015. "Player Migration and Talent Development in Elite Sports Teams. a Comparative Analysis of Inbound and Outbound Career Trajectories in Danish and Norwegian Women's Handball." *Scandinavian Sport Studies Forum* 6: 1–26.

Agergaard, Sine, and Nina Clara Tiesler, eds. 2014. *Women, Soccer and Transnational Migration*. London: Routledge.

Alvarez, J., D. Forrest, I. Sanz, and J. D. Tena. 2011. "Impact of Importing Foreign Talent on Performance Levels of Local Co-workers." *Labour Economics* 18 (3): 287–296. doi:10.1016/j.labeco.2010.11.003.

Andersen, Svein S., and Lars Tore Ronglan, eds. 2012. *Nordic Elite Sport: Same Ambitions – Different Tracks*. Oslo: Universitetsforlaget.

Andersen, Torben M., U. Michael Bergman, and Svend Erik Hougaard Jensen. 2015. *Reform Capacity and Macroeconomic Performance in the Nordic Countries*. 1st ed. Oxford: Oxford University Press.

Bale, John. 1991. *The Brawn Drain. Foreign Student-athletes in American Universities*. Urbana: University of Illinois Press.

Bale, John, and Joseph A. Maguire, eds. 1994. *The Global Sports Arena: Atheltic Talent Migration in an Interdependent World*. London: Frank Cass.

Baur, Dirk G., and Sibylle Lehmann. 2007. *Does the Mobility of Football Players Influence the Success of the National Team*. IISS discussion paper No. 217. Dublin: Institute for International Integration Studies (IIIS).

Beechler, Schon, and Ian C. Woodward. 2009. "The Global "War for Talent"." *Journal of International Management* 15 (3): 273–285. doi:10.1016/j.intman.2009.01.002.

Berlinschi, Ruxanda, Jeroen Schokkaert, and Johan Swinnen. 2013. "When Drains and Gains Coincide: Migration and International Football Performance." *Labour Economics* 21: 1–14. doi:10.1016/j.labeco.2012.12.006.

Carter, Thomas F. 2011. *In Foreign Fields. The Politics and Experiences of Transnational Sport Migration*. London: Pluto Press.

Castles, Stephen, and Mark J. Miller . 2009. *The Age of Migration. International population movements in the modern world*. New York: Palgrave Macmillan.

Christensen, Mette Krogh, Dan Nørgaard Laursen, and Jan Kahr Sørensen. 2011. "Situated Learning in Youth Elite Football: A Danish Case Study among Talented Male under-18 Football Players." *Physical Education and Sport Pedagogy* 16 (2): 163–178. doi:10.1080/17408989.2010.532782.

Cornelissen, S., and E. Solberg. 2007. "Sport Mobility and Circuits of Power: The Dynamics of Football Migration in Africa and the 2010 World Cup." *Politikon* 34 (3): 295–314. doi:10.1080/02589340801962619.

Darby, Paul. 2001. "The New Scramble for Africa: African Football Labour Migration to Europe." *European Sports History Review* 3: 217–244.

Darby, Paul. 2006. "African Football Labor Migration to Portugal: Colonial and Neo-Colonial Resource." *Analise Social* 41 (179): 417–433.

Darby, Paul. 2013. "Moving Players, Traversing Perspectives: Global Value Chains, Production Networks and Ghanaian Football Labour Migration." *Geoforum* 50: 43–53. doi:10.1016/j. geoforum.2013.06.009.

Darby, Paul, Gerard Akindes, and Matthew Kirwin. 2007. "Football Academies and the Migration of African Football Labor to Europe." *Journal of Sport and Social Issues* 31 (2): 143–161.

Elliott, Richard, and Joseph Maguire. 2008. ""Getting Caught in the Net": Examining the Recruitment of Canadian Players in British Professional Ice Hockey." *Journal of Sport and Social Issues* 32 (2): 158–176. doi:10.1177/0193723507313927.

Elliott, Richard, and Gavin Weedon. 2011. "Foreign Players in the English Premier Academy League: 'Feet-Drain' or 'Feet-Exchange'?" *International Review for the Sociology of Sport* 46 (1): 61–75. doi:10.1177/1012690210378268.

Engh, Mari Haugaa. 2014. *Producing and Maintaining Mobility : A Migrant-Centred Analysis of Transnational Women's Sports Labour Migration : PhD Dissertation*. Aarhus: Aarhus University, Department of Public Health, Section for Sport.

Engh, Mari Haugaa, and Sine Agergaard. 2015. "Producing Mobility through Locality and Visibility : Developing a Transnational Perspective on Sports Labour Migration." *International Review for the Sociology of Sport* 50 (8): 974–992.

Engh, Mari Haugaa, Rico Settler, and Sine Agergaard. 2016. "'The Ball and the Rhytm in Her Blood'. Racialised Imaginaries and Football Migration." Ethnicities 8. doi:10.1177/1468796816636084.

Esson, James. 2015. "Better off at Home? Rethinking Responses to Trafficked West African Footballers in Europe." *Journal of Ethnic and Migration Studies* 41 (3): 512–530. doi:10.1080/136 9183X.2014.927733.

Falcous, Mark, and Joseph Maguire. 2005. "Globetrotters and Local Heroes? Labor Migration, Basketball, and Local Identities." *Sociology of Sport Journal* 22 (2): 137–157.

Frick, Bernd. 2009. "Globalization and Factor Mobility: The Impact of the "Bosman-Ruling" on Player Migration in Professional Soccer." *Journal of Sports Economics* 10 (1): 88–106.

Galipeau, J., and P.Trudel. 2006. "Athlete Learning in a Community of Practice. Is There a Role for the Coach." In *The Sports Coach as Educator. Re-Conceptualising Sports Coaching*, edited by R. L. Jones, 77–94. London: Routledge.

Gelade, Garry A., and Paul Dobson. 2007. "Predicting the Comparative Strengths of National Football Teams." *Social Science Quarterly [H.W. Wilson – SSA]* 88 (1): 244–258.

Klein, Alan M. 2009. "The Transnational View of Sport and Social Development: The Case of Dominican Baseball." *Sport in Society* 12 (9): 1118–1131. doi:10.1080/17430430903137761.

Lave, Jean, and Etienne Wenger. 2001. *Situated Learning : Legitimate Peripheral Participation, Learning in Doing*. Cambridge: Cambridge University Press.

Magee, Jonathan, and John Sugden. 2002. ""The World at Their Feet": Professional Football and International Labor Migration." *Journal of Sport and Social Issues* 26 (4): 421–437. doi:10.1177/0193732502238257.

Maguire, Joseph, and R. Pearton. 2000. "The Impact of Elite Labour Migration on the Identification, Selection and Development of European Soccer Players." *Journal of Sports Sciences* 18 (9): 759–769.

Poli, Raffaele. 2007. "Migration of Football Players and Globalisation: From the World System to Social Networks." *Mappemonde* 88 (4): 1–12.

Poli, Raffaele, Loic Ravenel, and Roger Besson. 2010. "The Trajectories of African Footballers in Light of Globalization." *Cahiers D'outre-Mer* 250 (2): 235–252.

Pratt, A.C., and T.Hutton. 2013. "Reconceptualising the Relationship between the Creative Economy and the City: Learning from the Financial Crisis." *Cities* 33: 86–95.

Skjerk, Ole. 2001. *Dameudvalgets inderlige overflødighed : kvindehåndbold i Danmark 1900-1950. 1.* København: Institut for Idræt, Københavns Universitet.

Storm, Rasmus Klarskov, ed. 2008. *Dansk Håndbold: Bredde, Elite Og Kommercialiseringens Konsekvenser.* Slagelse: Bavnebanke.

Storm, Rasmus Klarskov, and Sine Agergaard. 2014. Talent Development in times of Commercialization and Globalization: The Pros and Cons of International Stars in Danish Women's Handball. In *Women and Sport*, edited by B. Saltin, 2–10. Stockholm: SISU Idrottsböcker.

Ungruhe, Christian. 2014. ""Natural Born Sportsmen". Processes of Othering and Self-Charismatization of African Professional Footballers in Gefrmany." *African Diaspora* 6 (2): 196–217. doi:10.1163/18725457-12341247.

Von Der Lippe, Gerd. 1994. "Handball, Gender and Sportification of Body-Cultures: 1900-40." *International Review for the Sociology of Sport* 29 (2): 211–231. doi:10.1177/101269029402900206.

Wenger, Etienne. 1998. *Communities of Practice: Learning, Meaning, and Identity, Learning in Doing.* Cambridge: Cambridge University Press.

Wenger, Etienne. 2014. *Learning in Landscapes of Practice: Boundaries, Identity, and Knowledgeability in Practice-Based Learning.* New York: Routledge.

We're all transnational now: sport in dynamic sociocultural environments

David Rowe

ABSTRACT
Sport has a deep, enduring attachment to nation as spatial anchor, governmental principle and romantic ideal while being simultaneously implicated in processes that strain, challenge and disrupt the sport-nation nexus. Sport institutions, practices and tastes move into new territories and, correspondingly, people relocate to national spaces where they must negotiate the terms of an established sporting-societal order in the context of a global 'media sports cultural complex'. Sport, therefore, is compulsively transnational, unevenly global, and reflexively national in character by means of multi-dimensional, dynamic interplay. This article focuses on how the lives of ethnically diverse, urban and mobile human subjects in Australia are interwoven with sport in ways that illuminate its capacity symbolically to bind and separate citizens/residents to extant national formations. In addressing sport's role in social inclusion/exclusion and cultural citizenship in demographically diverse societies, the article explores its positioning at the intersection of national symbols and material processes.

Introduction: sport within and beyond nations

Sport is a social institution and cultural form that derives much of its symbolic power from the idea of nation while, for over two centuries, increasingly exceeding the boundaries of the national in material and symbolic form (Bairner 2001). For this reason, to talk about sport in 'transnational contexts' is, in effect, to embrace all contemporary sport, including those that are highly local and more 'folk'-oriented (such as kabbadi, kho kho, jukshei and pelota) but cannot be isolated from external sporting forces. It may be more or less national, transnational or global in nature, but to be defined as sport – in short, rationalized, regulated, competitive physical play – is inevitably to be implicated in the realm of the supranational. This article is principally concerned with those sports that are most regulated, commercialized and mediated. Sport in the twenty-first century is pulled in different directions, appealing, especially when involving international competition, to nationalist frameworks and impulses, while, especially in the light of its digitally-facilitated mediation (Hutchins and Rowe 2012), creating myriad connections and points of identification. A double movement, therefore, is evident in the field of sport – one oriented towards nation, the other resisting and transcending it.

Sport has a deep, enduring attachment to nation as spatial anchor, governmental principle and romantic ideal. It is, therefore, naïve to talk of a post-national sport (Rowe 2011). One need only to consider the continuing salience of national sport leagues – such as the American Football League, English Premier League, National Basketball Association, J-League, Major League Baseball, Australian Football League, La Liga, and so on – to recognize the importance of the nation to the 'grounding', organization and collective identity formation of sport. Furthermore, international sport relies heavily on nations for its meaning – where, for example, would the Olympic Games or FIFA World Cup be, the tournaments with the greatest claim to being global, without the pivotal principle of a contest of nations? But the mere presence or invocation of the nation does not imply its absolute integrity, and should not be confused with the formal entity of the nation state. For example, the national leagues mentioned above are all deeply implicated in the 'New International Division of Cultural Labour' (Miller et al. 2001), with athletic labour circulating the globe in various directions. In some cases the involvement of sportspeople from outside the country causes a nationalist backlash, such as in the case of complaints that the domination of the English Premier League by foreign players, managers and coaches is negatively affecting the performance of the English national team (Football Association 2014). But this transnationalism is less problematic for cricket's Indian Premier League, which is designed to attract players from all over the cricket world (except those, in a sharp reminder of national geo-politics, from Pakistan) to its franchises on short contracts that range from the spectacular to the modest, with the former dominated by Indian players (Rasul and Proffitt 2011). At the same time, in individual sports such as golf, tennis and surfing, there are year-round global circuits in which, while sportspeople are invited as individuals, they are also routinely identified by their country of origin (e.g. in coverage of the rising performance of Korean golfers and Russian tennis players).

Thus, it can be seen that the nation is simultaneously asserted and implicated in processes that strain, challenge and disrupt the sport-nation nexus. The sports media are central to this development because they are increasingly, in the age of the Internet, unconstrained by national media systems (although, of course, these have not disappeared, especially in print media – see e.g. Horky and Nieland 2013). The growth of a global 'media sports cultural complex' (Rowe 2004) both reinforces and disrupts nation-based sporting systems. It is this multi-dimensional, dynamic interplay that constantly re-fashions the relationships of sport to the mythologies and ideologies that invest it with social meaning and animate its political-economic utility. Sport, therefore, is compulsively transnational, unevenly global, and reflexively national in character. It is caught up with processes involving the movement of sport institutions, practices and tastes into new territories and a corresponding relocation of people into national spaces where they must co-exist with, and negotiate the terms of, an established sporting-societal order that is itself in flux – not least because of their presence. Within a broader theoretical framework of mobility, this configuration of flow, friction and immobility reveals the constant interaction between what is extant and what is in the process of becoming in societies conceived as nations (Cresswell 2006; Urry 2000).

This article, instead of concentrating on the movement of sports, sports media texts and sportspeople around the world (Carter 2011; Maguire and Falcous 2011), will concentrate on the sociocultural implications of populations moving around the world and relocating in new national sporting environments. In some regards, therefore, it is not about how sport comes to people, but the ways in which people come to sport. This is inherently a matter of transnationalism – those engaged in global ethnoscapic flows (Appadurai 1996) pass (in most cases, except when in so-called 'failed states' or territorially disputed zones) into new nationally organized nation-state jurisdictions with pre-existing national-cultural orders. Sport's position in these countries is variable, but it is often significant, and the focus in this instance is on a nation where national sporting culture is especially strong – Australia. Findings from a current research project[1] are addressed here in examining how the lives of ethnically diverse, urban and mobile human subjects are interwoven with sport in ways that illuminate its capacity symbolically to bind citizens/residents to extant national formations and to reinforce existing – or to stimulate other – forms of affiliation. In addressing the extent to which sport promotes or obstructs social inclusion and cultural citizenship in demographically diverse societies, the article seeks to enhance understanding of the inter-section of national symbols and material processes as they pertain to the domain of sport.

Australia: sport and the (trans)national

Australia is a nation that is renowned for its attachment to sport. While there is no doubt that much is mythological about the typification of the country as *A Paradise of Sport* (Cashman 2010), it is persistently officially described as a sporting nation in its institutional and cultural – especially media – apparatus. For example, the most recent (50th) edition of *Australia in Brief*, which is produced by the Australian Government's Department of Foreign Affairs and Trade (2014) to provide 'an authoritative overview of Australia's history, the land, its people and their way of life', states in its 'Society and Culture' section:

> Australians love sport. There are more than 140 national sporting organisations and thousands of local, regional and state sports bodies.

> Community-based sport across the nation underpins Australia's remarkable sporting achievements at the elite level where many international champions have been produced in many sports. The nation unites when Australians play on the international stage. Sport is a powerful force in creating social harmony in a nation made up of people from so many different countries. (58)

Similarly, the latest version of *Australian Citizenship: Our Common Bond*, which provides 'All of the information you need to sit the Australian citizenship test' (Commonwealth of Australia Department of Immigration and Border Protection 2014, 2), opens the section on 'Australia's identity' with 'Sport and recreation' and proclaims that:

> Many Australians love sport and many have achieved impressive results at an international level.

> We are proud of our reputation as a nation of 'good sports'. Australian sportsmen and women are admired as ambassadors for the values of hard work, fair play and teamwork.

> Throughout our history, sport has both characterised the Australian people and united us. From early settlement, sport provided an escape from the realities of a harsh existence. Even during wartime, members of the Australian Defence Force organised sporting competitions to help relieve the stress of the battleground.

> Sport also provides a common ground that allows both players and spectators to feel included and a part of something that is important to Australian society. (43)

Sport is officially deemed to be so central to Australian national culture that its most important events – over 1300 in total (including multi-sport events) – are protected by law for free-to-air television through an 'anti-siphoning regime' involving 'events of national importance and cultural significance' that prevent them from being exclusively captured by subscription television (Rowe 2014a).

Such state-initiated endorsement of sport means that there is a clear association between sport and 'Australianness', and a general expectation that embracing sport is part of becoming an Australian as an expression of social inclusion and occupation of 'common ground'. This is an important matter for those seeking Australian citizenship despite the fact that detailed questions about sport are not asked in the nation's citizenship test. Australia is a country with a highly diverse demography, containing people from over 200 nations. A former British colony with a dominant Anglo population (explaining to some degree the historical importance of sport in the country) and Indigenous peoples, levels of immigration are high and characterized by increasing diversity. According to the Australian Bureau of Statistics (2015a):

> The proportion of Australians who were born overseas has hit its highest point in 120 years, with 28 per cent of Australia's population – 6.6 million people – born overseas …

> 'Australia traditionally had a high proportion of migrants, but we've now hit a peak not seen since the gold rushes of the late 1800s,' said Denise Carlton from the ABS.

> 'Overseas migration has been a large contributor to the total Australian population growth for several years – it has consistently been the main driver since 2005–06, contributing more than 50 per cent of population growth in Australia.'

> 'While the largest migrant groups were people born in the United Kingdom and New Zealand – with a total of over 1.8 million Australian residents being born in those two countries, the next two most common birth places were from the Asian region.'

> 'These were China and India, with around 450,000 and 400,000 people respectively …'

> 'In contrast, the proportion of the population born in the United Kingdom saw a drop, falling from 5.6 to 5.2 per cent over the last ten years …'

As Table 1 reveals, 5 of the top 10 countries of birth in Australia are in Asia, with some variability regarding both age and sex. Unsurprisingly, the median age from the population sources with rising numbers in Asia is lower than for those involved in earlier waves of immigration, while women outnumber men in all Asian origin countries in the top 10 apart from India.

This level of transnational mobility and demographic diversity in Australia, and its official commitment to multiculturalism, has caused some anxiety about social cohesion and the maintenance of Anglo cultural hegemony. Its notorious White Australia Policy, the Immigration Restriction Act, was brought into law shortly after the establishment of the Australian nation in 1901. It was not until the post-Second World War resettlement and immigration programmes that the policy was weakened, and the passing of the 1975 Racial Discrimination Act finally made racially-based immigration selection unlawful in Australia. Nonetheless, there have been various expressions of opposition to demographic diversity and multiculturalism since – usually directed towards immigration from Asia – including the 'Blainey debate' in the 1980s (Markus and Ricklefs 1985) and the rise and fall of the 'One

GLOBAL AND TRANSNATIONAL SPORT

Table 1. Top 10 countries of birth, selected characteristics – Australia – 30 June 2014(a).

Country of birth	Persons		Median age	Sex ratio
	No.	% of Australian population	Years	Males per 100 females
United Kingdom	1,221,300	5.2	54.4	104.6
New Zealand	617,000	2.6	39.7	105.2
China	447,400	1.9	35.5	81.9
India	397,200	1.7	33.2	119.7
Philippines	225,100	1.0	39.5	63.7
Vietnam	223,200	1.0	44.5	85.0
Italy	201,800	0.9	68.8	108.5
South Africa	176,300	0.8	40.9	99.8
Malaysia	153,900	0.7	38.6	88.3
Germany	129,000	0.5	62.9	92.4

Notes: (a) Estimates from June quarter 2013 onwards are preliminary.
Source: Australian Bureau of Statistics (2015a).

Nation' party in the 1990s (Leach, Stokes, and Ward 2000), and its subsequent resurgence in the 2016 federal election. The stance of long serving Prime Minister John Howard in seeing 'Anglo-Saxon culture as the "core culture" in Australia into which other cultures ought to "blend"' (Tate 2009, 109) is fairly typical of this Anglocentrism in Australia.

Sport – with its close association to the 'Britishness' with which both the Anglo-Australian elite and majority have traditionally identified – might be seen in this dynamic demographic context as a bulwark against the erosion of Anglo-Celtic historical dominance. This is not only a question of displaying an attachment to sport in general, or to the 'right' sport, but also, in an evocation of what has been described as the 'cricket test' by the British Conservative politician Norman Tebbit, to the 'right' national team (Malcolm 2001). Tebbit had famously asked, 'A large proportion of Britain's Asian population fail to pass the cricket test. Which side do they cheer for? It's an interesting test. Are you still harking back to where you came from or where you are?' (Farrington et al. 2012, 87). In the Australian context, a similar (though less confrontational) sentiment has been expressed by former Federal Treasurer Peter Costello (Hallinan and Hughson 2010). Such discursive interventions have particular salience in the site of the research for this article, Greater Western Sydney, which has an estimated population of 2.12 million; 680,000 of whom were born overseas (with India now the first-ranked country, followed in the top 10 by the UK, Vietnam, China, Philippines, Lebanon, New Zealand, Iraq, Fiji and Italy); with 17% of residents having arrived in the five years before 2011 (the most recent year for which census data are currently available), and with 39% of residents speaking a language other than English in the home (WSROC 2014). The research has involved qualitative interviews and focus groups with over 70 residents of Greater Western Sydney, most of whom have some connection to a community-based sports organization, exploring their relationships to sport, nation and cultural citizenship. Particular attention has been given to the ways in which overseas migrants to Australia orient themselves to sport in the Australian context and negotiate the aforementioned pressure to become fully engaged citizens in a 'nation of good sports'. In the following section an illustrative (rather than strictly representative) analytical sample is drawn from the project data in exploring various dimensions of the transnational experience relating to sport and people from different backgrounds and periods of residency in Australia.

Sport and the transnational experience

As was discussed above, in Australia attachment to sport is constructed both as a defining characteristic of being Australian and as the 'common ground' on which otherwise diverse social subjects are brought together. This harmonizing and integrative role of sport occurs at the level of practice for participants and spectators, and is held to be at its most symbolically potent at the moments in which (as quoted above) 'The nation unites when Australians play on the international stage'. At this point, the national, the transnational and the international meet in complex ways, as is revealed in interviews with a range of people from various backgrounds who are involved in sport in various formal and informal contexts. Research participants were selected on the basis that their origin or ancestry reflect the various currents of the experience of a settler-colonial nation containing Indigenous peoples; those of Anglo-Celtic background who have traditionally controlled the country's institutions (not least sport); the post-Second World War wave of European migrants (including Italian, Croatian and German), and the more recent, growing migrant groups of people from Asia (including China, Vietnam, Nepal, Lebanon and India). The sample was rounded out with participants from Africa and the Americas. While some had little connection to sport either as participants or spectators (both in-stadium and media-related), most of those interviewed had some connection to sport at the community level, as that link enabled a more detailed investigation of sport's role in everyday life in Australia. The resultant data revealed the complexity of human biographies, cultural identities and orientations to sport.

A case in point is Kat [a pseudonym, as is the case for all research participants quoted], a self-identified 'sport lover' in her late 30s, of Anglo origin with dual Australian-New Zealand citizenship, who is a player and administrator in rugby union, and a former youth worker who now works in the sports apparel industry. Kat was born in Australia but became a New Zealand/Aotearoa citizen by descent, and lived there until her early 20s. When asked about whether sport is important to Australian culture and identity, Kat emphatically agrees but also recognizes the problems associated with a hierarchy of sport that does not always sit easily with the transnational sporting experience:

> Definitely I think so, and I think it allows people to integrate into the community easier. So if you are a new immigrant to Australia or refugee – I used to do youth work, so I worked with some kids from Sierra Leone and they had a massive communication barrier, found it very difficult to talk and get to know the other kids. But through sport, particularly soccer being the world game, they were able to integrate seamlessly because it's a language they all understand, and you don't need to have the same. And for them it made them, it helped to make them feel like more, like citizens. It certainly made our life easier because the kids were less depressed when they felt that they could engage with other kids. So yeah I definitely think that sport is [an important part of Australian culture and identity].

> I think sometimes it can be a barrier, though, because if it's not things like soccer and swimming and athletics that are understood around the world, and it's more NRL [National Rugby League] or AFL [Australian Football League], the new kids, they don't understand. They don't know what it is, they don't get it, and so for them it can be a barrier to being part of the society. So it's a double edge really. I guess we need more soccer. (Kat)

Kat's personal experience is compatible with the Australian sport system in that her main sport, rugby union, is popular as both a participant and spectator sport in the country, as is its national men's team, the Wallabies. Tables 2 and 3 indicate patterns of sport participation and spectatorship that are distinctive in Australia, including widespread playing

Table 2. Top 20 sports and activities by regular participation rate.

	Age 6-13	(000s)	%	Age 14+	(000s)	%	TOTAL Age 6+	(000s)	%
1	Swimming	1198	48.8%	Swimming	1949	10.1%	Swimming	3147	14.4%
2	Soccer	1194	48.7%	Cycling	1419	7.3%	Cycling	2343	10.8%
3	Cycling	924	37.7%	Hiking/Bushwalking	847	4.4%	Soccer	1790	8.2%
4	Athletics/Track & Field	778	31.7%	Aerobics	623	3.2%	Dancing	1303	6.0%
5	Basketball	748	30.5%	Soccer	596	3.1%	Basketball	1088	5.0%
6	Dancing	743	30.3%	Dancing	560	2.9%	Hiking/Bushwalking	1079	5.0%
7	Cricket	631	25.7%	Tennis	471	2.4%	Tennis	961	4.4%
8	Netball	503	20.5%	Netball	343	1.8%	Cricket	959	4.4%
9	Tennis	490	20.0%	Basketball	340	1.8%	Athletics/Track & Field	874	4.0%
10	Gymnastics	444	18.1%	Cricket	328	1.7%	Netball	846	3.9%
11	Australian Rules	438	17.9%	Martial arts	242	1.3%	Aerobics	698	3.2%
12	Hiking/Bushwalking	232	9.5%	Body surfing	231	1.2%	Australian Rules	622	2.9%
13	Rugby League	229	9.3%	Surfing	211	1.1%	Gymnastics	569	2.6%
14	Softball	218	8.9%	Australian Rules	184	1.0%	Martial arts	457	2.1%
15	Martial arts	215	8.8%	Volleyball	133	0.7%	Rugby League	339	1.6%
16	Volleyball	189	7.7%	Gymnastics	125	0.6%	Body surfing	335	1.5%
17	Baseball	165	6.7%	Horse riding	122	0.6%	Surfing	330	1.5%
18	Field Hockey	144	5.9%	Rugby Union	113	0.6%	Volleyball	322	1.5%
19	Roller blading/skating	127	5.2%	Rugby League	110	0.6%	Softball	271	1.2%
20	Horse riding	119	4.9%	Field hockey	103	0.5%	Field Hockey	247	1.1%

Sources: Roy Morgan (2015) Single Source (Australia), January 2014–December 2014, sample *n* = 15,944 Australians aged 14+; Roy Morgan Young Australians Survey, January 2014–December 2014, sample *n* = 2404 Australians aged 6–13.

Table 3. Spectators at selected sporting events (a) (by sex).

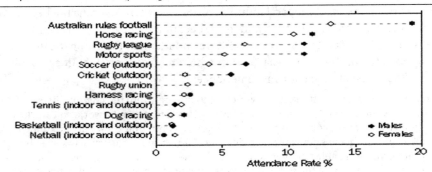

(a) The top 12 ranked sports in terms of total attendance.

Source: Australian Bureau of Statistics (2010).

and watching a game, Australian Rules Football, that is virtually confined (certainly at a professional level) to one country or, like rugby league, is played only in a few places in the world. But there are many other sports that are global in nature, such as association football (soccer) and basketball, or that are particularly popular in parts of Asia, such as cricket. Ironically, it should be mentioned, the most recent research questions Australia's official and popular image as an active sporting nation, with the Australian Bureau of Statistics (2015b) finding that:

> There has been a decrease in the number of Australians participating in sport and physical recreation … Overall, 60% of Australians aged 15 years and over participated in sport and physical recreation in 2013–14, compared with 65% in 2011–12.

This finding is consistent with the statistic that Australia has the world's fastest climbing obesity rates, with almost a quarter of children and almost two thirds of the adult population found to be overweight (Australian Broadcasting Corporation 2014).

The young people from Sierra Leone mentioned by Kat found sport, therefore, to facilitate both social inclusion and exclusion, certainly at the transitional point of new residency. Ironically but understandably, they felt more 'like citizens' through a shared interest with Australians of longer residency in soccer as the 'world game', rather than through sports that are more closely associated with Australia, such as Australian rules football and rugby league. In theoretical terms, this situated experience can be regarded, following the analysis of Bourdieu (1984), as an instance of how cultural tastes operate within a framework of 'distinction' that reinforces the structure of power relations – here the Australian sport field is reproducing the cultural capital that is associated with sports which assert a privileged attachment to 'Australianness' (Rowe 2016). Soccer, despite being one of the most popular participant sports in Australia, has had historical difficulty with being regarded as a bona fide Australian sport, sometimes attracting the ethnocentrically insulting descriptor 'wogball' (Hallinan and Hughson 2010). Nonetheless, the esteemed place of sport in general within Australian national culture is highlighted by Kat in addressing whether it might be regarded as 'un-Australian' (a term frequently used to emphasize otherness and even treason; see e.g. Frow 2007), not to like sport:

> No I don't think so … we don't have a rich artistic culture. So our culture has been built on sport and so other people would think they're un-Australian if they don't like sport because that's what so many people attach our identity to. But I don't think so. I've got friends who are terrible at sport and so they have no interest at all … (Kat)

Here is evoked a critique of Australia as too sport-loving and so excluding and repressing other expressions of Australianness – such as through art and science. While this is a highly-charged debate that cannot be adequately addressed here, it is noted that neither of the citizenship information documents of the United Kingdom and Canada – two countries with substantial sporting traditions – give as much prominence to sport in describing their national lives as the equivalent official Australian document (Rowe 2013). It might be suggested, therefore, that there is greater pressure – both at the more formal level of nation-state governance and at the informal level of everyday life in specific sociocultural environments – for migrants to Australia to assume a positive disposition towards sport and to identify with its national representative teams. This expectation showed through in Kat's response to the question of whether it is advisable for citizens and residents to be knowledgeable about Australian sport and its history:

> I think it makes life easier for them if they do. I think it makes you able to assimilate into your society easier. So especially for new Australians I think it's really important that they get an introduction to sport so that that way they are able to converse with the majority of Australians who are into sport. (Kat)

Kat noted that, at this level of quotidian social intercourse, a lack of engagement with sport in Australia can be exclusionary in its effect:

> Definitely. Definitely. Unless you attach yourself to a sub-group who's not involved in sport, then yes. I mean, as I said, all schools focus on sport so if you're a child it's going to be difficult

because the school will be involved in that. As an adult, yes, because the majority of people are going to be either watching it on telly, going to a match or talking about it, or watching their kids play on the weekends. So I think it does make it, yeah it is harder for them. (Kat)

Through her active involvement in women's rugby union, Kat is clearly supportive of sport participation and takes a strong position on gender inequality in the sport. It is important to register this manifestation of intersectionality in order to prevent simplistic, essentializing conceptions of ethnicity and nation. Kat had herself experienced some objection to playing a contact sport from within her own (Anglo) family on the grounds that it was 'gender inappropriate', and had also seen how restriction based on gender could be exacerbated by cultural, religious or national background, citing examples from her experience of girls from Samoan, Mormon, Muslim and Japanese backgrounds whose parents had disapproved of them playing sport. She had sought to overcome such barriers through, for example, successfully lobbying to change playing dress code regulations to reduce exposure of the female body. Kat was also acutely aware of another domain of intersectionality – social class – that prevents many children and adults from participating in sport because they cannot afford the costs of registration, uniforms, equipment, travel and so on.

This problem is also recognized by Assi, an Australia-born woman in her mid-20s from a self-described 'very bi-cultural home' (both parents being Lebanese born, but her mother having no 'cultural memory of Lebanon' after migrating when she was only three years of age, while her father moved to the country as an adult). She also reflects on the ways in which transnationalism interacts with a range of other intersectional factors in conditioning sport's sociocultural ramifications. An English- and Arab-speaking public servant, Assi plays association football, tag rugby and does CrossFit, but her main sporting involvement is through Australian rules football, having established a women's team in which she is also a player. Assi and her sisters were discouraged by their parents from participating in sport after school for reasons of gender, cost and logistics. But, on reaching a more independent stage of life, their involvement in sport became significant: 'So it was a long journey for us to go through because of the cultural barriers or the socio-economic barriers. Once we got there, I just discovered an untapped passion and energy for sport' (Assi). In addressing the role of sport as a facilitator of conversational opportunities between people of diverse backgrounds, Assi pithily sums up her own experience in different contexts in which she occupies minority status in various respects:

> I think it helps. It definitely helps. I can tell you as a public servant I work with a lot of Anglo Australians – majority Anglo Australians and majority male in my profession. In university I chose to go study in the city [rather than Western Sydney] so I'm still the minority in the minority. In a lot of hats – when I chose to play AFL, similarly I'm the minority in the minority. The minority being women in AFL but then the minority in the minority being a multicultural Muslim woman in AFL, and it really is an icebreaker to be able to have a conversation about sport because it's a common ground. (Assi)

A self-described 'confident person' who, as noted, is Australia-born, Assi can connect with other people in a variety of ways, 'It could be *Master Chef* or it could be anything. A TV show, what you are studying, the grind of life, family values or whatever it is. There is always room to find just something'. But she acknowledges that others (including recent migrants from countries where English is not the main language) may be more 'shy' and so reluctant to converse with others on sport and other subjects. Nonetheless, Assi is convinced of the social benefits of involvement in sport, especially among minority groups, and so of waiving registration fees for players – many of whom are young women from Muslim communities – who cannot afford them. She is almost evangelistic when describing the reactions of some players to their involvement in the team, and regarding cases where sport is deployed to promote peace in the 'international community':

> For us it's more important to get them involved in the club and for some of them, especially when you've got stressful financial situations, coming to football from week to week is almost like their lifesaver. I kid you not when I use that word. There have been players that have said to me 'Assi sport … this team saved my life' and it gives me goose bumps. That's such strong words to hear from one person to another. But I think that is the effect of sport and if you look at the international community, there are countless examples. I'll give you Melbourne, they run a Unity Cup event and they had a team called Mujew and it was Muslim Jewish kids playing together and there was also the Peace team that came over – a Palestinian Israeli peace team that came over to Australia and participated in the international cup for AFL. Those examples where they are really tackling some serious issues around racism, there are human rights issues and there is politics. When you can use sport as a vehicle to cut across [and] through all of those layers, that's remarkable. I'm a big advocator on engaging communities through sport and I think sport is the equaliser. (Assi)

Assi is most interested in encouraging participation in sport, but there are many other ways of interacting with it, such as through the media (especially television) or through family members. Kelil, a bank employee who was born in China and has been an Australian citizen since 2007, enjoys watching soccer and basketball on television, but is disappointed that top international leagues such as the EPL and NBA are not well represented on Australian free-to-air television:

> It's like quite strange … surprisingly when I arrived in Australia, I found that on the TV all the time is the rugby, is the cricket and tennis … well tennis is getting more and more popular, but you know the other two we have never, we don't even know how to play the game in China. It's not something we do in China at all so, but it takes like 80 per cent of the time on the TV in Australia for those kind of games, which we're not interested in unfortunately. (Kelil)

An emergent factor that helped shape orientation to sport for some interviewees was intergenerational influence – especially that of children. In part, this is a matter of formal schooling and sporting resource opportunity. As Vinh, a middle-aged bi-lingual Vietnamese-Australian citizen, notes:

> Here the youth, Vietnamese youth, got more opportunity to play any kind of sport they really like because they have the better life, and they have time and the family look after them carefully, and so they have more opportunity to play sports, any kind of sport, than in Vietnam. (Vinh)

Vinh was one of several of those interviewed with backgrounds in Asia who remarked on Australia's superior sporting infrastructure, especially for children. Kanchha, a Nepal-born Australian citizen who works in computing and speaks Nepali, Hindi and English, is directly affected by the opportunity afforded to many – though not, as already noted, all – children and young people in Australia to engage with sport, and especially those that have been culturally sanctioned at a national level. He plays racquet sports that are popular in his region of origin – table tennis, lawn tennis and badminton – and is not interested in or knowledgeable about popular sports in Australia like Australian rules football and rugby league. But Kanchha encounters them via his son, while also believing that different migrant sporting tastes are changing the overall Australian sporting taste 'palate':

> I think this is now changing the taste of that – I believe that you know – because I was watching last time and you know, in the AFL, the stadium was almost empty now, so why people are

saying, why is [it] like that? Because now most of the migrant people and including myself, so I don't love to go and watch AFL and NRL like though my son forces me to, I'm not really … So most [of] the people migrating I think [from] China and the Indian people, so Indian people love to watch cricket and Chinese people love to watch like table tennis, all these sorts of things, you know. So I don't think Chinese people will like to go and watch AFL … So I think [it's] changing … (Kanchha)

Similarly, Randhir, an Indian financial services worker who speaks four Indian languages as well as English, and who migrated to Australia after living in the Middle East, is drawn to a completely unfamiliar sport like Australian Rules Football because of his son:

You know, cricket in Australia is one of the sports … for me it is 'the sport' to play. I look at it, I grew up playing cricket, so now after coming here then I learn about tennis, I learn about golf. I start to accept[ing] the AFL and my son likes that game … it takes time for me to learn that game, and understand how it's played. And then when you see your own kids you start liking that game also – after all it's just a sport. (Randhir)

Although 'it's just a sport', AFL is not *any* sport – it is the most powerful football code in the country and the only sport that is defined through its nomenclature as 'Australian'. Here the dialectic of migration and transnationalism is evident. In a fluid sociocultural context involving high degrees of mobility, it is not only migrants who have to adapt to nationally dominant sporting tastes, especially in an intensely competitive sport and media market like Australia. This emergent complexity is highlighted by Kanchha when he takes his son to a sport site that is not Anglo-dominated:

And again it depends on the sports you're playing. Like I take my son to play table tennis, so [we] actually went to a couple of tournaments. So my son is only the odd one [out], you know – all Chinese and only his name is odd. (Kanchha)

This kind of transnational encounter (here between Nepalese and Chinese Australians) is the inevitable consequence of a diversity in which there is some necessary ceding of Anglo-hegemonic control over sport and social exchange. In this fluid context, the experience of Saili, a Nepal-born office manager who has been a permanent resident of Australia since 2007, may be interpreted as defensive: 'Yeah, sometimes I've been commented if I don't know AFL, people kind of comment that "are you Australian?" kind of that comment is over there, but that doesn't mean that I'm not Australian or anything'.

The question of symbolic fealty to the nation, not only through sports interest and knowledge but also international sports patriotism, becomes especially problematic when manifest not just as pressure to support a national team, but when incurring abuse for not doing so. For example, Kat, the dual-citizen who supports the New Zealand All Blacks over Australia's Wallabies, reflects 'Well, it can be awkward and you can actually be abused by people', in describing some responses to her not supporting the team representing the country in which she was born and resides – an experience that she shares with those migrants from other countries who continue to support national teams from their places of origin:

So I think, and you can get abused. Like even still as an adult people will say to me 'How come you go for the All Blacks? You live in Australia, you're an Australian, that's a disgrace and if you like them so much go and live in New Zealand'. And I've heard people say that to other people, especially like you'll have people who have moved over from England or Ireland, they'll still be going for their national rugby team and other people will feel that they are, they have the right to abuse them and say, 'You should be going for Australia or go back home', and I think that's disgusting. I think you should be allowed to go for whatever team you want but no, in Australia you can be made to feel extremely uncomfortable for doing that. I've seen friends as well who go to the cricket and they'll go support Pakistan, Sri Lanka, India, and they're just colourful, have their national flag and they've had stuff thrown at them. It's just appalling. It's so wrong. And so there is still a part of the society who won't let you do it. (Kat)

By contrast, Assi describes herself as being 'indifferent' to the outcome of a sports contest between Lebanon and Australia ('I mean I always just support Australia because I've got no connection to overseas'), while recognizing:

But certainly for refugee and recent migrant communities, that's quite a bind because you have a sense of pride in both. So I think – it's probably better that you ask someone else but my observations are that it is difficult for people depending on the attachment to their ethnic heritage or their homeland. Sometimes they probably will still lean – I think it also has to do with a sense of belonging. If they feel like they belong here, then there is more loyalty to support that country. I know with a lot of young Lebanese men, they feel so unwanted and rejected by society and the media, so if Australia was to play Lebanon, maybe they would go 'Well, it's not like Australian society really likes me. I'm going to go for Lebanon. At least the Lebos [vernacular term for a Lebanese person] love me'. It's kind of sad.

When considering the concrete case of Australia playing Italy (the source of many post-Second World War migrants in Australia) in the FIFA World Cup (see Rowe 2014b), Assi is quite comfortable even with Socceroos [the name of the men's national team] fans being in a minority:

I understand if I went to a stadium and it was in Australia and three quarters of the stadium were supporting Italy I would be like 'Oh, that hurts a little bit', because I have a sense of pride in my nation, but I understand equally that people lean different ways for different reasons. Maybe because I'm less emotionally involved and attached to the sport, I can go 'It is okay whatever way you go'.

For Randhir, however, the aforementioned intergenerational effect applies also to supporting Australian teams, because 'my son is a hard core Aussie' and 'because I like to please my son, so by default over a period of time, I have seen it with myself … I say yeah Australia is the great team'. This is the case even when India are playing Australia at his favourite sport, cricket, which in the past had created 'a lot of friction in the house between me and my kids', but the conflict has now been settled in Australia's favour because 'this is our home now'. As can be seen from such instances, the politics of sport under transnationalism is played out at both micro and macro levels, from nation state rhetoric to water cooler encounters, from formal school curricula to family dynamics. In all such cases, sport is deeply implicated in rhetorics of collective belonging and social subjectivity.

Conclusion: sport cultures and the transnational challenge

The discussion above has focused on how citizens and residents in Australia, mostly with culturally and linguistically diverse backgrounds, oriented themselves to Australia's national sport culture and system. Transnational flows of people, media and sports exert pressure for change in national sporting 'orders', while inevitably also incurring resistance and even hostility. These symbolic power struggles over sport's structure, practice, politics and meanings take place in many different sites, including among governments and sport associations at all levels, local communities and clubs, public and commercial media, and in transnational corporations. For example, Ugra (2015), in her report on the impact of the South Asian diaspora on Australian cricket, observes that:

There are hundreds of registered cricket clubs across Australia and each account of an exclusionary – or blokey, boozy – environment can be matched by examples of inclusion or attempts to change. Even so, there persists a mutual cultural dissonance that has led to the creation of new clubs centred largely around national or ethnic roots, which must be taken into account. Whether such clubs play in the mainstream or in breakaway Sunday Twenty20 competitions depends on the environment around clubs, the time available for the game, and personal preference …

… Club cultures vary but the exclusionary are easier to turn away from. [Chris] Harris [from Cricket Victoria], on his way to conduct a cricket information night, once walked through a club whose 'all Anglo-Saxon' football team was drinking at the time and 'looking at me not in a great light'. He could have had, 'any coloured face' but to the footballers he became 'the outsider to their sanctum'. Waiting for the cricket information night at the club, among white Australians families, were a group of Sri Lankans with their children. The footballers made the connection between Harris and the Sri Lankans and left Harris 'really concerned about the attitude of these footballers'.

Despite this hostility from one Anglo-Saxon football club towards a multi-ethnic group of people interested in cricket, Ugra (2015) is optimistic that 'The old status quo is no longer the normal in Australian cricket'. Clearly, though, overall progress is reliant on a long March through both state and civil society institutions. Earlier in this article there was a discussion of Anglocentrism and the White Australia Policy, and there are echoes of both in the paragraphs above. Sport can also not be isolated from the developments in other domains in political struggles over material and symbolic territory – for example, current debates about the human rights of the multitudes of refugees seeking asylum from conflict zones in Africa, the Middle East, and central and south Asia (Gatrell 2013). If in sport, as in other spheres of the social, 'we're all transnational now', this does not mean that nations and their borders are passing into history (Rowe 2011). Instead, national formations are constantly in the process of being made and re-made, and sport has an important role as both agent and symbol in constructing the field of national, transnational and global relations.

Sport has an uncommon ability to crystallize and de-stabilize all three relational logics, a capacity which only reinforces the imperative of exercising due analytical scepticism over the discursive claims made on its behalf and, as has been attempted here, to attend closely to the ways in which sport 'plays' in dynamic, complex sociocultural environments. The nation by no means monopolises the sport-identity nexus, with attachment to, and detachment from, sport in its many forms evident in the everyday articulation of multiple and sometimes conflicting identities and affective alliances (Brummett and Ishak 2014). As is evident in some of the above quotations from research participants, physical and symbolic transnational mobilities can help shape a sporting cosmopolitanism that is much more free-floating than the 'immobilising' demands that original place of birth and current residence would allow.

But cosmopolitanism itself takes a range of forms. As Giulianotti and Robertson (2007, 64) have argued in relation to association football, cosmopolitanism can be both 'thin' (a 'rudimentary politics of recognition') and 'thick' ('a decidedly more universalist orientation towards, and engagement with, other cultures'). They do not predict that there will be an inevitable move from the former to the latter through 'the cross-fertilization and hybridization of social practices across a transnational terrain', or that there will be a progressive eradication of 'more particularized forms of civic, ethno-national, ethno-linguistic or ethno-religious identification'. The Australian context is characterized by just such a co-existence and negotiation of sport-related and -unrelated sociocultural processes and

Note

1. *A Nation of 'Good Sports'? Cultural Citizenship and Sport in Contemporary Australia*, funded by an Australian Research Council Discovery Grant (DP130104502).

Disclosure statement

No potential conflict of interest was reported by the author.

References

Appadurai, Arjun. 1996. *Modernity at Large: Cultural Dimensions of Globalization* (Public Worlds, 1 vol.). Minneapolis: University of Minnesota Press.

Australian Broadcasting Corporation. 2014. "Australian Obesity Rates Climbing Faster than Anywhere Else in the World, Study Shows." May 29. Accessed May 18, 2015. http://www.abc.net.au/news/2014-05-29/australian-obesity-rates-climbing-fastest-in-the-world/5485724

Australian Bureau of Statistics. 2010. "4174.0 – Spectator Attendance at Sporting Events, 2009–10." Accessed May 18, 2015. http://www.abs.gov.au/ausstats/abs@.nsf/Products/4174.0~2009-10~Main+Features~Most+popular+sports+attended?OpenDocument

Australian Bureau of Statistics. 2015a. "Overseas Born Aussies Hit a 120 Year Peak" (Media Release, January 29). Accessed May 18, 2015. http://www.abs.gov.au/ausstats/abs@.nsf/Latestproducts/3412.0Media%20Release12013-14?opendocument&tabname=Summary&prodno=3412.0&issue=2013-14&num=&view=

Australian Bureau of Statistics. 2015b. "Participation in Sport and Physical Recreation Declines in Australia" (Media Release, February 18). Accessed May 18, 2015. http://www.abs.gov.au/ausstats/abs@.nsf/Latestproducts/4177.0Media%20Release12013-14?opendocument&tabname=Summary&prodno=4177.0&issue=2013-14&num=&view=

Australian Government Department of Foreign Affairs and Trade. 2014. *Australia in Brief*. 50th ed. Canberra: DFAT. Accessed May 13, 2015. http://dfat.gov.au/about-us/publications/Documents/australia-in-brief.pdf

Bairner, Alan. 2001. *Sport, Nationalism, and Globalization: European and North American Perspectives*. Albany: State University of New York Press.

Bourdieu, Pierre. 1984. *Distinction: A Social Critique of the Judgement of Taste*. London: Routledge and Kegan Paul.

Brummett, Barry, and Andrew Ishak, eds. 2014. *Sports and Identity: New Agendas in Communication*. New York: Routledge.

Carter, Thomas F. 2011. *In Foreign Fields: The Politics and Experiences of Transnational Sport Migration*. London: Pluto Press.

Cashman, Richard. 2010. *Paradise of Sport: A History of Australian Sport*. 2nd ed. Petersham: Walla Walla Press.

Commonwealth of Australia. 2014. *Australian Citizenship: Our Common Bond*. Canberra: Department of Immigration and Border Protection. Accessed August 1, 2015. http://www.border.gov.au/Citizenship/Documents/our-common-bond-2014.pdf

Cresswell, Timothy. 2006. *On the Move: Mobility in the Modern Western World*. New York: Routledge.

Farrington, Niel, Daniel Kilvington, John Price, and Am Saeed. 2012. *Race, Racism and Sports Journalism*. London: Routledge.

Football Association. 2014. *The FA Chairman's England Commission Report*. May. London: FA.

Frow, John. 2007. "UnAustralia: Strangeness and Value." *Cultural Studies Review* 13 (2): 38–52.

Gatrell, Peter. 2013. *The Making of the Modern Refugee*. Oxford: Oxford University Press.

Giulianotti, Richard, and Roland Robertson. 2007. "Recovering the Social: Globalization, Football and Transnationalism." In *Globalization and Sport*, edited by Richard Giulianotti and Roland Robertson, 58–78. Malden, MA: Blackwell.

Hallinan, Chris, and John Hughson. 2010. "The Beautiful Game in Howard's 'Brutopia': Football, Ethnicity and Citizenship in Australia." In *The Containment of Soccer in Australia: Fencing off the World Game*, edited by Chris Hallinan and John Hughson, 1–8. London: Routledge.

Horky, Thomas, and Jörg-Uwe Nieland, eds. 2013. *Quality and Quantity of Sports Reporting: An International Comparative Study of Print Media*. Hamburg: Horky Sport & Kommunikation.

Hutchins, Brett, and David Rowe. 2012. *Sport beyond Television: The Internet, Digital Media and the Rise of Networked Media Sport*. New York: Routledge.

Leach, Michael, Geoffrey Stokes, and Ian Ward, eds. 2000. *The Rise and Fall of One Nation*. St Lucia: Queensland University Press.

Maguire, Joseph, and Mark Falcous, eds. 2011. *Sport and Migration: Borders, Boundaries and Crossings*. London: Routledge.

Malcolm, Dominic. 2001. "'It's not Cricket': Colonial Legacies and Contemporary Inequalities." *Journal of Historical Sociology* 14 (3): 253–275.

Markus, Andrew, and M. C. Ricklefs, eds. 1985. *Surrender Australia? Essays in the Study and Uses of History: Geoffrey Blainey and Asian Immigration*. Sydney: Allen and Unwin.

Miller, Toby, Geoffrey Lawrence, Jim McKay, and David Rowe. 2001. *Globalization and Sport: Playing the World*. London: Sage.

Rasul, Azmat, and Jennifer M. Proffitt. 2011. "Bollywood and the Indian Premier League (IPL): The Political Economy of Bollywood's New Blockbuster." *Asian Journal of Communication* 21 (4): 373–388.

Rowe, David. 2004. *Sport, Culture and the Media: The Unruly Trinity*. 2nd ed. Maidenhead: Open University Press.

Rowe, David. 2011. *Global Media Sport: Flows, Forms and Futures*. London: Bloomsbury Academic.

Rowe, David. 2013. "Sport: Scandal, Gender and the Nation." *Institute for Culture and Society Occasional Paper Series* 4 (3): 1–17. Accessed May 23, 2015. http://www.uws.edu.au/__data/assets/pdf_file/0005/539123/ICS_Occasional_Paper_Series_4_3.pdf

Rowe, David. 2014a. "'Events of National Importance and Cultural Significance': Sport, Television and the Anti-Siphoning Regime in Australia." In *Sport, Public Broadcasting, and Cultural Citizenship: Signal Lost?*, edited by J. Scherer and D. Rowe, 166–187. New York: Routledge.

Rowe, David. 2014b. "The Mediated Nation and the Transnational Football Fan." *Soccer & Society* 16 (5–6): 693–709.

Rowe, David. 2016. "'Great markers of culture': The Australian Sport Field." *Media International Australia* 158: 26–36.

Roy Morgan Research. 2015. "The Top 20 Sports Played by Aussies Young and Old(er)." Accessed May 13, 2015. http://www.roymorgan.com/findings/6123-australian-sports-participation-rates-among-children-and-adults-december-2014-201503182151

Tate, John W. 2009. "John Howard's 'Nation': Multiculturalism, Citizenship and Identity." *Australian Journal of Politics & History* 55 (1): 97–120.

Ugra, Sharda. 2015. "Fawad Ahmed and the Vanishing of Billy Birmingham: How Ethnic Diversity and the South Asian Diaspora Became Front and Centre in Australian Cricket Policy." *The Fearless Nadia Occasional Papers on India–Australia Relations*. 1 vol. Melbourne: Australia India Institute. Accessed May 13, 2015. http://www.aii.unimelb.edu.au/sites/default/files/AII-Fearless%20Nadia-FA_0.pdf

Urry, John. 2000. *Sociology beyond Societies: Mobilities for the Twenty-First Century*. London: Routledge.

WSROC (Western Sydney Regional Organisation of Councils) 2014. *Community Profile* (profile.id). Accessed May 13, 2015. http://profile.id.com.au/wsroc?WebID=200

Index

1930 World Cup participation 81
1978 World Cup: Amnesty International reaction to Argentina human rights violations 97; Argentinean junta plan to blind the world to human rights violations 101; DFB and West German government opposition to using football for human rights advocacy 98–100; player responses to Amnesty petition 99–100; 'Yes to Football, No to Torture!' campaign 101–106

AAA (Argentine Anti-Communist Alliance) 97
Aboriginal assimilation of cricket 74
Academic Ice Hockey Club of Zurich 47
alliance among non-European countries post-Second World War 84
amateurism: cricket 63
Americanisation of basketball 20
Amnesty International Argentina campaign: player responses to Argentina human rights violations petition 99–100; recognition of human rights violations in Argentina 97; 'Yes to Football, No to Torture!' campaign 101–106
Anglocentrism in Australia 127–128
anti-English movement in India 70–71
Anti-Imperialist Information Bulletin support of 'Yes to Football, No to Torture!' campaign 102
Arbeiterturnerbund 38–39
Argentina: Argentine Football League 33; Dirty War 96–97; founding father of football 27–29; national re-interpretation of the arrival of football 30; social divisions in football 37; Swiss boarding school students transferring football 49
Argentina human rights violations: Amnesty International recognition of 97; DFB and German government opposition on using football for politics 98–101; junta plan to blind the world to human rights violations 101; 'Yes to Football, No to Torture!' campaign 101–106
Argentine Anti-Communist Alliance (AAA) 97
Arnold, Thomas 35
athletic immigration *see* sport labour migration

Atlantic borderlands: basketball 17–20; lacrosse development in England 11–17; ludic cultural transference and exchange 10
attachments to nations 124–125
Australia: Aboriginal assimilation of cricket 74; Anglocentrism 127–128; gender inequality 132; intergenerational influence on sports 133–134; migrants supporting national teams from places of origin 134–135; social benefits of sports participation/interaction 132–133; social inclusion/exclusion through sports 131; sociocultural attachment to sports 126–128; sports participation and spectatorship 129–130
Australian Citizenship: Our Common Bond 126

Barassi, Ottorino 86–88
basketball: Americanisation in South Wales 20; arrival in Britain 18; British Basketball Association 19; Christian roots 17–18; expansion beyond YMCA 18–19; first competitive league in British Isles 18; origins 18; post-war Americanisation of basketball 19–20; secularization 19–20
BBA (British Basketball Association) 19
Beckham, David: Chinese fan frenzy for 2
Beeche, Hector 82
Beers, George 14–15
Beeton, Samuel 13
Bensemann, Walther 49
Blickpunkt support of 'Yes to Football, No to Torture!' campaign 102
boarding schools spread of British sports 47–49
borderlands model 3; basketball 17–20; lacrosse 11–17; North Atlantic 9–10
bourgeois football clubs in Germany 38
brawn drain 112
Brazil: founding fathers of football 28–29
Bristol Lacrosse clubs 16
Britain: Americanisation of basketball in South Wales 20; basketball arrival 18; British Basketball Association 19; development of lacrosse 11–17; disbanding of lacrosse clubs 14; expansion of basketball beyond YMCA 18–19; football roots

INDEX

25–26; growth of lacrosse clubs 15; lacrosse tours from Canada 12–13; middle-class roots of lacrosse 16–17; National Lacrosse Association formation 13; re-emergence of lacrosse 14; resurgence of basketball in mono-industrial areas 19–20; strong Briton presence in Switzerland 45–46; well-educated middle class support 13–14

British Basketball Association (BBA) 19

British Isles: Beers 1876 lacrosse tour 14–15; Bristol Lacrosse clubs 16; British development of lacrosse 13; disbanding of lacrosse clubs 14; first competitive basketball league 18; growth of lacrosse clubs 15; lacrosse players' character 16; lacrosse tours 12–13; re-emergence of lacrosse in England 14; well-educated middle class support of lacrosse 13–14

British sports spread across Europe/North Africa: boarding school students 49; Swiss expatriates' popularization of football 51–52

British sports spread to Switzerland: boarding schools 47–49; British students establishing 46–47; ice hockey as winter tourist attraction 49–50; popularization of football 50–51; professionalization of football 52; professionalization of ice hockey 52–53; strong Briton presence in Switzerland 45–46; Swiss migrants 47; unorganized sporting activities 53–54

Burro, Enrique 81

Bulgaria: popularization of football 52

Buli, Hugo 52

Canada: lacrosse identification as sport 12; lacrosse tours across British Isles 12–13

Careless, James Maurice 10

celebrity culture: David Beckham fan frenzy in China 2

character: lacrosse players 16

China: David Beckham fan frenzy 2

Chowdhury, P. 67–68

Christianity: basketball roots 17–18

civilising mission English colonies: circulation of cricket 64

class divisions *See* social class

colonies of England: cricket 64

commercialization: Danish women's handball 115

communities of practice 113–114

competence and knowledgeability comparison 114

Cook, Nelson P. 19

cosmopolitanism 136–137

Cox, Oscar Alfredo Sebastião 28–29, 49

creator's game 11

cricket: amateurism 63; anglicised 61; Australian Aboriginal assimilation 74; class divisions 60–62; colonies 64; emulation of English play in colonies 64; Englishness 62–63; golden age

61–62; hard form 63–64; Indian nationalism 65; philosopher king 70; praise/criticism after India's independence 66; preservation 63; *see also* Indian cricket

criticisms of 'Yes to Football, No to Torture!' campaign 103

cultural brokering 4

culture; basketball across oceanic borderlands 17–20; gender inequality 132; inclusion/exclusion through sports 131; intercultural transfers 26–27; intergenerational influence 133–134; lacrosse across oceanic borderlands 11–17; migrants supporting national teams from places of origin 134–135; multiculturalism and nationalism 127–128; national identities 131; social benefits of sports participation/interaction 132–133; state-initiated endorsements of sports 126–127; Switzerland as British tourist destination 45–46

Danish women's handball case study: financial incentives 118; immigrant athletes as obstacles to domestic talent development 116–117; immigrant athletes as source of inspiration for domestic talent 118–119; immigration of foreign players 115; post-financial crisis sporting level decline 117; professionalization and commercialization 115; social practice adaptations 117–118; talent development across local and national communities of practice 118

de Loys, Treytorrens 47

de Regibus, Georges 52

decentralization of FIFA 84–85

Der Ganz Grosse Traum 30

Derby: first competitive basketball league 18

Deutsche Turnerschaft 38

DFB (Deutsches Fussball Bund): opposition to using football for human rights advocacy 98–101; support of Rudel and Argentine junta 105–106

diffusion-modernization models 8–9

Dirty War 96–97

domestic talent development: across local and national communities of practice 118; balancing professional player wide knowledge and established competence in local clubs 119; changing perceptions and realities of labour immigration 120; financial incentives 118; immigrant athletes as obstacles to domestic talent development 116–117; immigrant athletes as source of inspiration for domestic talent 118–119; media's role in shaping public perceptions 120; national sport governing bodies approaches 120–121; post-financial crisis sporting level decline 117; social practice adaptations 117–118; sport labour migration influence 111–112

140

INDEX

dual-citizens supporting national teams from places of origin 134–135
Dupuy, Luis 83

Eastern Europe: Swiss introduction of football 51–52
economics; basketball in mono-industrial areas 19–20; British presence in Switzerland 45; sport labour migration effects on domestic workers 112
educational system: football's role in reform 33–36; popularization of football in Switzerland 50–51
elitist football clubs in Argentina 37
English cricket: amateurism 63; anglicised 61; class division 62; colonial mimicry 66–67; colonies 64; Englishness 62–63; golden age 61–62; hard form 63–64; Indian folk culture 67–68; moral masculinity 69; preservation 63; rusticity 68; symbol of social cohesion and harmony 69
English language legacy in India 71–72
Escuela de Campeones 30
ethnic divisions: cricket players 60
European Champion Clubs' Cup 89
European football: 1930 World Cup participation 81; FIFA associations post 1950 86–88; loss of political superiority post-Second World War 84; South American conflict 82–83; UEFA 78–79, 88–90
exclusion through sports 131

father of lacrosse 14
FC Bari 51
FC Zurich 51
FIFA (Fédération Internationale de Football Association): 1930 World Cup participation 81; continental organizations requirement 78; decentralization 84–85; first non-European Executive Committee member appointment 81; marginalization of non-European countries 81; reorganization into continental groups post 1950 86–88; Second World War 83; South America-Europe conflict 82–83; South American challenge of singular control over international governance 83; South American request for equitable distribution of continental representation in Executive Committee 85; UEFA creation 88–90
First Nations: lacrosse 11
First World War: British POWs playing ice hockey in Switzerland 47; resurgence of basketball in mono-industrial areas 19–20
Fluminense Football Club 49
folk culture: Indian cricket 67–68
football: 1930 World Cup participation 81; Argentina founding father 27–29; Argentina

national re-interpretation of the arrival of football 30; Argentine Football League 33; boarding schools spreading in Switzerland 47–49; Brazil founding fathers 28–29; British students introducing to Switzerland 46–47; DFB and West German government opposition to using football for human rights advocacy 98–101; English roots 25–26; female Swiss 52; first continental tournament 80; German founding father 28; German national re-interpretation of the arrival of football 30; Germanizing 31–32; intercultural transfer 27–29; intercultural transfer through industrialization 32; nationalistic tones 26; popularization across Europe 51–52; popularization in Switzerland 50–51; professionalization in Switzerland 52; role in educational/social reform 33–36; social divisions in society 36–39; Swiss migrants transfer of football to Switzerland 47; UEFA 88–90; unorganized in Switzerland 53–54; writing out of history the English origins 30–31; *see also* European football; South American football
founding fathers of football: Alexander Watson Hutton 27–29; Konrad Koch 28; Oscar Cox and Charles William Miller 28–29
France: Swiss expatriate popularization of football 51
Frankfurter Allgemeine Zeitung criticism of 'Yes to Football, No to Torture!' campaign 103
Frankfurter Rundschau support of Yes to Football, No to Torture! (single quotes) campaign 102
French introduction to football 49

Gamper, Hans Joan 51
gender: ice hockey 53; inequality sociocultural impact 132; moral masculinity of cricket 69; Swiss football 52
gentlemanliness of cricket 63
Germany: contributors to Koch's transfer of football 32–33; football's role in educational/social reform 33–36; founding father of football 28; Germanizing football 31–32; gymnastics 34; national re-interpretation of the arrival of football 30; social divisions in football 37–39; Swiss boarding school students transferring football 49; *see also* DFB
giving cultures: intercultural transfers 27
global history 2–3
global solidarity of 'Yes to Football, No to Torture!' campaign 103
glocalization 11
Gloucester County Lacrosse Club 16
golden age of cricket 61–62
Grace, W.G. 63

INDEX

Grasshopper Club at Zurich 47
Griffith, Tom E. 47
gymnastics: Germany 34

Hammond, Wally 62
Hermann, August 32–33
Hobbs, Jack 63
Hockey Club Bellerive 48
Hughes, Thomas: *Tom Brown's Schooldays* 28–29
human rights advocacy and sports: DFB and West German government opposition on using football for 98–101; the last utopia 98; player responses to Amnesty petition 99–100; 'Yes to Football, No to Torture!' campaign 101–106
Hutton, Alexander Watson: Argentine Football League 33; introduction to football 27–29; national re-interpretation of his transfer of football 30

ice hockey: boarding schools spreading in Switzerland 47–49; British students introducing to Switzerland 47; professionalization in Switzerland 52–53; unorganized in Switzerland 53–54; as winter tourist attraction in Switzerland 49–50
identity politics: Indian cricket 67
immigrant athletes: balancing professional player wide knowledge and established competence in local clubs 119; changing perceptions and realities of labour immigration 120; financial incentives 118; media's role in shaping public perceptions 120; national sport governing bodies approaches to talent development 120–121; as obstacles to domestic talent development 116–117; post-financial crisis sporting level decline 117; social practice adaptations 117–118; as source of inspiration for domestic talent 118–119; talent development across local and national communities of practice 118
immigration: labour migration 111; supporting national teams from places of origin 134–135
inclusion through sports 131
Indian cricket: antidote to social evils 69; anti-English movement 70–71; class divisions 60; colonial mimicry 66–67; emulation of English play 64; English language legacy 71–72; equalizing class divisions 68; folk culture 67–68; identity politics 67; moral masculinity 69; national contempt of foreign game 72–73; nationalism 65; praise/criticism after independence 66; religious oppositions 69–70; rusticity 68; socialist party opposition 70–71; symbol of social cohesion and harmony 69
industrialization: intercultural transfer of football 32

Informationsbulletin support of 'Yes to Football, No to Torture!' campaign 102
Institut Auckenthaler 48
Institut Bellerive in Vevey 48–49
intercultural transfer of football: founding fathers 27–29; industrialization 32
intercultural transfers 26–27
intergenerational influence on sports participation/interaction 133–134
international fandom: David Beckham in China 2
Internazionale Milano 51
intersectionality: sociocultural impact of sports 132–134
Ireland: rise and fall of lacrosse 15
Italy: Swiss expatriates' popularization of football 51

Jahn, Friedrich Ludwig 34
Joint Lacrosse Committee 16
journalists support of 'Yes to Football, No to Torture!' campaign 102
juvenile ice hockey 53–54
juvenile street football 53–54

knowledgeability and competence comparison 114
Koch, Konrad: Germanizing football 31–32; introduction to football 28; national re-interpretation of his transfer of football 30; participation of others in transfer process 32–33
Konkret support of 'Yes to Football, No to Torture!' campaign 102–103
Kuhn, Gustav 51

labour economics: effect of sport labour migration on domestic workers 112
labour migration 111–112
lacrosse: Beers 1876 tour 14–15; Bristol Lacrosse clubs 16; British development 13; as creator's game 11; disbanding of clubs in England 14; father of lacrosse 14; identifying as Canadian sport 12; Joint Lacrosse Committee 16; Merchant Venturers' Lacrosse Club 16; middle-class roots 16–17; National Lacrosse Association formation 13; player character 16; re-emergence of lacrosse in England 14; rise in Scotland 15; tours across British Isles 12–13; well-educated middle class support 13–14
Lake of Constance boarding schools spread of British sports 47–49
Lake of Geneva boarding schools spread of British sports 47–49
landscape of practice 114; balancing professional player wide knowledge and established competence in local clubs 119; competence and knowledgeability comparison 114;

INDEX

financial incentives 118; immigrant athletes as obstacles to domestic talent development 116–117; immigrant athletes as source of inspiration for domestic talent 118–119; post-financial crisis sporting level decline 117; social practice adaptations 117–118; talent development across local and national communities of practice 118

the last utopia 98

The Laws of Football as Played at Rugby School 35

Lessons of a Dream *(Der Ganz Grosse Traum)* 30

Ligue Romande de Football 48

ludic diffusion 9–11

Margetson, Alfred James 16

Marylebone Cricket Club (MCC) 60

masculinity: Indian cricket 69

MCC (Marylebone Cricket Club) 60

media: nation-based sporting systems 125; role in shaping public perception of sport labour migration 120

Merchant Venturers' Lacrosse Club 16

Merchant Venturers' Technical College 16

metropolitan fallacy 8–9

metropolitanism: North America 9–10

middle class football clubs: Argentina 37; Germany 39

middle-class roots: lacrosse 16–17

migrants: influence on domestic population 111–112; supporting national teams from places of origin 134–135

Miller, Charles William 28–29

Monnier, Henry 49

mono-industrial areas: basketball resurgence 19–20

moral masculinity in Indian cricket 69

Moyn, Samuel 98

multiculturalism and nationalism 127–128

Naismith, James 18

Naples introduction of football 49

national identities: sociocultural environments 131

National Lacrosse Association 13

nationalism: attachment to sport 126–127; Australia and sports 126–128; immigrant players as obstacles to domestic talent development 116–117; Indian contempt of foreign games 72–73; Indian cricket 65; intergenerational influence 133–134; migrants supporting national teams from places of origin 134–135; multiculturalism 127–128; national identities through sports 131; nation-based sporting systems 124–125; sports role as agent/symbol of national, transnational, and global relations 136

nationalization of football 26; Argentina national re-interpretation of the arrival of football 30–33; German national re-interpretation of the arrival of football 30; Germanizing the game 31–32; writing out of history the English origins 30–31

Nazi Olympic similarities with Argentina human rights violations 103

Neuberger, Hermann: opposition to using football for human rights advocacy 98–101; support of Rudel and Argentine junta 105–106

Niclaes, Hendrick 69

North Africa: Swiss introduction of football 51–52

North America: metropolitanism 9–10

North Atlantic borderland: basketball 17–20; lacrosse 11–17

oceanic borderlands; basketball 17–20; lacrosse 11–17

Official Languages Act of 1967 71

opposition: Indian cricket 69–70

Pan-American football organization 84

Pan-Americanism: helping interconnect countries 83

philosopher king of cricket 70

Pianzola, Florida 52

politics: anti-English movement in India 70–71; Argentina Dirty War 96–97; British political affinities in Switzerland 45; European colonial powers loss of political superiority post-Second World War 84; Indian cricket 67; sports role as agent/symbol of national, transnational, and global relations 136; *see also* human rights advocacy

popularization of football 50–52

post-Second World War: alliance among non-European countries 84

Pozzo, Vittorio 49

Pragnell Mervyn Oliver 16

Prince George: basketball exhibition game 17

professionalization: Danish women's handball 115; football in Switzerland 52; ice hockey in Switzerland 52–53

Public School at Rugby 35

Rauch, Louis 51

receiving cultures: intercultural transfers 27

Reck, Friedrich: participation in transfer of football to Germany 32

religion: oppositions to cricket 69–70

Rous, Stanley 86–88

Routledge, George 13–14

Rudel, Ulrich 105

Russia: popularization of football 51–52

rusticity: English cricket 68

INDEX

Sabha, Arya Pratinidhi 70
Sachs, Edwin Thomas 14
Santiago Agreement 82–83
Scarfoglio Michele and Paolo 49
Schinz, Konrad 51–52
School of Champions (*Escuela de Campeones*) 30
Schwartz, Ebbe 88
Scotland: rise and fall of lacrosse 15
Second World War: alliance among non-European countries 84; Americanisation of basketball in South Wales 20; FIFA 83
secularization: basketball 19–20
Seefeld, Horst 104
Sillig, Max 48
social class: cricket 60–62; equalizing in Indian cricket 68; football 36–39; sports sociocultural impact 132
social cohesion: benefits of sports participation/interaction 132–133; cricket 69; gender inequality 132; immigrant and domestic athletes 117–118; inclusion/exclusion through sports 131; intergenerational influence 133–134; migrants supporting national teams from places of origin 134–135; multiculturalism and nationalism 127–128; national identities 131
social reform: cricket as antidote to social evils 69; football's role 33–36
socialist parties in India: opposition to cricket 70–71
sociocultural impact of sports: Australia 126–128; gender inequality 132; intergenerational influence 133–134; migrants supporting national teams form places of origin 134–135; national identities 131; social benefits of sports participation/interaction 132–133; social class 132; social inclusion/exclusion 131; sporting cosmopolitanism 136–137
Solidarität support of 'Yes to Football, No to Torture!' campaign 102
South American football: 1930 World Cup participation 81; challenging FIFA's singular control over international governance 83; continental tournament 80; European conflict 82–83; FIFA reorganization into continental groups post 1950 86–88; first non-European FIFA Executive Committee member appointment 81; influence on UEFA 88–90; national associations 80; Pan-American organization creation 84; Pan-Americanism helping connect countries 83; request for equitable distribution of continental representation in FIFA Executive Committee 85
South Wales: resurgence/Americanisation of basketball 19–20
Spiess, Adolf 34

sport as an alternative form of physical activity 34
sport education 5
sport labour migration: balancing professional player wide knowledge and established competence in local clubs 119; changing perceptions and realities of labour immigration 120; economic effects 112; financial incentives 118; immigrant athletes as source of inspiration for domestic talent 118–119; immigrant players as obstacles to domestic talent development 116–117; influence on domestic talent development 111–112; interdependency at both ends of the migration 111–112; media's role in shaping public perceptions 120; national sport governing bodies approaches to talent development 120–121; post-financial crisis sporting level decline 117; skills exchange between domestic talent and immigrant athletes 112; social practice adaptations 117–118; talent development across local and national communities of practice 118; talent drain from Global South to Global North 112; *see also* Danish women's handball case study
sporting cosmopolitanism 136–137
spreading of British sports across Europe/North Africa: boarding school students 49; Swiss expatriates' popularization of football 51–52
spreading of British sports to Switzerland: boarding schools 47–49; British students 46–47; ice hockey as winter tourist attraction 49–50; popularization of football 50–51; professionalization of football 52; professionalization of ice hockey 52–53; strong Briton presence in Switzerland 45–46; Swiss migrants 47; unorganized sporting activities 53–54
St. Petersburg Circle of Amateur Athletes 51
state-initiated endorsements of sports 126–127
Swiss expatriates' popularization of football 51
Swiss Football Association 48
Switzerland: boarding schools spread of British sports 47–49; British students establishing sports 46–47; expatriates' popularization of football in other countries 51; female football activities 52; female ice hockey 53; ice hockey as winter tourist attraction 49–50; popularization of football 50–51; professionalization of football 52; professionalization of ice hockey 52–53; strong Briton presence 45–46; Swiss migrants transfer of football 47; unorganized sporting activities 53–54

talent development: across local and national communities of practice 118; balancing professional player wide knowledge and established competence in local clubs 119;

INDEX

changing perceptions and realities of labour immigration 120; financial incentives 118; immigrant athletes as obstacles to domestic talent development 116–117; immigrant athletes as source of inspiration for domestic talent 118–119; media's role in shaping public perceptions 120; national sport governing bodies approaches 120–121; post-financial crisis sporting level decline 117; social practice adaptations 117–118; sport labour migration influence 111–112

talent drain from Global South to Global North 112

Thames Hare and Hounds 14

Thommen, Ernst 86–88

Tittle, Gerald 16

Tom Brown's Schooldays 28–29, 69

tourist ice hockey activities in Switzerland 49–50

Towerzey, Alec Reginald 16

transnational history 2–3, 26–27

Turin introduction of football 49

UEFA (Union of European Football Associations) 78–79, 88–90

unorganized sporting activities in Switzerland 53–54

urbanization: football 36

Valenzuela, Luis 83

Vollenweider, Eduard 51–52

Wagner, Ernst 28–29

Wales: rise of lacrosse 15

Wenger, Etienne 113–114

West Germany: opposition to using football for human rights advocacy 98–101; reaction to Argentina Dirty War 96–97

West-Berlin-based Chile-Latin America Documentation Centre published appeal support of 'Yes to Football, No to Torture!' campaign 102

Westdeutscher Rundfunk support of 'Yes to Football, No to Torture!' campaign 102

Wills' Staff Lacrosse Club 16

Wilson, Harold 70

women: gender inequality sociocultural impact 132; ice hockey 53; Swiss football 52; *see also* Danish women's handball case study

'Yes to Football, No to Torture!' campaign 101–106: activists' attempts to bring posters to Bundesliga games 101–102; criticisms of misusing sports 103; DFB support of Rudel and Argentine junta 105–106; global solidarity through references to 1936 Olympic Games 103; journalists support 102; parliamentarian support 104; population support 104; traveling exhibition 101

YMCA: basketball arrival in Britain 18